For Bucky,
whose wise and gentle spirit hovers patiently at my side,
and for Rob,
whose ability to simultaneously make money and sense
made this book possible.

MAY DAY

1982

I always knew I wanted to be somebody.
Now I realize I should have been more specific. — Lilly Tomlin

My obsession with my possible role in the end of the world reignited on a blustery Chicago day on my way to the Billy Goat Tavern for a cheeseburger.

All morning long my freshly manicured and caffeinated fingers pecked away at copy for McDonald's Happy Meal boxes. The words had to rhyme, be funny, and make kids want to eat nowhere else. When the clock radio on my desk flipped to noon, I stacked my papers, grabbed my handbag off the door and escaped down the elevator. But at the top of the concrete staircase leading down to the underground diner, a pair of anxious eyes leapt out at mine from the front page of the *Chicago Tribune*.

Bucky.

R. Buckminster Fuller, to be exact. Once upon a time, the iconic futurist locked onto my eleven-year-old eyes and said women like me were going to rescue humanity from

1

extinction. My framed *Time* magazine cover proclaiming him "the first poet of technology" still hung over my nightstand. I hadn't given him much thought for years, but the fear in his bulging eyes was palpable and had me fumbling in my purse for a dime.

I bought the newspaper and plopped down on a bench to read words so familiar they leapt off the page: "Humanity is undergoing its critical examination. Whether or not we make it will be up to the individual."

A blast of air whipped at the newspaper. I straightened it out and kept reading, transfixed by words and phrases I knew so well they swept me up into the déjà vu of a lifetime.

"Weaning ourselves off fossil fuels is humanity's most critical task. We must stop burning up the house to keep the family warm. We have all the technologies needed to tap vast available cosmic energies, but we are not allowed to do so because tax-hungry government and greedy big businesses can't find a way to put a meter on the sun."

Shadows swept across that same sun, which currently felt anything but powerful. A chill raced down my spine. My head pulsed. I pulled my navy blazer around me for warmth. A bus roared up Michigan Avenue, belching the poison that was still ruining the planet. Stray bits of rubbish swirled by in a squall. I coughed. A solitary pigeon hopped my way, pecking at a pebble, reminding me I was hungry.

The pigeon looked up at me and cocked its head.

"Holy crap," I said to the pigeon.

I tucked the newspaper under my arm and fled down the stairs to join a long line at the greasy spoon diner recently made famous on *Saturday Night Live*.

Bucky had always said, "Man knows so much, but does so little." It was long past time for me to do something.

But first, lunch.

Standing in front of a sizzling grill filled with burgers, two burly, sweating men in white hats yelled good-naturedly at customers. Their comic rudeness had been immortalized by John Belushi, Dan Aykroyd, and Bill Murray in a skit written by a former advertising copywriter.

The jowly waiter shouted at me happily.

"DOUBLECHEEZ? Wake up, lady!"

"Uh, I only feel like a single."

"No. DOUBLECHEEZ! You want DOUBLECHEEZ!"

I knew better than to argue. "Okay. And a Pepsi, please."

"NO PEPSI, COKE!"

I knew they only had Coke. "Okay, Coke."

"CHEEPS OR NO CHEEPS?"

"Chips, thank you."

He turned and yelled to the grill man like a performer on stage. "DOUBLECHEEZ. COKE. CHEEPS. FOR LOVELY LADY IN BLUE!"

The *SNL* skit had been written by Don Novello from Leo Burnett, who had also created and played the character of Father Guido Sarducci, a hilarious chain-smoking priest in tinted glasses who critiqued the Vatican and other purveyors of hypocrisy. Novello was proof to me that advertising copywriters could go on to become something more. Maybe I hadn't given up journalism after all. Maybe I was just on a temporary detour.

With my spirits lifted by that thought and the greasy burger bag in my hand, I dashed back to my office to call the hotel where the newspaper said Bucky was staying.

▽▽▽

"Conrad Hilton. May I help you?"

I put on my most professional voice. "Yes, could you please connect me to the room of Buckminster Fuller?"

"One moment, please."

I held my breath. Would they put me through?

A tidy male voice answered. "Hello, Buckminster Fuller's room."

"Uh, yes, is this Mr. Fuller?"

"No. You are speaking to his assistant. And it is *Doctor* Fuller. To whom am I speaking, please?"

"Oh, sorry. My name is Patricia Field. I'm a freelance writer working on a story about Buckminster Fuller for *Chicago* magazine, and I am wondering if I could interview him."

"One moment."

I took a bite of the cheeseburger. It wasn't totally a lie. I was a real news writer in my old radio reporting job at WSJM in St. Joseph, Michigan. I'd even won a Michigan School Bell award for a documentary I wrote and produced about the Benton Harbor Schools desegregation case. How much I'd loved that job, especially the remote broadcast vehicle I could take out at lunchtime for man-on-the-beach reports.

But without a college degree, there was not much of a path for me to leap from a small-town Michigan broadcasting job to one in Chicago, without first going through Fort Wayne or Cleveland, or both, and moving to Chicago became my number one goal when escape became necessary from a messy but at least blissfully short marriage.

Yes, I know, stupid. I was only twenty-one. Even my mother had suggested I live with him first, but instead I had rushed into marriage with an attractive and successful general manager of a plastics company, who had taken literally the famous advice from *The Graduate*. I didn't know until after I said "I do" that what I was expected to do was stay home and throw dinner parties until the babies came. On the airplane ride to our honeymoon, he told me he didn't want me working, let alone in a high-profile job like radio news. When my feet touched the ground on the tarmac in St. Pete's Beach, an all-knowing man's voice boomed inside my head. "You have made the biggest mistake of your life."

Less than a year later, the day the divorce was final, I was browsing through a bookstore to find a new life when I spotted a paperback called *How to Put Your Book Together and Get a Job in Advertising.* I bought the book and did just that, landing on my feet in Chicago, a city I'd fantasized about since my fifth-grade field trip there was cancelled after a freak spring snowstorm. Back then I'd cried myself to sleep knowing I was missing out on the great city all the older kids had visited, but life was long and I was getting even.

First off, I had doubled my radio salary and was more than "making my age," *Money* magazine's definition of success, at $24,000 a year. I had stumbled onto a perfect condo rental smack-dab on Lake Michigan in an elegant black curved building called Harbor Point. My seven hundred square foot studio on the eleventh floor overlooked Grant Park and the Chicago Yacht Club. The building had everything. An indoor pool. A hot tub. A grocery store. A doorman. And nobody to tell me what to do.

There came a click on the line.

"So, Miss Field, you say you are a writer for *Chicago* magazine?"

I nearly choked on a lump of cheeseburger. "Well, um, actually I am a freelance writer, but I plan to write a story about Mr. Fuller's ideas and submit—"

"Dr. Fuller."

"Dr. Fuller, yes, of course, so sorry."

"One moment."

Muffled voices rose and fell in the background.

I took another bite and examined Bucky's photo up close. He was getting really old. He might not be around much longer. If they said no, maybe I would have to walk down to the Conrad Hilton after work and wait for him.

What could be taking so long? Were they debating whether I was worthy of Bucky's precious remaining time? The *Tribune* said he was eighty-six. Eighty-six. What happens when you "eighty-six" something? Not a good thing. I popped open my can of Coke, needing something to calm my nerves. Maybe they were calling *Chicago* magazine. Maybe they were learning that nobody had ever heard of a writer named Patricia Field, that there was no such person on any list of actual writers.

He cleared his throat.

"All right, then, Miss Field. Dr. Fuller will see you at two p.m. tomorrow at the John Hancock Center, at the Sky Deck, on the ninety-eighth floor."

"Yes, sir, thank you. Thank you very much."

"Do not be late."

"I will. I mean, I won't. Thank you again."

I hung up before he could change his mind. How had he known I was always late?

THE END IN THE BEGINNING

1964

Children are our elders in Universe time. We are privileged to see a new world through their eyes. — Buckminster Fuller

The world first ended by my hand when I was seven. On my new purple Spyder bike, I cruised down the road next to the man-made lake where we lived in Riley, Indiana. My rampant freckles had nearly merged in solidarity as they did every summer, which created the ideal camouflage for hiding out with turtles, frogs, rabbits, and other magical creatures living along the shore.

I pedaled like the dickens to make my long sun-streaked hair lift off my back as the astoundingly beautiful blue and green world rolled by. I raised my hand to my face to push up my glasses, and when they weren't there I knew I was dreaming. In real life, I couldn't see much beyond my hands without my glasses, but now I could make out the individual feathers on the Canadian geese flying high above me, without even squinting.

Being awake inside a dream was my favorite place to be, so I laughed and let my hair grow long and thick until it morphed into great wings that lifted me high over the lake. The geese caught up with me and squawked their compliments for my wings made of hair.

On the road below I spotted a huge yellow sunflower. Thinking I would decorate my bike with it, I dropped back down to earth, hit my brakes, and leaned over to pick the flower.

As I grabbed its fat hairy stalk, the voice of an angry giant boomed out of nowhere inside my head.

"What right do you have to end a life?"

I looked around for the source of the voice. Nothing. I figured it was just part of the dream, so no harm could come of it. It was just a flower. In a dream.

"Silly old man!" I called out to the sky. "Flowers don't have feelings!" I tugged at the stalk with both hands, but it held tight to the ground. Not one to let a mere flower get the best of me, I twisted and tugged until the entire root ball popped out of the earth like a cork. Dirt flew everywhere. A fat red earthworm popped out and screeched into my face, "What have you done? What have you done?" Foamy white spittle flew out of its mouth. Time slowed down, as if nature or God or whoever was in charge wanted me to understand the idiocy of what I had done. I opened my mouth to apologize to the worm when a massive mushroom cloud exploded and sucked it all away — the road, the grass, the sky.

My bike clunked me on the head, and I woke up.

▽▽▽

My eyes came to rest on the glittering sunlit waters beyond the sliding glass doors of my bedroom. Without my glasses, the lake was nothing but a shimmering slab of light, fuzzy daytime fireworks put on by nature herself under a cloudless morning sky. The birds sang out but I shut my eyes quickly to capture the dream before it got away. The bike. The birds. The flower. Its message made my heart sink. I had ignored a powerful voice inside my own head that seemed to know exactly what it was talking about—and in doing so, I had single-handedly caused the end of everything.

The whole crazy idea planted itself like a tiny seed inside my mind that one day I might have something to do with the end of the world. But the birds chattered happily through the open screen door as if they also had crazy dreams to share. The brilliant green leaves of the sycamore tree next to the water rustled in the cool breeze. It was an ordinary Saturday morning in spring. I threw off the covers, put on my glasses, picked up my cat Jasper from the foot of my bed, and ran down to the beach to check on the tadpoles.

THE WORLD GAME

1969

All children are born geniuses, but the process of living de-geniuses them. — Buckminster Fuller

It was the summer of 1969 when everything seemed to happen at once. The *Age of Aquarius* was supposedly dawning, which meant peace and love would finally guide the planet. But not only was my brother Roger attacked by a muskrat, but on the television more than a half million Americans were fighting in the Vietnam War, which my father called "bloody bogus." And then, right before our eyes, on July 20, a Sunday, an American astronaut in a puffy white suit floated down a metal ladder and stepped onto the surface of the moon.

Daddy, still wearing his red plaid pajamas, stepped onto the gray slate coffee table in the family room, raised his glass and saluted the "bloody huge leap forward for all mankind." All four of us kids took turns making our own momentous leaps from the couch onto the coffee table until my mother came in from doing the breakfast dishes and made us stop.

My parents had immigrated to Terre Haute, Indiana from London, England two years before I was born. They thought it hilarious that the first word I ever spoke was "why," which I never understood until I learned that babies imitate whatever they hear. Moving to America had been my mother's dream, but she'd envisioned palm trees and movie stars, not smokestacks and tire factories, so they'd moved us out to the country, to Riley, population 409, where they designed and built a redwood and glass house on a small man-made lake, called Lakewood Lake, in Lakewood Subdivision.

My father, an architect, created something so unusual our neighbors nicknamed it "the California house." Instead of sitting tidily up on the berm like the other boxy houses in the subdivision, it jutted brazenly out over the water, the same way my parents' English accents did.

To save trees Daddy crafted openings in the eaves for them. Curious people would ring the doorbell to ask if they could see the trees growing through our roof. The answer was always no. English people didn't entertain the idea of a drop-in visitor, let alone the reality of one.

I knew we were different but I didn't know how. After being laughed at in first grade when I stood to read aloud from the book *How Now Brown Cow,* I worked hard to get rid of my silly English accent. The arrival of the Beatles that same year made such an accent cool in some parts of the country, but not in Riley, where sticking out was the worst possible fate.

Everyone seemed happy in our new home on the lake until my father, who could be so charming and make everybody laugh when he wanted to, went a little crazy when

President Kennedy, and then his brother Bobby, and then Martin Luther King, were all shot and killed. He started making us sit down and watch the news on the television every night, filling in the parts he said they weren't telling us.

Mummy constantly worried he was "going 'round the bend" and she didn't just mean in his tiny convertible Austin Healy Sprite.

On the afternoon of the moon landing, Daddy and some other men who lived around the lake rowed out into the middle and circled their boats in celebration. At one point he stood up in the boat to amuse the boisterous men with his account of the moon landing, and when he got to the part about "one small step for man," he walked right off the back of the boat.

Laughter roared out over the water as he splashed and flailed about, pretending to drown. Roger and I were watching from the beach. I stood up and applauded them. I loved seeing adults goof off and have some silly fun for a change.

Roger, still cranky from his stitches, wasn't so sure. "How embarrassing. They're drunk." He picked at the scar on his upper arm.

"But they're funny! Daddy's a riot." I swatted at his hand. "And quit picking."

Earlier that summer, Roger and I had chased a muskrat into the garage and cornered it under the station wagon, hoping to turn it into a pet. Roger lay on the concrete floor to reach for it while I blocked its passage on the other side. The muskrat, still dripping wet from its morning swim and super mad at being cornered, lunged out at Roger and latched onto his shoulder with its needle-sharp teeth.

Roger recoiled in pain, but the muskrat clamped onto him. The terror in both their eyes gave me the courage to swat at it with the back of my hand. It released its grip and darted off into the woods, but blood spurted everywhere. Roger was in shock. I placed his other hand over the wound, told him to hold it tight and ran inside to get Daddy, who bolted up out of his chair. When he saw the blood gushing out of Roger's arm, he whipped off his dress shirt and tied the sleeve just above the ripped pink flesh that was about to make me throw up.

By now, Roger's bandages were off and the stitches out, but he was convinced a piece of thread or a muskrat tooth was still stuck inside his arm. He couldn't stop picking at it.

The boats on the lake banged up against one another as the men took turns trying to walk on water. They swore and laughed and nearly capsized every time someone tried to climb back into their boat. Every now and then water skiiers would go by. A girl in a red bikini waved an American flag. The men whistled and cheered her wildly until the wake behind her nearly tipped their rowboats over.

"You're intoxicated, you fools!"

It was our next-door neighbor, Mrs. Hockett, standing on the grassy bank in her apron, her fists clenched against her wide hips.

"We know that," shouted one of the men.

"David! Get in this house at once!" Mummy appeared up on the deck, cigarette in hand, showing off her most haughty English accent, the one nobody could ignore.

The men grew quiet and rowed back in. Daddy went inside to take a nap.

Later that evening, my two sisters cuddled up on the couch and watched *Lost in Space* while I took one last swim out to the new dock Daddy had built over the weekend. It was made of redwood and Styrofoam and had chicken wire all around the foam to stop the muskrats from gnawing at it. Floating on my back in the cool, shadowy water, I

stared up at the sliver of the moon and felt the expansive-
ness of a new world, where humans were way out there,
walking around on a big rock, proving that anything was
possible.

Up on the deck, the sliding glass door scraped open.
Daddy emerged and turned up the radio for one of my favorite songs, "In the Year 2525," about how it had been ten
thousand years, man had cried a billion tears, but maybe
now his reign was through. Ice clinked in his glass.

Roger sat glumly on the beach next to the fishing dock
since he wasn't allowed to swim. Fresh sand had been de-
livered that week — a dump truck full of hidden treasures
in the form of tiny fossilized fish bones. Daddy had even
taken us to the quarry so we could pick out the best sand,
whichever had the most fossils. Next to the little beach, the
bank was lined with rocks the whole family had carried
down one by one from the back of the station wagon earlier that summer. We had all complained wretchedly at the
time, but in the moonlight, the smooth round rocks holding back the water made me feel proud to have helped.

The door scraped open again and Mummy stepped outside in her long flowery dressing gown, unlit cigarette in
hand, her lips painted a dark red, her short hair as black as
coal.

"David, turn that down." When he didn't budge, she
did it herself.

"So, what do you think?" he said.

"About what?"

"About Woodstock."

She sighed. "I think it's the most daft idea you've ever
had, is what I bloody well think. What on earth's gotten
into you? I think you've gone a bit soft."

Daddy's metal Zippo lighter clicked. The fire lit up his
face, which was tan and handsome but covered with frown

lines. He took a drag off his Kent and extended the lighter to Mummy's Pall Mall.

"The children aren't learning anything in these bloody stupid American schools," he said. "For Chrissakes, they're ducking down beneath their desks to prepare for an atom bomb."

"Well at least they won't see it coming," she said matter-of-factly.

"Do you think anyone has bothered to tell them that the only country to ever drop an atom bomb was theirs? And that they did it twice? That America is the world's biggest bully?"

"You mean *we* did it twice. It's our country too. We live here now, remember?"

"America is a bloody mess," he said. "We should have never come."

"But I love living here on the lake. It suits me. The children are happy. And your new buildings at the college are beautiful. Can't you ever be satisfied?"

He took an angry puff off his Kent and blew it out like he was some ancient English dragon. I missed what they said next so I rolled over on my side and strained my ears to hear.

"How can anyone be happy when things are such a mess?" he said. "All these assassinations, and now this damn sham of a war..."

"You don't know about any of that. It's only a conspiracy theory. And why trouble yourself over things over which you have no control?" She flicked the ash off her cigarette.

"I'll tell you why: because America is being ruined by some disgusting, evil assholes."

"David! The children!"

"Oh sorry, children," he called out to us. "I didn't mean to say 'assholes.'"

Roger laughed.

"David, didn't you already put on enough of a show for one day? Do you really want the whole subdivision knowing you want to take your children to some free love concert?"

I wasn't sure I'd heard right. I sat up. "A free love concert?" My voice echoed over the lake. This was the best idea I'd heard all summer.

"Let's go!" Roger yelled.

"Amen to that," I said.

"Peace will guide the planet," Roger said, holding up his jar of twinkling lightning bugs for me to see, his round face grinning in their flickering light.

"Love will steer the stars," I sang out, not sure we had the words right, but it didn't matter.

"Absolutely not. Your father has no idea how to raise children," Mummy said, flinging her lighted cigarette butt through the darkness, which fizzled out in the water not far from where I lay.

"Mummy!" I shouted. "Don't do that!"

"Yeah, Mummy, the lake is not your ashtray," said Roger. "You will poison the fish."

"Both of you, stop being cheeky to your mother or you'll get a clip across the ear," Daddy said. He scraped back his chair and stood to go inside.

My mother had the last word as always. "You're not taking the children to Woodstock."

By the following weekend Daddy had come up with another idea for a road trip, to Carbondale, Illinois, where a genius with a funny name was hosting an exhibit of something called the World Game. Even Mummy approved.

The night before the trip, I found him in his office doing his stamps. He had a huge stamp collection from all over the world which took forever to sort and catalog, but he stopped working when I came in to show me a picture book called *The Dymaxion World of Buckminster Fuller*. It was filled with black-and-white photographs of mind-blowing inventions. There was a lozenge-shaped three-wheeled car that transported eleven people, went fifty miles on a single gallon of gas, and could turn on a dime. A miraculous pop-up Dymaxion house hung on a pole and could be installed anywhere in a day, even in a jungle or a desert, even over the water. This meant people didn't need to be stuck in one place, but could transport their home by helicopter anywhere. And then there was his most famous creation of all, the geodesic dome, a dumbfoundingly beautiful bubble in the sky; one of them big enough to fit a train inside. Daddy called it a signature of God, even though he didn't believe in God, because it used the same design principles nature used.

I didn't understand most of it, but to me these ideas were even better than the Jetsons because they were real. I took *The Dymaxion World* to bed and read aloud to Jasper until Mummy came in and made me turn off the light.

The next morning, I leapt out of bed before dawn, not caring that the sky was overcast and threatening rain. Bucky's ideas had lit up my mind, and I couldn't wait to see the World Game, not to mention spend the whole day with my father.

Daddy slid the picnic basket and some blankets into the back of our powder blue Ford station wagon while we piled in. As always, Roger claimed the front seat, which made me want to scream.

"That's okay," Mummy said, in answer to my protests. "Roger is the only boy."

I was constantly being reminded that the existence of a floppy pink appendage between a pair of skinny legs somehow made all the difference in the world. "We're from England," my mother would say. "English men are not expected to help with the cooking, or the dishes, or the washing." This meant Roger got to take out the garbage and rake leaves, greatly preferable tasks since they needed doing only occasionally and were done outside in nature, where a person could think.

"But we are not in England," I stated matter of factly enough. "We live right here in America. In Indiana no less. And the Smith boys next door always do the dishes."

My temper had gotten to be a problem over this and other issues. One night while Roger sat on the couch and Sarah again dictated that I would dry and put away the dishes instead of the easier job of washing them, I pulled a huge carving knife out of the sink and waved it at her.

"I'm tired of drying. I want to wash!"

"Mummy, Pat's got a knife!" Sarah shrieked.

All hell broke loose and I was sent to bed, but at least I got out of drying the dishes. Ever since, they all seemed a little afraid of me, which made me feel awful. I was apparently the only one in the family who knew I would never intentionally hurt anyone or anything.

Giving up, I slumped into my regular spot in the car, the same position I held in the family: smack-dab in the middle, sandwiched between my two sisters and right behind Roger, who turned around and grinned, then hunkered down next to beloved Mummy. It took all my strength not to swat him.

Sarah, only thirteen months older than me, looked positively ancient in her pale blue cardigan and perfect dark brown ponytail. On the other side of me, sweet baby Sheila clung to her pink-checkered blanket with her thumb in her mouth, beaming at me from under blond ringlets splayed out over her head like sunshine itself.

Daddy climbed into the car and started the engine. He reached up and pulled down the visor for his Ray-Bans, put them on, then cocked his head at me in a jaunty way.

"Guess what, Pat?" he said. "I have realized that Bucky's World Game is the exact opposite of Monopoly."

"I hate Monopoly!" I yelled without thinking.

"Pat, must you always shout?" asked Mummy.

"That's why I'm telling you it's the opposite, silly Pat," Daddy said.

"Yeah, the opposite, silly Patty," said Roger, who knew I hated being called Patty.

"In the World Game," Daddy said, ignoring Roger, "people come together to figure out how to make things work for everybody. Instead of competing against one another, you win by creating success for everyone else."

I leaned back against the cool vinyl seat to think. The opposite of something I hated had promise. "Monopoly should be called 'Ruin Everybody,'" I announced to the car, crossing my arms across my chest.

"You're a smart girl to be concerned about such things," Daddy said.

Mummy looked up from her *McCall's* magazine and made her *tsk* sound.

"But it's true, Barbara. For example, Bucky says the only reason we are not allowed to enjoy solar power is because nobody's figured out a way to put a meter on the sun."

"Don't be ridiculous. If solar power was so possible, why wouldn't it be happening? Believe you me, if there's money to be made in America, someone would be doing it."

"They're not letting it happen."

"Who's not?"

"Big Oil, of course—which is in cahoots with your love-ly American government."

"Why is it always Mummy's government?" Roger often asked questions nobody answered.

Mummy offered up a deep sigh, the one that said she knew better than everybody about everything. "So you really think they're all working together on this? That there's some big conspiracy?" She picked at a shiny red fingernail with her thumb. Green ribbons of corn fields under a darkening sky rolled by outside the car windows. "Children, pay no attention to your father. Life is too short to bother yourself about things over which you have no control."

"Children," my father's eyes met mine in the mirror, "do not become an ostrich-with-its-head-in-the-sand type of human being as your mother has done. We must all stay awake and not fall for the silly side shows put on to de-ceive us."

"Poo!" Mummy twisted around to face her riveted backseat audience and rolled her eyes. Everybody laughed except me. I was still thinking about what Daddy had said about Monopoly, which was a big deal at our house. On a typical Sunday night after roast beef and Yorkshire pud-ding, my father would sit like a king at the head of the din-ing room table, dole out all the properties and play money then proceed to win them all back. One by one, all four of us children would sulk away from the table, either in tears or shouting, which would sometimes get us sent to our rooms, or maybe even to bed for the rest of the night, if we swore.

One evening while I awaited the others on skid row (the couch in the family room), I looked up Monopoly in the *Encyclopedia Britannica* and learned that the inventor was a woman who wanted to warn people about the dangers of

America's capitalistic "land grab" system. I wasn't quite sure what that meant, only that it felt deliciously wicked to snatch away other people's properties until you were lying in bed later thinking about what you had done to them.

Daddy would come into my room after those stormy nights of fighting to tuck me in. He talked patiently about lessons that needed to be learned and said not to worry, that I would figure everything out because I was the smart one, that the Iowa Basic Skills Test had proved I could accomplish anything I set my mind to. This made me so happy I threw my arms around his neck and kissed his face until he pulled my arms down and said English people didn't behave that way.

Fine. I was still the smart one. He still believed in me.

The windshield wipers scraped against the glass as noisy rain started falling. A large white truck skidded sideways in front of us. Daddy slammed on the brakes. Everyone flew forward. The car stopped just in time, barely avoiding the truck, which was filled with terrified cows— massive, wide-eyed black-and-white creatures with pink steaming nostrils.

Just past the cows on the side of the road stood the cause of all the commotion, a majestic buck with antlers like trees, frozen in place. His eyes looked like they might pop right out of his head. The hair on my arms stood straight as cornstalks as our eyes connected and we both realized our lives could have ended in that moment.

Nobody spoke for some time after that, giving me a chance to think. My father's words made perfect sense. Why would anyone expect oil companies to support the end of oil? Of course they would defend themselves and shut down the competition, just like in Monopoly.

When at long last we pulled into the leafy parking lot at Southern Illinois University, I was first to spot the signs for the World Game. We stretched ourselves like cats and followed the signs along a tree-lined sidewalk next to a glittering little lake, where ducks and their babies glided by, nibbling their way along the shoreline.

Inside the huge, sunlit hall, drifting clouds of cigarette smoke floated overhead. A large paper map of the world was spread out over the floor. Men in dark suits stood around on the map, talking and smoking, their hands jingling keys and change in their pockets. My father looked relaxed and handsome in his soft comfortable sweater, which seemed much smarter than a suit and tie. I couldn't understand why men agreed to wear ties around their necks. They were like self-imposed nooses, and seemed especially out of place on a Saturday. The few women in the hall wore flowery summer dresses, as if to make it official they existed only for decoration. There weren't any other children anywhere to be found.

There was also nothing resembling a game, although I figured it had something to do with the map on the floor. I wondered if there had been some mistake. Disappointed, I made my way back toward the lobby, wanting to escape all the smoke and men in suits. Maybe I would sneak out to visit the ducks.

I was about to exit through the double glass doors when I was stopped in my tracks by words printed on a tall brass easel:

It is now highly feasible to take care of everybody on Earth
at a higher standard of living than any have ever known.
It no longer has to be you or me. Selfishness is unnecessary.
War is obsolete. It is a matter of converting
our high technology from weaponry to livingry.
Humanity has a choice.
It is Utopia or Oblivion.
— R. Buckminster Fuller

My feet cemented themselves to the floor. I took in the words again, and a third time. Of course, this was all possible. It was simple common sense. But why was it taking so long? It was 1969 already. The Age of Aquarius was supposed to be well underway.

"Pat, my girl, there you are!"

Daddy's voice startled me. His forehead had that Chinese house look, lined with worry.

"Daddy, look. Read this." I reached for his hand.

A man's voice came over the speakers "Ladies and gentlemen..."

"It's starting," he said.

"But—"

"Let's go hear what the amazing Bucky has to say."

I let him take me by the hand and lead me back into the hall, where a tall mustached man spoke into a microphone. "Our distinguished host and creator of the World Game has earned more than thirty honorary degrees and not a single traditional one. He has written some twenty books, invented countless artifacts for living, and is most assuredly doing more than any other human being alive to help our species evolve. I am honored to present to you the one and only Richard Buckminster Fuller."

A stocky older man in a brown suit marched into the room carrying a plywood box, something like a fruit crate. He reminded me of the banker man on the Monopoly cards, almost totally bald, but instead of a mustache he had bulging eyes from behind thick black-rimmed eyeglasses that made him look way too intense.

He stopped in the middle of the room, set the plywood box down on the floor not too far from where we stood and stepped up onto it. He touched his fingers together lightly as if he were trying to create an invisible ball with them, and while holding his hands that way he turned around slowly in a circle, while looking carefully at all of us.

People laughed nervously as he circled around a second time. His eyes came to rest on Roger and then on me. He stopped. I wondered if he was soaking up our energy or maybe even reading our minds. I tried to think good thoughts, so he wouldn't know I was judging him a rather odd little man, what with his comically protruding eyeballs and roundish belly.

He took a silver pocket watch out of his vest, closed his eyes for a moment, then snapped them open. "It's five minutes until midnight!" He nearly shouted, as if he were the white rabbit in *Alice in Wonderland.* "What are we going to do?" He threw his arms out wide.

There was nervous laughter from behind us. A man coughed, then couldn't stop coughing. I hoped Bucky would mention the stupidity of all the cigarette smoke, but he had even bigger problems on his mind.

"Humanity is undergoing its final examination." He smiled as if that might ease the pain of the bad news. "Whether or not we pass this test will be completely up to the integrity of the individual."

I felt like I was falling into a hole. I had no idea what integrity was, which probably meant I didn't have it. I squeezed Daddy's hand. His crinkly eyes met mine. He squeezed back.

"Survival of humanity will be up to each of us, each individual." Bucky's eyes came to rest on Roger, who then, unbelievably, shouted out like an idiot.

"Don't look at me!"

The crowd roared with laughter. I thought I might faint, but Bucky just smiled. "All children are born geniuses, and you, young man, are no exception."

Roger elbowed me hard in the ribs. His face turned a ridiculous shade of pink as Bucky went on to explain that everyone, young and old, must focus on the big picture and view the universe all at once. We must become comprehensivists, he said, because overspecialization would cause our extinction.

He looked down at Roger and me again. "You children will still be breathing this sweet Earthian air long after I am gone. You will lead the way to a new world beyond war. You will prepare for peace by converting our resources from weaponry to livingry. If we only prepare for war, that's all we'll ever know."

I imagined fighter jets delivering food and medicine to the naked children we'd seen running through the streets of Vietnam on television. Massive cruise ships with overflowing buffet tables could serve the starving African children in *National Geographic* magazine. How good would it feel to be an American if we did these things instead of dropping bombs on people?

"We are the first species to understand we have the potential to destroy all life on our planet," he said. "The first species to understand we have this choice."

I looked over to see if Mummy was paying attention, but she was stooped down listening to Sarah, who wasn't much interested in Bucky sorts of things, once you got past the geodesic dome and other eye candy like his three-wheeled car and hanging house.

"Now, I know there aren't many women here today," Bucky said. "But women's leadership is very important for the future. Men need to understand this. Only women are continuous. Only women are hardwired for compassion and empathy."

His eyes landed on me. Staring right at me, as if to make sure I was paying attention, he said, "Tomorrow's women have the future of humanity in their hands. They must step up and lead the world."

His words flowed into my brain as clearly as sparkling water. Everything inside me lit up at the thought that women had an edge in the long run, and that I might be part of a great revolution. It was my turn to jab an elbow into Roger. Never had I heard anyone speak with such authority about things that mattered. Maybe those thick glasses of his gave him such perfect vision he could see into the future.

A few minutes later Roger started complaining he was hungry. Daddy eventually rounded us all up and we headed back outside. I didn't want to leave, but Mummy promised we'd come back after lunch. On the way to the car, under a brilliant blue sky with trees dancing in the breezes, I looked around to see if anybody else's feet were hovering off the ground, but nothing had changed except inside me. My brain had expanded like a helium balloon to hear Bucky's visions and I was certain it would never return to its original size.

Daddy grabbed the picnic basket and blankets from the car, and we walked over to the lake where the ducks were still gliding around aimlessly, having no idea it was five minutes until midnight on humanity's clock.

I didn't think I would be able to eat, but I loved cucumber sandwiches on Wonder Bread, and Mummy poured Tang into paper cups from a red plastic jug — the same orange drink astronauts had taken to the moon. How thrilling it had been to learn on television that sugar was so important to healthy nutrition. It almost seemed too good to be true.

After lunch, Roger and I bounced and rolled around on the grassy banks of the lake, practicing to be astronauts, while our parents took a nap. Sarah sat under a tree reading to Sheila. The polka-dot bow on her ponytail bobbed up and down as she read aloud from her Bobbsey Twins book, *Freddie and Flossie at the Beach.* Sheila's eyes were closed, her thumb in her mouth.

I was skipping stones into the lake when Daddy awoke from his nap and opened his sketchbook. I ran up to sit with him. He flipped through the pages to show me his Bucky-inspired drawings. There were complicated shapes made of triangles that somehow showed Bucky's ideas about nature and the future. The shapes were called isohedrons and tetrahedrons. Even though I didn't understand it, I knew it somehow made sense, because it was beautiful. When something's beautiful, it feels like it was meant to be.

"Bucky figured out that nature builds in spheres." Daddy's long tanned fingers traced over his drawings. "Imagine all the bubbles in all foam, on all the rivers, lakes, oceans, and even in the bath. Each bubble is a miraculous formation of nature, made by millions of single atoms. Bucky figured out how nature creates. It all starts with sixty-degree triangles."

I threw my arms into the air and announced, "It's a miracle, ladies and gentlemen!"

Mummy's eyes flew open. I'd startled her.

"Pat, why aren't you down playing with the others? David, really? Can't you give it a rest?" She stretched like a cat, extending her legs to admire her black velvet shoes.

The secrets to all life on earth were being revealed, and Mummy was interested in her shoes.

"Mummy," I said. "Do you really think it's all right to glide through life like a duck on a lake when amazing and difficult challenges are facing the whole human race?"

She gave me a blank stare. "Do you really think it's all right to be so cheeky to your mother?" She picked a blade of grass off her shoes.

I didn't answer her. Instead, smoke came out my ears. I wanted so badly for Daddy to keep talking, but he sighed and put his sketchbook away. Why did the doors always slam shut just when the conversation got interesting?

"You can't take care of everyone in this life, Pat the cat," Mummy said. She lit her cigarette and took a dainty sip of it. "You'll do well enough to look after yourself."

Daddy looked at me, lifted his hand to his temple, and pretended to shoot himself. I took one look at the expression on Mummy's face and let out a shriek of laughter. She awkwardly stood up in a huff, nearly falling back on top of me, and then she said it was time to go. I thought she meant we'd go back into the World Game, like she'd promised, but she stuffed everything into the picnic basket and announced we'd stop for ice cream on the way home. The others went running after her. Daddy and I slumped along after them to the car, holding hands, both of us surely thinking the same thing, that humanity was cursed.

Hours later, we finally crunched onto the gravel driveway, and I dragged myself into bed without even brushing my teeth. Jasper purred a greeting and snuggled up to me, glad I had made it home safe.

Many hours later I awakened to the moon splashing its light over the foot my bed like it was a stage. I sat up, feeling oddly electrified. Knowing sleep would not return any time soon, I put on my glasses, picked up my madly purring Jasper, and slipped out my sliding glass door.

The stepping stones were cool and damp to my bare feet. Crickets and frogs greeted us joyfully as always, their voices rising and falling like a choir over the low rhythmic base of my father's snoring, which drifted toward me through the open screen door.

I tiptoed as quietly as I could over to my favorite place on the entire planet. Under the massive arms of the ancient oak tree stretching out over the water, Daddy had hung a porch swing. It was already magical to live in a place where land and water met, but nothing compared to the views of all creation from the swing. From there I could keep watch over my magical kingdom, and if I looked closely enough, for long enough, I could witness more life than I had even imagined possible when we lived in the city.

I flipped over the damp cushion and hoisted Jasper up onto the swing. The full moon hung low in the ink black sky, ready to make its exit. Tiny pinpoints of starlight shined bright and sharp. Not a breath of wind broke the velvety surface of the lake, the water was so still it even reflected the stars. I rubbed Jasper's head, which made him purr madly. The crickets and frogs settled down to a gentle hum.

It seemed the most natural thing in the world when the stars began to rearrange themselves in the sky to create what looked like a spiral staircase. A rhythmic clicking sound came from somewhere high above me. The crickets started shrieking. Jasper's back arched. His fur shot straight up as he cried out and tore off my lap, his claws puncturing my legs. I winced in pain and squinted up to the sky, not quite sure what we were seeing, only that I'd never seen anything like it before.

The tiny shape of a tuxedo-clad man appeared at the top of the staircase. He wore a top hat and carried a cane, which he tapped in a haunting rhythm as he danced down the stairs toward me. There were no words, just a rhythmic pattern that somehow made perfect sense. It seemed he was tapping out secrets just for me, in some kind of gibberish language just beyond my understanding. He came a little closer, making me think he was waiting for me to acknowledge him, so I did.

I sat up straight, lifted my face to the star-studded sky, and whispered, "I promise I will do whatever I can to help."

The surface of the lake rippled to life, caused not by a breeze, as I first thought, but by hundreds of starlings. They flew in perfect formation, zigzagging in unison and then hovering together over the water, casting moon shadows, making glittering, rippling patterns that swept over the surface. It was as if the birds were showing off just for me, a dance of nature created to show the breathtaking potential of living beings coming together.

I looked back up at the little man, but he had turned away and was dancing back up the staircase. There was no tapping of his cane this time, just the soft shuffle of his shoes. And then he was gone.

The frogs and crickets sang great praises for the performance and then settled back down to a low hum. I'm not sure how long I sat there, my head suspended as if by invisible silver threads. I had no idea what the man in the stars was trying to tell me. All I knew at that moment was that everything was made of stardust, even me. The swing, the lake, Jasper, the crazy starlings flying in unison. We were all one and the same. I also knew if I paid close enough attention, one day all the secrets in the universe would be revealed and I would know exactly what I needed to know when I needed to know it.

I took a deep breath to gather myself, feeling relieved to have at least partly figured things out. I felt my body rise from the swing. I picked up Jasper, still cowering in the shadows of the oak tree.

We were two tingling balls of glittery stardust floating back along the pathway.

How much easier it was to move silently past my sleeping parents' bedroom now that I was almost weightless.

UNRAVELING

1970

Nature is trying hard to make us succeed,
but she does not depend on us. — Buckminster Fuller

The following summer, the lake wore a brilliant green algae collar like some enchanted eco-priest. The world's first Earth Day had occurred. We watched on television as millions of people from all over the world took to the streets to demand a less polluted world. A place called Love Canal in New York had water so thick with poison the people who lived nearby were dying, but now people everywhere were finally waking up. The Age of Aquarius was happening. Bucky's better world was on the way.

One Saturday Roger and I decided to do our share for the planet by rowing across the lake to capture some of the beautiful painted turtles that lived there, on the wild side. Our plan was to feed them and keep watch over them, protecting them from the muskrats, who were now public enemy number one. Our parents were playing golf at the Terre Haute Country Club. We were strictly forbidden from going out in the rowboat when nobody was home, but Sarah was babysitting and it was also strictly forbidden to have boyfriends in the house, and since Billy Brown was already watching television in the family room, we figured we had a truce.

Roger rowed first while I filled him in on what I'd read in the *Encyclopedia Britannica* about turtles.

"In ancient cultures, turtles were known for their wisdom," I lectured, pushing my glasses up onto my nose. "Native Americans believed that all of North America was created on the back of a turtle. They believe that Father Sky's wife fell through a hole in the sky and that to keep her from drowning, a muskrat dug up a handful of soil from the bottom of the ocean and placed it on the turtle's wide back. That's what made land, how America was formed—on the back of a turtle."

"No way should a muskrat get credit for that," Roger said. "That's ridiculous."

We glided silently toward the shore. The shade of the willow trees drooping lazily along the water's edge gave us some relief from the muggy heat of the sun. I scanned the bubbling and shimmering algae all around the boat, watching for the turtles' tiny heads.

"There's one!" Roger said.

I spotted it too—an intricately fashioned green, red, and yellow head about the size of my thumb, resting atop a warm algae pillow. It was sleeping.

"Okay, I'm getting out." I said, and lowered myself into the foamy algae, which was nearly hot on the surface. "It's like turtle soup," I said, sinking in up to my neck, watching spindly, sunlit water bugs skitter away from my hands. I glided smoothly atop the water to keep myself afloat, dog paddling gently to sneak up on the turtle, not wanting my feet to find out what the bottom was like. I could handle the algae but the oozing sludge underneath it all reminded me of death.

I crept up behind the slumbering turtle. His cute little neck was stretched out luxuriously in the sun, his intricately painted head like a statue. I raised my hand slowly up through the water and snatched him up.

His shiny black eyes popped open. His tiny feet and hands swam frantically in midair for a second or two and then he snapped everything away, like doors slamming shut.

I laughed and held up the closed shell for Roger to see. "The perfect creature! When it sees trouble, it hunkers down and waits for it to pass."

"Yeah, like you should do, instead of always yelling at everyone," Roger said.

I let his comment go and held the miraculous turtle on my open hand. How brilliant nature was. Together we waited and watched, not uttering a sound. After a few minutes, the turtle's head crept out. "He's looking right at me," Roger whispered. He leaned over to look more closely, and as he did the turtle extended a tentative foot and shot off my hand like a rocket. It landed in the water with a cartoonish plop, which made us laugh like crazed hyenas and agree that nature put on the best show on the entire planet.

We caught many turtles that day — twenty-three, to be exact. They came in all sizes, from as small as a quarter to one as big as a cereal bowl. We added just enough water and algae to the boat to keep them cool and happy and they clunked around on the aluminum bottom while our great turtle harvest continued.

Mummy's voice careened out over the water.

"Children! Pat! Roger! What on earth are you doing over there? Get back here right now. It's tea time!"

Roger took up the oars as I climbed back into the boat. "Ah, man, does she really have to call it that? And then yell it out over the whole lake? Doesn't she know everyone can hear her?"

Mummy stood next to the fishing dock in her yellow polka-dotted dress, waving her arms like a mad woman. Her short dark hair was newly frosted, and her lips were painted such a bright red I swear I could see them all the way across the lake. The wind picked up against us when we reached the middle so I took over the rowing. Roger may be a boy, but I was almost two years older and still stronger than him. I shifted in my seat. The aluminum was so hot it burned my legs. Roger splashed in some water to keep the turtles cool. They banged away happily on the metal bottom. Mummy was still waiting when we glided up onto the little beach in front of our house. There were rings of sweat under her arms. Her face was red.

"You naughty children, how dare you go out in the boat while we were away." Her arms were crossed over her chest, a cigarette in her hand. "You wait until your father gets home."

"We were bored," Roger said. "You're never here."

"We were fine," I said. "We know how to row and how to swim. Where's Daddy?"

"Your father had to go to the office. And it's not fine. You two are always breaking the rules." She dropped her cigarette onto the grass and rubbed it out with her flip-flop as if that's what she would like to do to us.

We pulled the boat far up onto the shore so it wouldn't blow away. While climbing out, I noticed algae still clinging to Roger's legs and sticking to his hair, which made him look like a swamp monster. I looked down and saw that I too was draped in moss. We pointed at each other and laughed uproariously.

Even Mummy giggled. "Look at you two," she said. "You filthy little monsters. In the bath, both of you!" She rubbed Roger's head and smiled at me, so apparently all would eventually be forgiven. We jumped into the cool lake to rinse off and went inside to take a bath and then gorged ourselves on shepherd's pie.

Roger went to baseball and I fell into a coma onto the couch, feeling like a snake with a massive rodent inside me to digest. I lay there with my sisters watching *The Beverly Hillbillies* and *The Andy Griffith Show* until Daddy joined us when he got home and changed the channel to *Star Trek*.

▽▽▽

Many hours later I awakened to a pink sky with a dull ache in my stomach. Something wasn't right. And then I remembered—the turtles. I leapt out of bed and tore open the sliding glass door, not even trying to be quiet. It was still warm. A washed-out moon hung full and heavy in the dull grayish pink sky.

The rowboat was right where we'd left it. I approached slowly. Tiny waves lapped at its back, but there was no thumping. I peeked into the boat. The turtles had gathered themselves into a circle, all tucked tightly into their shells. I prayed that they were sleeping.

"Please, God, please..."

I picked up one of the smaller ones, its shell tightly closed. I plopped it into the water. It floated for a moment, then tipped sideways and sank to the bottom, its shell remained closed.

One by one, I checked each turtle, but every single intricately painted masterpiece of nature sunk like a rock and came to rest on the sandy bottom.

They had cooked because of me. The heat of the aluminum had apparently done them in. I had joked about turtle soup. I had lolled around the house like a pig doing nothing except eating shepherd's pie and watching television all while an entire community of innocent creatures had gathered together in a loving circle—to die.

I dropped down onto the beach and let out a deep, choking sob. To think that, in the end, they had hunkered down together, a whole town full of turtles, and they had died by my hand.

Jasper jumped up into the boat and started sniffing around. I shouted and swatted him away, wanting to take my anger out on somebody.

That made me cry even harder. What kind of devil was I? Now I was hitting my own cat, who I loved to death.

When I finally pulled myself together, I decided at first not to wake Roger. I would go back to bed and try to sleep forever. But then I realized I couldn't let him find them the same way I had, so with tears streaming down my face, I put all twenty-three dead turtles carefully back into the boat, picked up Jasper and went inside to wake Roger. We sat at the end of his bed and I tapped him on his good shoulder and tried to be patient while he struggled to wake up. It always took him awhile.

He rubbed his eyes, not understanding what I was saying at first.

"They're dead, Roger, all of them."

He snapped upright.

"The turtles? Dead? Great, just great, Pat. You murdered them!"

"But you caught them, too."

"You said you would set them free. How could you forget?"

"Well, you didn't remember either."

"I was at baseball. Losing! And I did think about them."

"You did?"

"Yeah, during *Star Trek.*"

"Why didn't you say something?"

"I don't know." Tears filled his eyes. "I figured you'd let them go already."

"But why didn't you at least say something?"

"I said I don't know. I trusted you to do it."

"But..." I broke down again.

"Look, they were probably dead by then anyway."

"How do you know? Maybe we could have saved them."

"The heat killed them. They cooked."

"I know. I know. I know." I dropped my head into my arms and cried some more.

"Stop crying like that, you're getting snot everywhere."

But I couldn't stop. Roger and I were the two people in the world who were most determined to save it, and now we were destroying it. Human beings were ridiculous. Doomed.

"Okay. Well, whatever," he said. "So what if we murdered a couple dozen turtles? It's not the end of the world."

But in a way, it was. We never again caught another turtle—or any other creature, for that matter. Never again would we scoop up handfuls of wriggling tadpoles in the muddy pond down the hill, or sit for hours waiting for a rabbit to peek out of his grassy hut. The next time we ventured out in the boat, it would be to sneak across the lake to drink beer and smoke cigarettes.

I had read that people who harmed turtles were in for some serious bad luck, so I hunkered down to wait for whatever was coming next. It didn't take long. One night I awakened from the depths of a dark dream to the sound of my mother crying through the shared wall of our bedrooms. I got up to use the restroom and rallied the courage to go in and check on her. Her bedroom door was wide open. Moon shadows from the sycamore tree spilled over their massive king-sized bed, which was empty except for my tiny mother, curled up on her side. Her spikey short hair, now frosted a wide range of colors from silver to orange to black, was all I could see.

She stopped crying and rolled over when I sat down on the bed.

"Are you okay, Mummy? What's wrong?"

She sniffed and took a deep breath. "He's gone."

"What? Daddy? No. He'll be back. He's probably just at work."

"No, he's gone. He's fallen in love with his secretary. He's moving out."

"No, Mummy, no way."

"Go on, my lovely, back to bed. I'm fine. We'll all be fine. He has to support us or they can send him to jail. Don't worry. Go on. Back to sleep."

I walked around the bed to check my father's closet, thinking how much he would hate to be in jail. The white louvered doors were flung open and most of his clothes were gone. His soft wool sweaters, his sharp black suits, the racing cap he loved so much—it had all vanished, along with the only person who believed in me.

On his nightstand, under a book by Ralph Waldo Emerson, lay the February issue of *Playboy*. I picked up the glossy pink magazine sneakily and hid it at my side, kissed the back of my mother's head, and told her good night.

I slipped quietly back into my room and closed the door, then climbed into bed and turned on the reading light. I opened the *Playboy* to the centerfold, a full-color nude photograph of a beautiful blond woman with hot-pink lips. Her perfect nipples on her perfect breasts were the exact same color as her lips and the satin sheets. This must be the kind of woman my father had fallen in love with. Maybe she was the best way to be, all pink and frosty and loving, surrounded by silky satin sheets.

Jasper snuggled up to me and I flipped through the magazine, trying to work it all out in my head, when I turned the page and found an interview with R. Buckminster Fuller — I kid you not. But I didn't even bother to read it. Something about his ideas seemed too far out there, pure fantasies about an impossibly perfect world that was obviously not going to happen.

COSMIC
SURFING

1982

Life is but a dream. And I can prove it.
— Buckminster Fuller

I wore the same navy suit as the day before, since I had only one and couldn't fathom meeting a famous genius wearing anything less than a suit. I arrived at the ninety-eighth floor of the John Hancock Center twenty minutes early to make sure I would not be late. I seated myself squarely on the brown leather bench across from the elevators and prepared to meet the modern-day Leonardo da Vinci.

A constant stream of tourist families and businesspeople emerged from the elevator, distracting me from my thoughts. What a nuisance the children were, screaming and running all around. I had pretty much decided I would never want to have them, which was probably a convenient thing since, so far, I was entirely unlucky in love.

The shiny brass elevator doors dispensed tourists again and again, until they finally slid open to reveal the one and only R. Buckminster Fuller.

I sprang up from the bench to greet him. There was something immediately charming in the sight of his smiling face and bulging eyes, his large head barely fringed with neat white stubble. A camel's hair coat hung loosely over a brown vest and khaki dress slacks. He held a tan fedora hat in his hands and wore a Burberry scarf around his neck.

Our eyes connected through his thick glasses; his pupils were like enormous gray sea anemones whose depth I could not imagine. He reached out his massive hand, ridged with mountainous purple veins, as if great wisdom had built up there. When our hands touched, I felt a surge of energy shoot through me as surely as if I'd touched a wall socket.

"You must be Patricia Field," he said, as if I were the special one.

"Yes, Dr. Fuller. It is an honor to meet you."

It occurred to me that his scarf and coat seemed too bankerly for the man who had coined the term "Spaceship Earth" and hung out with hippies in Golden Gate Park, but give him a break. He was, after all, eighty-six years old.

"Please, call me Bucky." His eyes danced with mine. "Everybody does."

"Okay. And everyone calls me Pat."

"Then Bucky and Pat it is."

The pale man standing next to him, who I had barely noticed until now, introduced himself as Dr. Fuller's assistant—no doubt the same man I'd spoken to on the phone. He looked at his watch. "Very well, then," he said to

Bucky. "I will return for you at six p.m. to take you to your signing at Barbara's Bookstore."

He turned to me. "Miss Field, enjoy the lesson of a lifetime." He gave me an odd wink, then turned away and pushed the button for the elevator. It occurred to me he was happy to be making an escape.

Four hours? What were we going to talk about for four whole hours? I had read somewhere that Bucky spoke at a rate of seven thousand words an hour, which meant twenty-eight thousand words were about to hit me. I reached into my briefcase, feeling for my notebook and pens. I knew from my reporting days that notes were like gold, especially if was something complicated. I could always look it up later.

Bucky set an alarm on his pocket watch, tucked it away into his vest pocket, and in a gentle, cultivated New England voice, he said, "It is very nice to see you, Pat. One day, you will come to understand the odd time and space continuum of our meeting here today."

What? Had the planet's friendly genius just launched us off a paranormal cliff?

"I know it is a difficult concept to grasp," he continued, "but time is not linear, and our paths will cross again and again."

I nodded, mesmerized by his words. I wanted to follow up with a question, but my mind went blank so instead I just smiled and nodded and pretended like I understood. Not exactly my most shining moment as a reporter.

He furrowed his brow. "As you already know, just because you don't understand something doesn't mean it's not true."

I gave him a small smile. "I feel like I've heard those words before."

"And it is certainly no reason not to keep listening."

"Yes, of course. But you know, I never really expect to understand anything anyway." Realizing how stupid that must have sounded, I willed myself to just stop talking and listen. I was a reporter after all. I reached for my pen. I would get it all down then figure it out later.

"You are exactly right," he said. "We can never be sure of our comprehension, since almost all physical realities are incomprehensible by humans, at least for now."

I couldn't resist trying. "But surely we know what we ourselves comprehend?"

"Aha, not quite — but you are on the right track. One day, we will. One day, humans will have that capability. We are evolving in that direction."

Another noisy group of tourists poured out of the elevator.

He gestured toward a staircase and gallantly held out his arm for me. "I want to start up on the rooftop. There is something I want to show you."

He led the way out through a thick metal door at the top of a concrete staircase. Behind us the door slammed shut, sending us aloft into a brilliant blue sky dotted with tiny cotton balls of clouds. A tiny river of traffic streamed far below on Lake Shore Drive.

As he led me to the north side of the roof he turned to me to make sure I was listening. "The first thing you should know is that I am here with you today because you will still be breathing this sweet Earthian air long after I am gone."

The hair on the back of my neck stood up. I knew I had heard these exact words before.

"There are great breakthroughs coming, an awakening of sorts, which your generation will lead us to," he said, reaching out his hands as if to capture the entire universe in them. "Human consciousness is evolving to where we will be able to use our minds to make the world work for one hundred percent of humanity."

I pulled out my notebook and my best pen.

"To make this happen, we must all begin to live lives of conscious evolution, bearing responsibility for all that we are, which is nature's finest and most complex experiment."

"Conscious evolution—nature's finest experiment" were the first words I wrote, feeling very much like an imposter, despite the quality of my pen. Surely someone really smart should be taking notes about something as important as the evolution of humanity. I wanted to apologize right then and tell him I wasn't sure why I was there.

Bucky seemed to sense my nervousness because he stopped to think a minute, then pointed northward up Lake Michigan. "This is where I want to start, at what was going to be the end for me. Right there, in Montrose Harbor." He pointed along the lakefront.

"It was a freezing day in November of 1927. My wife and I had just had a new baby. We'd only recently lost our four-year-old daughter to meningitis, which was at least partly my fault. I had been out gallivanting around like some big-shot architect and inventor, jabbering on and on about how to improve living conditions for all humanity while my own four-year-old daughter died in our drafty apartment."

I looked down at the shoreline. It seemed hard to imagine that such a famous genius had once thought himself a failure, responsible for his own child's death. I scribbled furiously to get it all down.

"I turned out to be a terrible businessman, never bothered enough about money. My new business went belly-up just as Anne gave birth to another daughter. I realized that if she got my life insurance money, she would have what she needed to take care of the baby."

The sun felt overly warm, but I didn't want to take the time to struggle out of my jacket. "How were you going to do it?" I asked, a bead of sweat running down my back.

His eyes locked onto mine. "Well, I was just going to jump into the water and swim out as far as I could." He stopped for a minute, letting himself float back to his fifty-year-old memory. But I saw no sadness in his eyes. His face was alight with the passion of a superb storyteller.

"Something amazing happened then," he said. "A voice inside my head spoke to me, saying, 'What right do you have to end a life? You do not belong to you. You belong to all of humanity.' I made a bargain with myself that I would allow myself to live, but only if I set out to serve all of humanity. I would discover the principles operative in Universe, the design laws of nature, and I would turn them over to my fellow man. I would make every day of my life an experiment to see what one ordinary little person could accomplish if he set out to work for the good of everyone."

He'd saved himself by latching onto a passion. That certainly sounded familiar, although I wasn't sure interviewing a genius whose ideas I barely understood was going to help me find mine.

"I went back home and took a vow of silence," Bucky continued. "I would not allow myself to speak. I would only let myself read and write and think until I understood the truth about things. When I reflect on all those months and how Anne put up with me through it all—especially since we had just had another baby and I had no money coming in—well, I'm not sure what I did to deserve her. But that is a story for another day."

Now he was talking about love, something I knew nothing about. I could not fathom how it would feel to know you were loved even though you had contributed nothing for two whole years except to be physically present, especially with a needy baby in the house.

He held his fingertips together to divine his next thought. "I stripped away everything about myself and got down to the truth of things. I asked myself the most fundamental of questions: What is the nature of Universe? My understanding of math brought me to realize that nature is governed by relatively few principles, and that only by understanding these principles can we secure our future as a species."

The mere mention of math made me worry the conversation was about to fly over my head. I had loved geometry in junior high, but recoiled from high school algebra and then never went back to math. It just didn't seem like a worthy use of a perfectly good brain, I told anyone who asked. But of course, it was more that I didn't have the aptitude or the attitude for grasping the hard stuff.

Bucky was still talking. Time to quit wool-gathering. "The next thing I want you to realize," he said, "is that ninety-nine-point nine percent of all that is now transpiring in human activity is taking place within the realms of a reality which is utterly invisible, inaudible, unsmellable, and untouchable by humans."

Now he was talking a language I understood. He had cracked open an invisible window in my mind. I had always sensed there was more going on in the world than anyone knew.

"The essence of Universe is not about matter but about design," he said. "Everything we can touch and see is nothing but patterns of continually moving electrons and protons, including you and me."

His words had a rhythm that made perfect sense. "Nothing is solid. There is no matter. Life is but a dream, you know. And I can prove it."

I laughed to be caught up in the perfect storm of such an astonishing brain. It made me feel disconnected for a moment, but then he circled around to pick me up, as a parent would a child.

"You see, humans use only a small part of their brains and have not yet come to understand the collective mind. They don't realize the human mind has possibilities beyond their wildest dreams. But once you write all about it, people will begin to pursue these possibilities. And eventually, humanity will evolve to a whole new level. They will become syntrophic, not entropic, and will begin to make all the right choices for all the right reasons."

Once I write all about it? And what did he mean by "life is but a dream and I can prove it"? Why did he keep referring to humans as "they"? Was he trying to distance himself? Was he reading my mind, knowing how little I understood of what he was saying? A dozen questions swirled around in my head, but I just kept writing, trusting it to eventually make sense.

"Humans have been discouraged from seeking their own inner, deeper natures. They must begin to live lives of conscious evolution and reconnect with the natural world. They must evolve on purpose, consciously. Do you understand?"

"Um, yes, kind of. I guess I do." But I didn't, not really. How could a person choose to evolve? And what on earth did nature's design principles have to do with any of it? It was a thick bramble of ideas, invisible patterns he wove in the air with his hands. I could sense that it all made sense, even though I didn't understand it—because, of course, it was beyond human capability to do so. But if that was the case, how was I ever going to write about it?

He must have sensed my doubt. "As long as you keep listening, you will eventually understand everything you need to know, exactly when you need to know it."

Now he was right inside my head.

"I know," I said. "Of course." Although of course I didn't. Not really.

The heat overwhelmed me. I took off my jacket and slung it over the railing. A cool breeze wash relief over my arms.

Bucky went on to explain that humans had been conditioned, especially recently, to believe in false, outdated notions. He said our language must become more precise to assure we were not mistakenly accepting lies as truths.

For instance, there is no up or down in *Universe*, he said, which should always be capitalized and used without an article like *the*, since there was only one of them. He said we must take care to speak accurately, that it was critical to our success.

We should not talk of going *up* or *down*, but rather *in* and *out* from Earth's center of gravity. And instead of the sun *rising* or *setting*, which of course it did neither, we should call it what it really is: a *sunclipse* in the evening and a *sunsight* in the morning.

"When we tell children to '*watch the sunrise*' and '*enjoy the sunset*,' we replace their natural-born genius with conditioned ignorance," he said.

He stopped for a moment to let me finish writing. My hand had cramped up, and he sighed when I stopped to shake it out. Was he becoming impatient with me? His ideas were shooting out of him with the force of a fire hose, and it was my job to capture every drop.

"The old Newtonian world will soon be replaced by a true grasp of Einstein's ideas," he continued. "Newton said in the first law of motion that a body persists in a state of rest except when it is affected by other bodies. Normal was at rest. Einstein flipped all of this on its head. There is no such thing as rest. Everything is moving, always."

Of course the earth was always moving, both rotating and orbiting around the sun. But what difference did that make to the future of humanity? At this rate, I was pretty sure I would never be able to write convincingly about things I didn't understand.

He seemed to sense my bewilderment. "Would you like to try a little cosmic surfing?"

I nodded enthusiastically, relieved at the chance for any change of subject, even though I was pretty sure "cosmic surfing" was what we were already doing.

He told me to put my notebook aside and stand straight and tall, but to relax my shoulders, which I realized were scrunched up around my ears. He had me face west and told me to close my eyes and hold my arms straight out at my sides. I did as he said and took a slow deep breath.

"Find your balance now, as if you were standing on a surfboard—because that is exactly what you are doing all the time. You are on a continually moving spaceship called Earth, and you are cruising through Universe at about a thousand miles an hour as Earth spins on its axis."

I peeked out to see that Bucky's arms were also out-stretched, his eyes also closed. An older couple with a camera eyed us curiously, but I didn't care. I closed my eyes again and sensed myself spinning on Spaceship Earth, the sun warming my face.

He gave me a moment. Then his voice grew softer. "Now, with your eyes still closed, sense that while you are spinning around Earth's axis, you are also simultaneously sailing around the sun at a rate of about sixty-seven thousand miles per hour."

My arms were splayed apart, and I forgot all about the onlookers and had a momentary awareness of myself as a tiny speck in a huge universe, one small human body fully conscious of itself. I was a goose bump–covered cosmic surfer in the full light of day, gliding through the galaxy, feeling the magic of my own radically profound existence. This was the education I'd been waiting for.

I almost forgot Bucky was there until he spoke again. "Humans must have faith in their own inner natures to guide them. They must understand they are interconnected with nature, that they continue to exist only at her pleasure. They must realize the power to destroy nature is also the power to destroy themselves. Even the best of intentions will lead to terrible outcomes if they are not aware of this power."

I wanted badly to write it all down, yet didn't dare open my eyes and ruin the moment. Not yet. He had taken me to another plane, a calm and golden place inside my own mind that I never wanted to leave. It was like my brain was resetting itself.

Something clicked. I got it. It wasn't just a cool idea that humans were swirling balls of energy. This idea was essential to humanity's future. I may not be able to get the math behind it, but this idea was as clear as could be.

A cool breeze hit my arms and I was beginning to wonder if goose bumps had taken up permanent residency on my body.

I opened my eyes and grabbed for my notebook and pen.

Bucky laughed. "I think you're starting to understand. Using your intuition is cosmic fishing. You feel a nibble, then you've got to hook the fish."

"By George, I think I've got it," I agreed with a laugh.

He let me write until I got it all down. It was starting to make sense. The world was fixable. Humans could do it — even those who had failed to live up to their potential. It wasn't too late. Enlightenment, which would come from understanding these global and profound ideas, would save the world — and I would help bring it all to light. I knew I had to tell Bucky's whole story.

"So, what happened after you saved yourself from suicide and went silent for two years?" I asked.

"Oh yes, of course. Well, by about 1929, I was feeling much better and had had some breakthroughs in understanding nature's design principles. I decided to celebrate by going down to Navy Pier to see an exhibition of Henry Ford's new cars, and while I was walking along Michigan Avenue near the Water Tower, I got a sparkly feeling all over, a sensation that my feet were floating off the ground."

His face lit up like a child's, an ancient and wise son of the universe. He splayed out his hands and made his fingers dance like he was playing the piano. This was the most animated I'd seen him yet.

"As I was floating along the sidewalk," he said, "a voice came into my head that said, 'You no longer need temporal attestation of your thoughts. You think the truth.'"

"What does 'temporal attestation' mean?" I underlined the two words.

"It meant I no longer needed to look beyond myself for validation. The very idea of this launched me into the greatest creative period of my life. I believed in my own insights. This outlook helped give rise to most of my inventions."

I couldn't fathom having that kind of confidence. If you believed your own thoughts were the absolute truth, wasn't that like believing you were some kind of god? He stopped talking and stared out at the horizon. A warm light seemed to float above and around his head. Were my eyes playing tricks on me? Whatever it was, I needed no temporal attestation to know that I was in the presence of someone extraordinary, some kind of wizard. A modern-day Merlin in a brown suit. No wonder he referred to humans as "they."

Just then, the sun disappeared behind an ominous gray cloud. A chilly wind whipped in off the lake. I shivered and put my jacket back on. Bucky suggested we go back inside for a cup of tea. We walked side by side, our heads down against wind. He insisted on pulling the heavy metal door open for me. As we entered the stairwell, the door slammed shut with a ferocious boom and echoed off the concrete walls.

"This wind is crazy," I called out too loudly.

He chuckled. "You do know that wind doesn't actually blow, right? Wind sucks."

I couldn't help laughing and said in my best radio newscaster voice, "Yes, Dr. Fuller, wind certainly does suck, especially here in Chicago."

"But it actually does," he said, close behind me on the stairs. "Wind happens when low pressure creates a vacuum. Air sucked into that vacuum is what creates the sensation of wind. The idea that wind 'blows' is just one more of man's failures in thinking, inadequate language that keeps us in the dark."

I excused myself to the restroom, thinking "wind sucks" would make a great Chicago punch line. I settled on a toilet and flipped through my notes, trying to figure out what to ask him about next. Everything felt jumbled again.

What good was it to know we were insignificant specks of swirling matter surfing along on a great rock hurtling through space? It seemed like a huge idea, but how was it relevant? I couldn't see how a new, higher level of consciousness based on this revelation would do anything to improve humanity's relationship with nature and thereby help us to survive.

And then there was the matter of how it all related to me. Throughout our conversation, moments of self-doubt volleyed erratically against a growing sense of grandeur. Was I being chosen? It felt almost like I was being anointed, or at least appointed. But was I the one brilliant person who would understand Bucky's genius enough to share it with the world, or merely a big talking Indiana girl who had smooth-talked her way into an interview?

AHEAD OF HIS TIME

1982

Ninety-nine percent of who you are is invisible and untouchable.
— Buckminster Fuller

Back in the cavernous two-story dining room, Bucky was seated in a booth under massive west-facing windows. Hazy sunlight luxuriously drenched the room and lit up his nearly bald head. He was writing his own notes on a yellow legal pad with four different colored pens lined up at its side. A waitress was approaching with white china cups on saucers and stainless steel pots of hot water.

He looked up as I scooted into the booth and thanked the waitress with a smile then put a tea bag into his pot of hot water.

"I'm not quite sure where to start," he said simply.

Start? Surely we were about to start wrapping up?

He snapped the top onto a red pen and slipped it into the plastic protector in his shirt pocket. Why did he carry so many different colored pens? And why did he have three watches, one on each arm and another in his vest pocket? I also wanted to get him talking more about his inventions, and I needed clarification on the whole conscious evolution thing. Did he mean we needed to evolve our level of consciousness? Or consciously evolve our whole selves? Or both?

But Bucky had his own agenda. "I have a great deal more to tell you, Pat, and I am happy to see you take such thorough notes. They will be important one day."

Right. No pressure. I pulled out my notepad and pen and flipped to a blank page.

"Okay, what's next?"

"Well, I guess I should tell you that America is likely to fail."

He said this as matter-of-factly as if predicting the sun would appear again tomorrow.

"That's awful," I said. The words came tumbling out. "How? Why? I love America. How could it fail?"

I wrote at the top of a new page in all caps: "AMERICA COULD FAIL."

"It's not really that awful, but inevitable and probably necessary. There are two hundred and forty captains on this planet all running different ships, and we need to integrate and work together as one United Spaceship Planet Earth. But thus far, America's intense sense of nationalism is making it impossible for us to integrate with the rest of the world."

My stomach tightened. I remembered the most frequently uttered phrase of my childhood, always from the lips of my father: "Bloody stupid Americans." He had railed about how foolish Americans were to support a warmongering government with an insatiable military industrial obsession, which was constantly creating new enemies in every corner of the world. It was all too easy, he said, for evil leaders to sell their well-crafted lies to all the bloody stupid Americans.

But my father had created his own pack of well-crafted lies, and in doing so he had lost all credibility in my eyes. His complete lack of integrity somehow negated everything he had ever said. All his talk about Bucky's revolutionary ideas now seemed hypocritical. Yet here was the real thing, the famous genius himself, saying exactly what my father used to say.

"Because we think we are too big to fail, failure is the likely outcome," Bucky said. "Americans are being deceived in many ways. But the world is changing fast. Communism is about to fall, and America will have the opportunity to lead in the creation of a new world government. But it's not looking like we will rise to the occasion." He pushed up his glasses by scrunching up his nose and leaned in across the table so he could speak more quietly. "We are becoming a great bully in some parts of the world, launching more wars than any other country. Those we have oppressed will revolt against us. Future wars will not be waged between countries, but by oppressed rogue groups who will organize and create new ways to attack us to bring the whole system down, starting with the economy."

I expelled the breath I didn't know I was holding. "But exactly what would happen if America failed?"

"Well, most likely, we would break up into a series of smaller nation-states. The East Coast might form its own nation-state, then the Southern States, the Great Plains, and of course, California."

A smile came over his face. He said he lived in California now, in a beautiful home near the ocean with his wife of sixty-six years. The weather there was rarely too hot and never too cold; he called it Goldilocks weather. I could scarcely believe such a place existed. In the Midwest, most days were too hot or too cold or too humid or too windy or too hazy—always too something.

Bucky leaned toward me and lowered his voice. "Once the United States dissolves, California should consider joining with Mexico and Alaska. That would create a true Pacific Rim Empire rich in farmland, energy, and labor. It would be a great place from which to steer our great planetary ship forward. It might also be a good spot for weathering a deteriorating atmosphere, since Pacific winds will help clear the air."

"It all sounds so... scary," I said, also lowering my voice so the young children in the booth behind him would be spared. "You're telling me the country I love is likely to fail?"

"Well, of course I don't know exactly what is coming, only what is likely based on what is happening now. But look, don't fret over these things. You mustn't get upset. The trick is to stay determined and know that if you keep an open mind, stick with the truth, and share what you know when the time comes, everything will turn out fine."

When the time comes? What did he mean by that? And how could he possibly know what was coming? I was saddened by the possibilities and wished they seemed a little more farfetched than they did.

"I cannot imagine how failure could be fine." I turned my head away so he wouldn't see me blinking back tears like a baby.

His voice remained calm. "America must learn to integrate with the rest of the world. If this great planetary ship of ours is to be righted, the divisions between nations must almost imperceptibly vanish. Selfish and short-term pursuits will be no longer welcomed or workable in an increasingly interdependent world society. Traditional power structures and their reign of darkness must be rendered obsolete."

He stopped to let it sink in. It sounded like revolution was inevitable, and I suspected it would be ugly. I envisioned him atop a proud white stallion on some mountaintop, wearing a red cape and brandishing a glittering sword, leading humanity onward to something better.

I put my teabag into the now lukewarm water of my teapot.

"Another way humans dwell in the dark ages is by believing that man was meant to dominate nature," he continued. "This is false and dangerous thinking. We must go along with nature's principles and let her run things. It is important for you to understand that humans are teleological."

My mind went blank. I looked up the word later. Both Plato and Aristotle had talked about teleological concerns, that human behavior is largely determined by nature. In other words, the reason behind most everything we think and do is that we're programmed by our nature.

For example, humans will do anything to protect their children, even when they behave like little turds as were the two little boys wriggling around in the booth behind Bucky, swinging at each other with their fists to torture their poor mother. The grimy one sneered at me, snot running from his nose, while the embarrassed mother grimaced and gently shushed them. It would be my teleological nature to swat them, since I had no interest in having children at all. Children were meant for people who had given up on living their own dreams.

Bucky was forging ahead, reintroducing a seemingly contradictory idea that had opened a door in my mind long ago.

"Whether humanity makes it will be up to the individual."

His eyes locked onto mine, and I wondered if he could see in my eyes that I had sold out any integrity I might have had by leaving journalism. That instead of saving the world, I was now telling kids to keep their eyes on their fries.

"It's true," he continued, his voice softening. "Something hit me very hard once, thinking about what one little person could do. Just think about a ship like the Queen Mary. The whole great ocean liner goes by, and then comes the rudder, and then there's a tiny thing on the edge of the rudder called a trim tab. Moving that little trim tab builds a low pressure that turns the whole ship. Takes almost no effort at all. So I say that the ordinary individual can be just like a trim tab. Society thinks it's going right by you, that it's left you behind altogether. But if you're doing dynamic things mentally, the fact is that you can just put your little ideas out there and make the whole big ship of state turn around—all because of you."

Growing up on the water, he explained, he'd marveled at how much control he could have over an entire boat using just the tiny rudder all the way in the back. "People believe they have no power, but that is just one more false assumption we have come to accept. For example, we have been conditioned to believe in scarcity, that it always must be *us* versus *them*. Because of this, we have come to accept that poverty, disease, and war are inevitable. Forever."

He shook his head sadly. "This is only true if we believe it to be." He linked this notion back to Darwin's idea of survival of the fittest, which I recognized, and said that's what has made us assume competition to the death is the best we could hope for. "Those who say a utopian world is not possible have been preconditioned to expect less of humanity. Malthus was wrong."

I had no idea who Malthus was—another thing to look up later, when I learned he was a renowned British scholar and economist who said that human beings would always have to compete for resources since resources would always be limited.

But now Bucky was saying the new reality could be the opposite of that, that we could live in a world of abundance if only we set out with that as our objective. "Man has the capability, through proper planning and allocation of natural resources, to forever feed himself and house himself and live in workless leisure."

Bucky had proven this mathematically back in 1940, he said, in a study published by *Fortune* magazine. He'd shown that only slight changes in how the world's resources were managed would be necessary to permit one hundred percent of humanity to thrive. The trick was to focus on creating livingry, as he called it, instead of weaponry. We had to shift our energy and resources toward life-supporting technologies. It sounded like a mathematically provable loaves-and-fishes story.

"But we must choose," he concluded. "It's either all of us, or none of us."

It made perfect sense. Suddenly I had a thousand questions about how to make all this happen, but Bucky's pocket watch made a loud beep. It was six o'clock. Four hours had passed.

How could that be? Hadn't we just sat down?

I was afraid if he stopped talking now, it would all fly right out of my head. Moments of absolute clarity were sandwiched between folds of unrelatable words and ideas. Every time I felt I was about to stitch it all together, the meaning would slip away.

And I still hadn't even asked him why he had three watches and carried so many different colored pens.

He reached for the check and I tried to grab it, but he insisted on paying, calling it an investment in the future. When I laughed and said I sure hoped I'd been worth four hours and a cup of tea, he sighed. I saw a staggering weight in his eyes. What a burden it must be to know you had important, even critical wisdom to convey to a world that was more interested in making money than making sense.

He put a ten-dollar bill into the leather holder. A random question escaped from my mouth. "Do you have any regrets about your life?"

He thought for a moment. "Only one. If I could do it all over again, I think I would have been a song and dance man."

That stumped me. The idea of a Hollywood version of Bucky dancing in a tuxedo like some nerdy version of Frank Sinatra made me smile. "Really? Why a song and dance man?"

"Well, as you will come to understand, is it difficult to get people to listen to the truth when it's painful or if their paycheck depends on their not listening. I've thought many times that if I could have sung and danced my ideas and maybe even been funny, I might have gotten more attention."

It was inconceivable to me that this great man could feel like a failure. The regret in his gentle eyes made me want to lift him out of the booth and break into song and dance — not that I had any talents whatsoever in that regard.

I scooped up my own belongings. "But people do listen to you, don't they? Haven't you spoken all over the planet, hundreds of times, to hundreds of thousands of people? You've been on national TV and on the cover of *Time* magazine."

He stood and gathered up his coat and scarf. "Ah, but that was some years ago. Times have changed. There are

powers at work now to delegitimize me and make my ideas invisible — or at least unbelievable. They're calling me a
quack."

"Who is? And why? Why would anybody want to make
you invisible?"

He shook his head. "Ah, well, my darling, that is a story
for another day. Suffice it to say we are entering something
of a dark age in America today."

He ambled slowly toward the elevators as I scrambled
to make sure I had everything and catch up. A gray-haired
woman in an expensive cream-colored suit converged on
his path, and her face lit up when she recognized Bucky.

"Why hello there, Dr. Fuller," she cooed in a Southern
accent.

Bucky stopped and graciously shook her hand. My
heart leapt to see his gentlemanly nature and warm man-
ner with a complete stranger. He really did seem to think
himself as an ordinary man.

The woman followed us to the elevator, chatting on
about Bucky's domes and his Old Man River project for
East St. Louis, which she said she had followed with great
interest because she lived nearby. It would be a whole new
kind of self-sustaining community, she said, and while I
didn't doubt she was right, I resented her intrusion, especially since I knew my time with him was running out.

The elevator arrived, and Bucky held the door open for
me. He beamed like a young boy as the elevator zoomed
weightlessly down — or more precisely, inward — toward
the center of the earth. His eyes lit up, and the decades fell
away from his face as he raised his hands over his head as
if we were on a roller coaster.

"Isn't this new world miraculous?" he asked me.

I didn't know what to say or how to thank him. I made
some lame crack about how impossible it would be to fit

all his ideas into one magazine story, that I would probably need to write a whole book. He dropped his arms and took on a newly serious tone. "I don't want you to worry about any of that right now. Everything will unfold as it should, and you will know exactly what you need to know when you need to know it. You are a good listener, Miss Pat, and an excellent note-taker. You will do just fine."

"I will do my best, Bucky." It was the first time I had called him by his preferred name.

He smiled. "Don't do it for me. It's not about me. Do it for all of humanity."

"Oh. I will—I mean, I will try my best. But don't forget I'm no genius, just an ordinary person. The idea that one day I'll be able to bring your amazing thinking back into the mainstream—well, it seems a little crazy right now."

"Ah, but ordinary human beings are magnificently endowed with creativity. We are mysteriously more capable than anyone thinks possible."

I smiled. "Well then, if ordinary equals magnificent, then I might have a chance."

Bucky gave a decisive nod of his head.

The elevator stopped and the doors slid open, but nobody got on. It was an odd moment that puzzled him, and he looked at me and said, "Never forget that you are one of a kind. If there weren't any need for you in all your uniqueness to be on this earth, you wouldn't be here. And never forget, no matter how overwhelming life's challenges and problems seem to be, one person can make a difference. In fact, it is always because of one person that the changes that matter most come about. So be that one person."

It was the best thing anybody had ever said to me. It seemed to be proof he believed in me.

The elevator sped down, or inward. I had time for one last question, which I regretted the moment it flew out of my mouth. "What kind of weather do you like best?"

Duh. My last chance to unearth the ideas of a great genius and I asked about the weather. Good going, Miss Star Reporter.

But he surprised me once again. "I love all kinds of weather, but my favorite is when it rains and the sun shines at the same time."

The elevator doors opened, and I stepped out behind him. Beyond the floor-to-ceiling glass windows of the huge lobby there fell a misty rain, all lit up by the late afternoon sun—Bucky's favorite weather, right on cue. Had he ordered it up just for me? Was he trying to demonstrate just how magnificently endowed human beings were?

We stood together and watched the sun and rain dance together in a mist that rose in the canyons of air between the high-rises. We stepped outside through the revolving door, and Bucky reached out his hands as if to catch the luminous drops and then he presented them to me like some metaphysical gift, a feast on a platter of air.

"Isn't she beautiful?"

"Who?"

"Nature, of course. Just look at her. She is like humanity's situation right now, rainy and sunny at the same time."

We walked toward a black sedan waiting for Bucky at the curb. A scruffy hobo on the sidewalk next to a lamp post held a sign proclaiming The End is Near.

Bucky glanced at me to make sure I had seen it. "Now there is a man ahead of his time."

I laughed. The man glowered at me, his red-rimmed eyes cold and unforgiving.

The pale man from earlier emerged from the sedan and opened the door for Bucky, who adjusted his scarf and reached out his hand to shake mine. He looked me squarely in the eye, the way you do when you have just shared mind-blowing secrets with a good friend. I wanted to hug him but didn't dare in front of the other man. The sunlit raindrops pirouetted around us. The planet's friendly genius climbed into the sedan and was gone.

I dug out a five-dollar bill and dropped it in the hobo's hat.

A FEW
FORGOTTEN
THINGS

In nature, empty vessels play a critical role. They carry things forward in time. — Buckminster Fuller

Barry the doorman jumped up off his stool and gave the revolving door a push.

"Hello there, Miss Pat. Did you have a fabulous day?" A wide grin lit up his face.

"Hi, Barry. Um, yes, incredible! Intense, though. Really intense."

"A good kind of intense, I hope?"

This was the moment I realized Bucky's ideas would never make good small talk. What was I supposed to say? *I've just spent the afternoon with a great genius who says America is collapsing and that our survival as a species requires we evolve consciously, starting right now, or else?* Or I could even go all metaphysical on him: *Yes, Barry, I've just learned on*

*good authority that we are not matter at all but overlapping se-
ries of energy events, and that knowing that really does matter.*

Instead, I took a deep breath and said, "Yep, all's good,
Barry, thanks. How are your kids?"

Barry always had something nice to say. Just having a
doorman was enough to make me want to throw my hat
into the air, but his thousand-watt smile made me feel like
a million bucks. He had looked out for me ever since the
rainy day last October when I became the first person, according to Barry, ever to move into Harbor Point with my
belongings in a pickup truck.

Since then, Barry had rescued me from a couple of overly enthusiastic dates who tried to follow me up the elevator even after I said goodnight. Once he'd even bailed me
out when I didn't have enough money for cab fare. Barry
was a like a protective father who ran off the jerks and
slipped me a twenty when I needed it.

Up in my eleventh-floor studio, I kicked off my shoes,
sank my toes into the thick shag carpeting, and looked out
through the curved wall of floor-to-ceiling windows that
framed my view of the harbor. The masts of yachts swayed
in the evening breeze. The street lights across Grant Park
along Michigan Avenue flickered to life.

My stomach growled with hunger. I mindlessly popped
a Lean Cuisine into the microwave, poured myself a glass
of Chardonnay, and picked up the princess phone from my
bedside table to call my father. I had bought a twenty-five-
foot extension cord for the phone so I could talk wherever I
wanted to, even in the bathtub. Affordable cordless phones
were supposed to be available soon, but I wasn't holding
my breath.

I hadn't talked to him in ages. We hadn't ever really
patched things up. I knew I would never forgive him for
how he'd mangled and pummeled our entire family just to

be with some busty blond secretary at his office. But he and I still saw eye to eye on world events and politics, and I knew my meeting with Bucky was something he would appreciate.

"You interviewed the one and only Bucky? Wow, Pat, that's incredible," he said. "That's fabulous, bloody excellent."

I told him all about it, leafing through my notes. When I mentioned the words "conscious evolution," he interrupted me.

"He said those exact words way back when, don't you remember?"

"Kind of, I guess I do."

"You were about eleven or twelve, I think. It was around the time..."

"When your troubles began?" I'd never challenged him before.

He stammered. "Well, um, yes, I suppose you're right about that, it was right around that time."

There was silence. I waited. He had never apologized. I really wanted an apology. I wanted to give him another chance to be open and honest, to have a dose of that individual integrity Bucky had spoken about. But he stonewalled, like always.

"What a day we had, huh?"

"Yes, Daddy, it was an amazing day, but—"

"He looked right at you. Remember? He said you would be the one to save the world."

"Roger didn't much like that."

He laughed.

Memories flooded back, but not of Bucky. Instead I saw my mother's anguished face and perpetual flood of tears following her discovery of his affair and then the fresh deluge of misery upon his eventual return. I wasn't quite sure how or why Mummy had taken him back, only that she had joked that he'd returned home because he liked the way she laundered his shirts. Leaving our friends and lakefront home to move to Mishawaka was one more torturous death march I would never forget.

I gave him one last chance. "Daddy, do you remember what Bucky said about individual integrity? That owning the truth was what mattered most to the entire future of humanity?"

"I do."

"So how do you reconcile that with what you did? You had four children. Do you have any idea how awful you made things for us back then?"

He mumbled something about needing to get back to work, said goodbye, and hung up.

The microwave beeped again, apparently my signal to let down and cry, and to let Bucky's ideas fly right out of my head. Something about Daddy's unwillingness to face the truth made me think nobody would ever care what a benevolent old genius had to say about the plight of humanity. It was no longer the seventies, when people embraced big ideas that might actually change the world. Life in 1982 was all about the money. At night we got high on free cocaine readily available in nightclub bathrooms and mindlessly danced to Donna Summers and the Bee Gees, if not home watching *Lifestyles of the Rich and Famous* and *Dallas* on television.

I picked up my copy of *Critical Path*, changed into my swim suit, and took my dinner down to the pool. I sat in a chaise lounge and tried to read, but my mind was having have none of it. A couple giggling in the hot tub reminded me of what I was missing. I forced myself into the pool and sloshed out fifty laps just to stop myself from thinking. I was exhausted when I dropped into bed, but I still thrashed around like a fish on a dock until rousted by the phone the next morning.

▽▽▽

The clock radio read 7:01 a.m. Who could be calling at this hour? The clunky black radio tumbled to the floor as I grabbed the receiver.

"Hello?" My mouth was dry and my tongue thick from last night's wine.

"Is this Patricia Field?"

"Um, yes. Who is calling, please?"

"This is Buckminster Fuller's assistant."

"Oh, yes, hello. Is everything all right?" I wondered if they had found me out. Had they discovered I actually wrote ad copy and not magazine articles at all?

"Dr. Fuller says he enjoyed meeting with you yesterday, but that there were a few things he forgot to tell you, and he's wondering if you could meet with him again today."

I sat up and tried to think straight. I was still traveling a thousand miles an hour as the Earth spun around itself while rotating around the sun and simultaneously flinging itself through space at a gazillion miles an hour. America was still on its way to failure. Humanity was still hurtling toward oblivion. I was woefully unprepared to do anything about any of it, yet was being called to duty once again.

"Um, sure, but... but I do have to work today." I couldn't skip out again. My Happy Meal copy was due, and Norma would be looking for me at 9:00 a.m. sharp, especially since I had snuck out early yesterday. "But I could meet him sometime this evening. Would that work?"

"One moment, please."

To the now familiar muffled voices in the background, I swung myself out of bed and dragged the phone over to the windows. The sunrise (or sunsight, as Bucky preferred) danced on the water below me. I cranked the window open to let in a breeze. The air was cool and smelled of the freshly mowed grass in Grant Park. A glittering row of silver masts clinked and clattered in the early morning breeze. A seagull flew past my window.

Bucky's assistant came back on the line.

"All right, then, Dr. Fuller will meet you in the dining room at the Conrad Hilton at seven p.m."

I thanked him, hung up the phone and made myself a small pot of coffee in my new Mr. Coffee machine. This was no big deal. Bucky had forgotten a few things and wanted to see me again. He would simply like to entrust me with a few more ideas he considered essential to the future of humanity.

I stared out the window while I drank my coffee and ate a piece of toast. I showered and blow-dried my hair and was putting on eyeliner when the realization struck. This was actually a huge deal. The great planetary genius, with so little time remaining on his beloved Spaceship Earth, wanted to spend more time with me.

Bucky trusted me.

Holy shit.

I rummaged through my closet. I needed something new to wear. Not the same old navy suit. I would have to go shopping at lunchtime and buy something new to celebrate my stature as a soon-to-be-important writer. I practically flew out the door, thrilled with my new life. I might be a divorced advertising copywriter from a broken home, but I was about to become someone relevant in the world.

At noon, I took a bus up to I. Magnin on North Michigan Avenue, where I tried on a ridiculously expensive champagne Calvin Klein suit made of one hundred percent silk. It hugged my body like a rich lady's glove. A perky blond saleswoman watched me step out of the dressing room to check myself out in the three-way mirror and said, "That's not just a suit—it's a dream."

I laughed at the thought. "Well, I am living a dream, so I guess I should dress for it."

I bought the dream of a suit despite its nightmarish price, relieved and a little surprised that my American Express card even accepted the purchase. Hugging it to my chest, I sat on the bus and daydreamed out the window. Forget *Chicago* magazine. Maybe I would write about Bucky for *The New Yorker*, or maybe *The New York Times*, or maybe I would write a screenplay and turn Bucky's ideas into a blockbuster movie. Nothing could stop me now.

At the office, I floated past a conference room inexplicably filled with men in dark suits. Norma's sharply raised eyebrows telegraphed that the clients were here to review my Happy Meal copy. Her eyes narrowed to slits when she noticed the I. Magnin bag.

She called out to me through the open conference room door. "We've been waiting for you, Miss Pat."

"So sorry! I'll be right there." I flung the suit on my desk, searched for the right file folder, and raced back to the conference room.

A pinstriped army of brand managers awaited with their backs to the wall of windows. Untouched water pitchers and glasses sat on a tray in the middle of the table. My mouth went dry. I slid into one of the big leather chairs and faced what felt like a firing squad. It was not like me to totally flake on a meeting. I felt like an idiot.

"Sorry I'm late."

Norma sighed.

A heavyset man I had not previously met, who had stopped talking when I walked in, reached up and adjusted the knot in his tie the way men do when they're about to let someone have it. His stomach pressed against his white shirt like a helium balloon. I wondered if it was painful to have a stomach that looked like it might explode.

"I like this copy"—he paused for effect—"except for one small problem." He looked at Norma and then at me. I looked down at my papers to check for a typo. He waited patiently, as if I were a child searching for a hidden image in a *Highlights* magazine picture. I wished that were true so I could find the knife in the picture and cut my way right out of that meeting.

He finally tired of waiting and picked up the copy in front of him, slid his glasses down to the end of his nose, and read aloud.

"Good times are flying high,

Ronald's circus is alive.

Swinging with ease on the flying trapeze,

the French Fry Guys have the crowd on its knees!"

He paused and looked around. I thought it sounded great—just the kind of nonsensical fun kids loved.

"The crowd on its knees?" the brand manager asked and looked around the room with a sarcastic smile. He took off his glasses and rubbed his eyes wearily, as if the entire future of humanity was at stake.

It was all I could do not to scream at them about how humanity's clock was at five minutes till midnight and how could they be worried about selling more junk food to more children at a time like this. But of course, that was out of the question.

"Uh," I began, "well..."

"Why isn't the crowd up on its feet?" He sighed heavily.

How awful it must have been to bear the burden of believing yourself the smartest person in the room, especially when you weren't. It was all I could do to hold myself together. "Um, well, because 'feet' doesn't rhyme with 'trapeze'?"

Norma raised her eyebrows again. I could see she was in no mood to support a copywriter who had flaked on a meeting.

The whole thing ended quickly. It was back to the typewriter for me. I was directed to solve not only the rhyming problem but to squeeze more mouthwatering taste appeal into the copy.

I grabbed a coffee from the break room and worked straight through the afternoon until time to meet with Bucky again. At six thirty, I pulled a fresh legal pad and a couple of pens out of my desk, stuffed them into my purse, grabbed my new suit off the door, and slipped into the women's room to change.

When I came out of the stall, Norma was standing at the sink washing her hands.

"Wow, great suit, Pat." She looked me up and down. "Big date tonight?"

"Ha! That's funny," I said. "Maybe. A date with destiny."

"A job interview? At seven o'clock at night?"

"No, more like the interview of a lifetime, with *the* Buckminster Fuller."

She shut off the faucet and shook the water off her fingertips. "Wow, really? Bucky is amazing. I saw him speak when I was at Columbia. So, wait—is this why you've been acting a little goofy lately?"

I nodded. "Sorry about that. I met with him for several hours yesterday, and then his assistant called me again this morning—"

"Really? Just the two of you? Are you sure he's not, you know, into you?"

"What? Come on, Norma, he's eighty-six years old. The only thing he's into is saving the planet—or more specifically, the human race. He's radical. You'd love him."

While Norma considered this, I took the opportunity to excuse myself. Already running late, I bolted to the elevators, then ran down Michigan Avenue in my heels. I was out of breath when I arrived at the Hilton, so I stopped to gather myself and breathe for a moment before pushing through the revolving doors of the brightly lit art deco dining room.

Bucky was seated in a red vinyl booth along the wall. His black suit, crisp white shirt, and red tie made him look sharper than the dull brown banker attire from yesterday. He looked a little like Fred Astaire, ready to go dancing.

His head was bent over a yellow legal pad as he scribbled away furiously. I held back so as not to interrupt him, and it dawned on me. He was superhuman. He knew practically everything there was to know that was important to know. He had the intellect of a laureate, the discipline of a scientist, the creativity of a poet, and the kindness and civility of a gentleman—surely the greatest man I would ever meet. He deserved the smartest, best audience possible for his ideas, especially now, nearing the end of his life. I knew I was not that audience. Not even close.

I slowed my approach to his booth, wondering if I should just slip away before he saw me, but it was too late. He looked up.

"Well, hello, Miss Pat. I've been waiting for you."

His impeccable suit and tie made me realize again how much he was expecting from me.

He started to rise, but I slid into the booth to spare him the considerable effort of getting up.

"Hello, Dr. Fuller," I said, still not comfortable calling him Bucky. "How are you?"

"I am just fine, thank you. But I realized last night that I'd forgotten to tell you a few important things, so I wanted to start off by talking about—"

"Um, Dr. Fuller—Bucky—I'm really sorry, but..."

He sat back, a little startled, not used to being interrupted.

"You see, I'm not actually a writer. Not a real writer, anyway. I'm not even a journalist, not anymore. My job right now is writing advertising copy. Sales promotion stuff. I didn't finish college. I'm worried I won't know how to begin to write about the things you told me yesterday. I'm afraid you could be wasting your time."

His eyes pierced through me just as they had yesterday. "Why, none of that matters to me at all. That doesn't bother me in the least."

A waitress appeared with menus and asked me if I wanted something to drink. Bucky had a cup of tea. I badly wanted a double vodka—anything to calm my nerves—but I settled for something new on the menu, a Diet 7Up.

"But why me?" I asked after the waitress was gone. "What if I'm not able to do anything with your ideas?"

"Well, you seem to be very good at taking notes," he said.

He was right about that. I was a good note-taker. I had filled an entire reporter's notebook yesterday.

"Look," he said in his gentle way, extending a large hand across the table. "I am eighty-six years old. I know how to spend my time. I didn't finish college, either. Didn't even really go. I think my own thoughts, and yesterday, I could see that you were thinking yours."

"Well, thank you," I said. "Your ideas seem so brilliant to me, so obviously true, that they should be considered common sense."

His eyes locked on mine. "Yesterday, I could see that you were an empty vessel."

Ouch. I thought of how my sisters and I had made fun of our Barbie-like friends, saying "the light is on, but nobody's home." Did he think I was an airhead?

He must have read my mind. "But that's not a bad thing at all. Empty vessels are essential. In nature, a leaf turned upward captures the rain to nourish the life that stumbles along later. You will be able to carry my ideas forward, to a time when they will be critically needed."

Goose bumps shot down my neck, a feeling I had become accustomed to yesterday. I hugged my arms to my chest. The idea of not having a deadline had a certain appeal. I had enough of those already at work. And maybe given a little more time, I would understand his message better. Maybe I worried too much.

"I realized yesterday," he continued, "that your mind was open. You have not been indoctrinated to believe what they teach these days in so-called schools of higher education. You have not been conditioned into false ways of thinking. I have spoken to many sharp young college graduates who have accepted modern economic theories that are simply incorrect and contrived to serve the wealthy. All the nonsense about Adam Smith's magical hand and the power of trickle-down wealth — it has been passed on to your generation by almost every major college and university in America. It's based on falsehoods and is designed to create a compliant workforce that will march in lockstep while the wealth goes the other way."

Trickle-down economics had always seemed entirely suspect to me, and it was certainly true that I had no higher education to get in the way of my own thinking. The public schools I had attended in Indiana had left plenty of space in my brain for new ideas.

I took out my notepad. He believed in me. I could do this. I sipped my soda, glad I'd resisted ordering a vodka.

"And you are especially right for the task because you are a woman," he said. "Only women are hardwired for compassion and empathy. Because women give birth, only women are continuous. Women tend toward greater compassion, cooperation, and sense of community than men, who see life as a competition to be waged. This new feminine paradigm of leadership will be urgently needed in the future."

"But isn't that sexist, in an opposite sort of way?" I asked.

He put down his cup. "It's not that all men are bad or all women are good, but women have allowed themselves to be held down for too long. They must step into their natural roles and speak their minds openly, as the true leaders of humanity that they are."

The waitress returned, and we ordered dinner. In a brand-new champagne dream of a suit, the girl who was going to save the world ordered chicken cordon bleu and braced for whatever was so important one of the world's greatest living geniuses had summoned her for another meeting.

I was still smarting over the empty vessel remark, but I got what he was saying. My mind was open. Wide open. Surely that wasn't such a terrible thing.

THE DARK SIDE

We are imprisoned in these dark ages simply by the terms in which we have been conditioned to think. — Buckminster Fuller

Bucky held up his knife and fork and prepared to tackle his steak.

"Yesterday, I mentioned we were entering into a dark age. This is what I want to talk about, especially about how much of it stems from the energy conundrum."

My first bite of chicken cordon bleu reminded me there was still plenty of good in the world. A crispy delicious chicken breast stuffed full of melted cheese and ham was the perfect backdrop for a scary story. I took tiny bites to make it last.

"The dark ages reign over all humanity, and the depth and persistence of this domination are only now becoming clear. This dark ages prison has no steel bars, chains, or locks. Instead, it is locked by misorientation and built of misinformation. We are caught up in a plethora of conditioned reflexes driven by the human ego. Both warden and prisoner attempt meagerly to compete with God. All are intractably skeptical of what they do not understand. We are powerfully imprisoned in these dark ages simply by the terms in which we have been conditioned to think."

I put down my fork. "But who is creating the misinformation? And why? And how?"

"Well, corporations, especially the oil companies, are now working hand in hand with our government to stop environmental progress. Reagan's not just deregulating corporations. He is inviting them into the henhouse by asking them to help write new laws that will protect them, not the people, and definitely not the environment. They have decided not to allow a transition to clean energy, even though they know it is both entirely feasible and necessary to our long-term survival."

"You mean they're killing renewable energy on purpose? Just because of money?"

"That is exactly what they are doing."

I shook my head. I had wondered if Jimmy Carter's act of installing solar panels on the White House was destined to remain only a symbolic one. There hadn't been much news about the environment at all since back in 1970, when twenty million people took to the streets on the first Earth Day. It was as if on that one day, the whole world had walked outside, raised their voices to the sky in protest, assumed they'd been heard, and then had gone back to living their lives, trusting their government would now do all the right things.

It was hard to believe anyone could be so selfish. "You mean that just for their own measly profits, they're willing to risk the future of us all? Of all life on Earth?"

Bucky nodded and held aloft another bite of his steak. "But it's not anything evil, really. It's simply the nature of corporations. They exist only to create short-term profits for shareholders."

"But don't those businesspeople have children too? Children who will also have children?"

"I am not telling you this to frighten you but to give you the power of knowledge. I have great confidence that humanity will evolve into a higher state of consciousness in which all people will care about all people. Even the rich guys can get into the idea of a conscious evolution, of becoming a class one species."

I wondered what that would take. Class one wasn't exactly how I'd define the specimens of the male of our species I had known so far.

Bucky's accusations about the oil industry executives and government working together had turned my mood dark. All I could think was how stupid people were to put their own bank accounts above the welfare of everyone else. Did they think they were somehow exempt from the end of the world? It made no sense.

"Venus." It was the first one-word statement I'd heard from him.

"Pardon?"

He leaned in and lowered his voice. "Venus. It's a possibility."

"How?"

He touched his fingers together, which I had come to realize was something he did to connect with himself. "Do you have a brother?"

"Um, yes." Roger was now in the Navy. He'd fled home to escape all the misery when he was just seventeen.

"Did he ever make jokes about passing gas and then being able to light it on fire with a match?"

I struggled to keep a straight face. Yes, that had been an actual thing. "That sounds about right."

"Well, it's a massive oversimplification, of course, and only one of many possibilities, but if Earth passes enough gases into the atmosphere, the sun could become the proverbial match, and *poof!* Earth could go the way of Venus."

The waitress appeared with a water pitcher. "Are you okay, hon? Can I get you something else?"

"No thanks, I'm fine," I lied. I'd finished every bite of my chicken. I thought about inviting her to have a seat so we could talk about anything other than the dark ages that were swallowing up the world and creating an Earth that might explode into Venus.

But the waitress left, and I took a long, slow sip of my Diet 7Up and returned to a subject I didn't understand.

"So, what does conscious evolution have to do with fossil fuels?"

He explained it simply and clearly. Through conscious evolution, humanity would eventually reach the point where each of us would put the good of the whole first. Everyone, even those who ran the fossil fuel industry, would realize their own survival was at stake. This would transform us from a selfish class-two species into a magnanimous class-one species.

He continued along this line for some time, explaining that the transition would not be an easy one since people might not see the problem coming until it was too late.

"The problem with the environmental crisis is that it is emerging almost too slowly. People have a hard time getting out of the way of something they cannot see."

It worried me every time Bucky referred to humans as "they," as if he preferred not to identify with such a flawed species.

A new waitress appeared. Shifts were changing; time was circling onward.

"Betty's off duty, and I'll be taking over. Would you angels like anything else?" Her golden hair was piled high on her head in a poufy bun. She looked entirely too cheerful for the lateness of the hour.

Bucky asked for more hot water for his tea. His steak was still half-eaten.

"Do you have any chocolate cake?" I asked impulsively.

"Sure do, honey, got a delicious devil's food. I'll bring you a slice?"

"Yes, please."

So, okay, cake wasn't the most evolved choice a person could make, but my brain felt as if it were being carved out with a grapefruit knife. I needed something. America was failing, the world might be exploding, and an advertising copywriter with a weakness for chocolate and a lingering craving for vodka was being drafted to save it.

Let me eat cake.

The waitress brought me a huge wedge of devil's food oozing with fudgy icing and topped with a big dollop of whipped cream. I took the first miraculous bite and offered some to Bucky, who declined.

He had returned to an idea from the day before, one he said was the most important of all: the power of the individual. Our destiny as a species, he said, would be determined by nothing more than the collective actions of individuals. We are so many bees in a hive, so many starlings in a murmur, each of us with the power to dance in perfect unison. We could swoop harmoniously over the beach, aligning ourselves in artfully coordinated flight, or we could ignore our innate abilities and crash and burn in a fiery mess. It depended on nothing more than the collective action of us all as individuals.

"Our collective will is a real and measurable thing. It is something that grows from individual integrity—or the lack of it. You will see signs that we are either all moving together in the right way, or something that indicates the reverse. Watch for the signs."

I took another bite of cake, wondering what the signs might be, and hoping that individual integrity and will-power were not one and the same. My stomach and mind were filling in unison. My heart was already full. This sincere man sitting before me obviously cared intensely about every little thing that affected the prospects for humanity. He was entirely lovable.

The sugary chocolate had gone to my brain and my notes were getting sloppy, but Bucky smoothly navigated us into a whole new subject area. He wanted to give me some personal advice about how to live a successful and happy life.

"If you simply apply yourself to the good of all humanity and don't worry so much about your own financial prospects, you will find the energies of Universe open up to you. The more you work to give advantage to others, the more energy you will possess to give. It is only self-seeking activities that come with the potential for loss and fear and, eventually, failure."

"So, the more we do for others, the more the universe will do for us?"

"Exactly. You won't know how much you have to give until you start trying. Great powers will become available to support you."

"Like what kind of powers?"

"We sometimes fall into the delusion that power is elsewhere, that it belongs to a different group, that we do not have access to it. But nothing could be further from the truth. Universe swirls with miraculous power waiting for anyone who wishes to harness it to just take it and go. Once we learn, in time, to accredit weightless thinking over physical values in our affairs and to understand that there is an overwhelming superior efficacy of the mind, as compared to muscle, then the particular team of humans now aboard Spaceship Earth will survive to perform their highest function. They will evolve into a syntrophic species."

My brain hit a wall. Chocolate was apparently not one of the syntrophic forces. I put down my pen and pressed the last crumbs of the cake onto my fork. I had no idea what he had just said.

The clock read 1:45 a.m.

Bucky extended a hand across the table. "I do believe that humanity will turn things around, given time. The youth of Earth are moving intuitively toward an utterly classless, raceless, and cooperative humanity. Your generation will lead the way into an utterly new era, one of a compassionate and fully joyful human experience."

I had lost any utopian impulse I might have felt earlier. To my mind, Americans seemed happily dazed and consumed with an obsessive pursuit of material wealth. Nobody I knew gave a darn about any of this conscious evolution stuff or putting the needs of someone else first.

"For instance," he continued, "technology is emerging so fast that one day soon, you'll be able to vote just by clicking Yes or No on a gadget on your wrist. We can do more and more with less and less. The simple trick is to steer all that technology toward advances in livingry instead of weaponry."

Voting on my wrist sounded like a novel idea, so I jotted it down. But the simple, undeniable truth was that my entire being was voting for sleep. There was no space left in my head. The empty vessel was stuffed full and shutting down.

Before he could get started again, I said I was sorry but that I had to work early the next morning, that Ronald

McDonald's vast corporate army of suits would be looking for my Happy Meal copy.

I thought this would make him laugh, but he didn't even smile. I saw disappointment cross his face. Had it just occurred to him that he could have spent the evening with someone much smarter? I wanted to reassure him, even though I wasn't at all sure of myself.

"I do promise I will work hard on this," I said, not wanting him to regret his investment in me. "I will do everything I can to share your ideas, if it's the last thing I do."

A typical overstatement. I sounded desperate. He looked at me over his glasses. "You will need to work hard to find the courage to speak out. First work to understand the truth, and then find the audacity to speak it. Wield your mighty typewriter and make people think, Miss Pat. Make them think about things, and then tell them what they can do about it."

"I will. I promise." I had never felt so resolute as I put away my notebook and pen and slid out of the booth. Bucky stood to say goodbye. It was an awkward moment. I wanted to tell him his ideas were miraculous and that one day I would surely understand them. I wanted to hug him, to tell him everything would be okay, that there were no doubt many truly smart people in the world he could rely on.

He must have read my mind, because he opened his arms. I leaned in for a hug. He squeezed me hard and patted me on the back. "You will do just fine, Miss Pat. You have taken excellent notes. Watch for signs that things are changing. There will be an emergence through an emergency. You'll know when the world is ready."

Plates were clanging in the kitchen. A busboy stacked chairs on a nearby table. There was the hum of a vacuum cleaner. Lights flickered. Time was spiraling onward.

I considered his trusting eyes, which even at this hour danced with the light of a much younger person. "I will, Bucky. I will do everything I can."

"That's my girl." He put his hand on my shoulder. "You'll be amazed at what you are capable of."

"Thank you. Nobody has ever told me that before. Good night, Bucky."

"Good night, Miss Pat."

I stepped out onto the misty sidewalk and took the shortcut home across Grant Park. A heavy dew on the sprawling lawns was lit up by an almost full moon, making the grass glitter like silver. Despite overwhelming fatigue and the chocolate monster growling in my gut, the world felt miraculous. My life had just changed forever. I would now devote myself to keeping Bucky's ideas alive. In exchange, he had agreed to let me go home and get some badly needed sleep, so I wouldn't lose my job tomorrow. We had sealed our deal with a hug.

It seemed like a fair trade.

The closer I got to my condo on the lake, the quieter the world became. Very few cars were out this late. I checked my watch; it was 2:17 a.m. If I added the two days together, I had listened to Bucky for a total of just over eleven hours.

Surely his better, smarter world would be coming soon. How hard could it be? Bucky's design science thinking would make it obvious that clean, free energy was both possible and necessary. Clean energy would raise the quality of life for all human beings while protecting the environment from the destruction wrought by fossil fuels. It would surely all happen soon. It was already 1982.

As I crossed the light at Lakeshore Drive, it struck me that I had made a colossally important promise to one of the greatest human beings alive. He had told me the future of all of humanity rested on the individual—me—and that I had the responsibility for making sure everyone else knew it. What had I gotten myself into?

A BUCKY LIFE

How often I found where I should be going only by setting out for somewhere else. — Buckminster Fuller

That first Saturday morning after Bucky, I bounced out of bed, made a pot of coffee, and slipped into my blue jeans and Keds. With a quick wave to Barry, I set off for downtown.

I had always loved getting around the city on my own two feet, but now, after Bucky, it felt downright revolutionary. My life would be forever divided into before and after. Learning about Bucky's way of thinking was like suddenly discovering I had a new engine underneath the hood of my car. There was just so much more to think about. So much I didn't yet understand, but I knew I would. All I had to do was keep thinking. And keep reading.

At the crosswalk on Lakeshore Drive, I caught the weathered eyes of an elderly woman under a white crown of hair. She was barely visible above her steering wheel, but the way she peered out at me through her windshield gave me a profound sense of connection, a powerful bond with this other living, breathing creature of nature. We smiled at each other.

Grant Park was lush and green under a brilliant morning sun. Two joggers ran by me on the path, a couple, talking and laughing while steam rose off their bodies. A hobo rifled through a trash can. A perfectly coiffed, fur-collared woman hurried by with a large Louis Vuitton bag. They were all the same, all fully connected indigenous parts of the natural world whether they knew it or not.

I reached the massive Harold Washington Library on State Street just as a security guard was lowering the heavy chain locks on the metal doors. I said a bright good morning to him and took the marble stairs two at a time up to the nonfiction department. In the small wooden drawers of the card catalog, I found several books by R. Buckminster Fuller.

I stacked a pile of them on the table, feeling like a kid at Christmas.

One large picture book I recognized from my childhood, *The Dymaxion World of Buckminster Fuller*. How strange it felt to see it through my older and wiser eyes. The massive dome he had designed and built for the 1967 World Expo in Montreal. His Dymaxion home, with a smiling old-fashioned family standing at the front door. There were other ideas I didn't remember. One was for a dome that would cover all of Manhattan, harvesting the sun's energy to control the climate inside. Another of the grandest domes ever built, commissioned by Henry J. Kaiser for use as a concert auditorium in Honolulu, took only twenty-two hours to completely assemble, yet could seat an audience of 1,832.

Bucky's invention of a floating breakwater would harvest the energy of the waves while also holding back rising waters. There was even a design for an all-in-one bathroom, with a fog gun that could clean a whole person with less than a gallon of water. His synergetic geometry was a whole new kind of math. He'd written poetry. He'd even written a children's book called *Tetrascroll: Goldilocks and the Three Bears, A Cosmic Fairy Tale.*

He had written so much, and even more had been written about him. I combed through files of press clippings from *The New York Times* and the *International Herald Tribune.* I was looking for a fresh angle for my story, something that had not been written about before. The whole renewable energy conundrum seemed most important, but would anybody want to publish an article about that?

All too soon, the clock on the wall read noon. I was already late for my lunch date with my new friend Jan. For the past few weeks, we had met every Saturday at Marshall Field's, the famous old department store on State Street, where Jan did her weekly shopping and I did my weekly wondering about whether my life would ever measure up to hers.

With her trim, tailored clothes and perfect nails, Jan had a way of making life look glamorous and easy. She didn't like it when I was late, so I hurried to reshelf the books, but as I was about to return the all too familiar *Dymaxion World,* I noticed there were three other copies on the shelf. I did not have a library card. There was no time left to apply for one, especially since I was running late. I really wanted that book.

Almost without thinking, I slipped *The Dymaxion World* right into my large leather purse. It wasn't that I was a kleptomaniac, but I was an "ends justify the means" sort of person, so without really thinking I walked down the massive marble steps with my heart in my throat. The security guard awaited me. Would he check my bag?

Squaring myself off, I gave him my most confident smile. He smiled back. I descended smoothly down the steps, careful not to look as if I were trying to escape. Adrenaline rushed through my veins. I hadn't stolen anything since the Snickers bars at the J & F Market when I was a kid. Now I had pinched a book by a world-famous genius who had told me to my face that individual integrity was the key to humanity's future.

I practically ran down State Street, but no matter how fast my Keds took me, I couldn't outrun the realization of what I had just done, and how it was just like me to take the easy way out. Maybe I would go back after lunch to apply for a library card, but no, I didn't see that happening. The moral compass of the person upon whom the future of humanity rested was a bit wobbly at best.

Jan was waiting for me on a bench next to the elevator. Her face was perfectly made up as always, her highlighted hair cropped short. But the biggest development was her newly rounded tummy.

She stood to greet me with a peck on the cheek from her polished pink lips. Jan lived with her husband on the Gold Coast in a luxurious condominium decorated in furry whites with touches of apricot to match their two toy poodles. Until I had seen it, I didn't even know apricot was a color, let alone a dog color.

"I am famished," she said with mock despair. "Pregnancy makes me hungry enough to eat someone's arm."

I held out my bare arm out as an offering, which made her laugh. "Sorry I'm late. I, um, needed a library book."

"No problem. You okay? You look... scared? Tired?"

"Just working on something, lost track of time."

"You're forgiven."

"You look beautiful, Jan. I know it's a cliché, but you are actually glowing."

"Well, I can tell you that it is a very cool thing to know you are creating a new life right inside your own body. It's a total trip."

The Marshall Field's dining room clinked and hummed happily. White tablecloths and thick Asian carpets absorbed the chatter of shoppers, most of them well-coiffed women with bulging shopping bags tucked next to their chairs.

We both ordered chef salads with iced teas. Jan showed me samples of the pink-and-white striped fabric she planned to use on the window coverings in the nursery.

"Do you like it?" she asked.

"It's pretty. I like stripes, but will it darken the room enough? Surely the most important thing is keeping the little bugger asleep for as long as possible, right?"

"Hmm, I didn't think of that." She held the fabric up to the light. "Guess it's back to the drawing board on this one."

We talked about her husband's job and Jan's family in Michigan before coming around to the regular subject of my lack of a boyfriend.

My father's shenanigans had made me highly suspicious of men in general. I felt destined to fail in the romance category, but now that seemed almost okay. I had bigger fish to fry.

I changed the subject and breathlessly told Jan all about my two days with Bucky.

She listened for a long time, nibbling at her salad, but when I got around to Bucky's warnings about fossil fuels and the environment, she held up one hand.

"Oh, come on, he sounds crazy now. As if there's enough energy available from the sun to power all this?" She reached out to indicate the big, brightly lit dining room. "Have you noticed how gray and cold it gets out there? This guy sounds a little nutty."

I tried to explain, but she cut me off. "What good are these ideas even if you do understand them? How do they change anything?"

I didn't have an answer. "You're right, I guess, but it seems important to know —"

"And anyway, how old is this guy? He's probably already senile."

That thought had not even occurred to me, since he seemed like the most intelligent being I had ever encountered.

"And besides, don't you have enough stress at work?"

I let out a long sigh. She had me there. I still hadn't solved the Happy Meal copy problem. I was also up against some senior writers for the furniture polish commercial. If I won, there would be a winter trip to LA for production. I would be ordering lunch poolside under a palm tree just as Jan hunkered down against another ridiculous Chicago winter with a new baby.

I nodded. "It's true, I do have some massive competition."

"And you are going to kill it, Pat. You are so creative. Just focus and don't get all caught up in some Bucky-saves-the-world business. You'll do great."

"But don't you see how important Bucky's ideas are?" I held out my hands to weigh the options. "On one hand, the future of the planet. On the other, a rhyme about French fries, which I still haven't come up with." I shrugged.

"But the future of the planet's not up to you. Come on. You're not a scientist or even a politician. There must be thousands of people already working on the problems he's talking about. Geez, you are so intense, I swear you're making the baby kick harder."

I swallowed some iced tea. Was that who I was? Someone crazy enough to freak out an unborn baby?

"No wonder you don't have a boyfriend—you probably scare them all to death," she said nonchalantly.

This rattled me. She was right. Why couldn't I be all smooth and polished and happy to be alive, like her? I lifted my purse off the floor for my checkbook. The weight of the secret stolen book in my bag pulled me down even further.

"You're just one little person, Pat. Leave the future of the planet to the boring old scientists and engineers. They'll figure it all out soon enough. Fall in love. Get married. Have babies. Don't worry, be happy."

This knocked the wind out of me. We split the check and stood to go. I walked home feeling torn in half.

How I hated the expression "don't worry, be happy." My father had said it when he moved us away to Mishawaka, on my first day at a new school, half way through my junior year. What nobody ever seemed to get was the intent of this quote. When the Indian mystic Meher Baba first said it, his words were: "Do your best. Then, don't worry, be happy." Everyone conveniently forgets the "do your best" part. How had Daddy been doing his best? How was Jan doing her best by picking out stupid curtains? And how was I doing mine by stealing a library book, which had grown so heavy in my bag, I wanted to toss it into a trash can?

The wind picked up. It started to rain. I ducked into a coffee shop to wait it out since I didn't have a coat or umbrella. I stared out at the pelting rain and thought of Jan's happy life, overflowing with her handsome husband's love and her decorating and her dinner parties, and how in a few short weeks, a real live baby would be in their midst.

But maybe there would time for everything.

First things first. Get something published.

▽ ▽ ▽

When I got home, I got to work right away, and for the next couple of weekends, I devoted every free minute to writing and editing my story for *Chicago* magazine. Sitting at the dining table with my iced tea or coffee, I stayed ramped up on caffeine into the wee hours, writing it all out in longhand on a yellow legal pad, and ending up with a ten-page article I called "Buckminster Fuller's Urgent Warnings for Humanity."

When it was done, I went to the office early that Monday morning, typed up a clean copy along with a cover letter, and slipped it into a manila envelope addressed to *Chicago* magazine.

Two weeks later, I'd heard no reply — the worst rejection possible. I worked up the courage to call the editor. The secretary said my submission was in a large pile still waiting to be read, which might not happen for weeks since everyone was busy working on the Tylenol poisonings story. Someone had laced some bottles with cyanide at a Walgreen's on the near north side, and seven people had died. They were very busy, she said. I felt sorry I'd troubled her, but before I hung up I got the name of another editor who might be interested in my story.

I edited some more. Proofread it again. Tightened it up. Each time I made changes, I had to retype the entire page. Then I sent it off again. But still no reply. Maybe, like Bucky had said, his best days were behind him. Maybe all the excitement over President Reagan's new trickle-down economics made Bucky's ideas irrelevant. Or maybe my writing wasn't good enough.

Or maybe the third time was the charm. One day after work, a crisp white linen envelope awaited in my mailbox. The moment I saw the *Chicago* magazine logo, my heart leapt. I ripped open the envelope. Barry looked on from the lobby, where he sat on a stool at his podium.

I read the letter to myself.

Dear Ms. Field,

Thank you for your submission, but you should know that we do not accept unsolicited manuscripts. We have a couple of excellent staff writers who are quite well-versed in all things Bucky and have an excellent grasp on his philosophies. In addition, we have given the great genius some good coverage recently.

Best of luck in your writing.

The Editors

Not even an actual signature.

I scrunched up the letter and shot it down the trash shoot with an anguished grunt and let the door slam. Barry called out to ask if I was okay. I punched the button for the elevator and was relieved when it opened right away. I couldn't even bring myself to answer him. No way would I let Barry see me cry.

Once my tears dried, I decided it obviously was not meant to be. Just like Jan said, if he was such a great genius, many other people were surely working to keep his ideas alive. And how egotistical was it for me to think I was somehow essential to anything this important? I was an ad writer, not a real writer, and even though my notes were good and I'd quoted Bucky accurately, there was obviously something else wrong. Probably my crappy writing. It's hard to know what you don't have, but the bottom line was I apparently didn't have whatever was required.

To stave off my sense of failure, I reminded myself what Bucky said about there being no hurry, that I should watch for signs, and that I would know exactly what I needed to know when I needed to know it.

That night I downed nearly a whole bottle of wine and the better part of a pint of Bresler's Double Fudge Walnut ice cream. Not my best night. A hundred laps in the pool the next morning was my punishment, along with a firm decision to put Bucky out of my mind, at least for now.

BUCKY
EVERYWHERE

1983

Integrity is the essence of everything successful.
— Buckminster Fuller

No matter how hard I tried to push thoughts of him away, Bucky's ideas weren't going anywhere. They had hijacked my brain. He kept coming back. His voice would pop into my head when I least expected it, always reminding me I had promised to never forget.

In mid-February, on Valentine's Day weekend, I was sitting by myself poolside at the Westwood Marquis Hotel in Los Angeles on break from production of a Pledge furniture polish commercial. I had won the assignment with an idea the client had loved, even though the agency hadn't recommended it: a simple monologue by a young woman crediting the lasting beauty of her parent's antique dining room table to weekly dustings with Pledge, "for twenty-eight years and counting." Pledge was being falsely accused by a competitor, Endust, of causing wax buildup. Market share was falling and the competition for a good idea was intense. Nobody at the agency liked my idea. They said yuppies were all about instant gratification, that nobody would care one bit about making things last.

Jan had been right about one thing. When I concentrated at work, I could occasionally hit it out of the park. Even if I wasn't saving the world, I was making dining room tables beautiful and giving spoiled yuppies some credit for giving a damn about the future. It wasn't exactly Bucky's idea of "think globally but act locally," but I was trying.

And advertising was a fun business. You got to pretend you were making real movies, doing casting and choosing wardrobe and other Hollywood sorts of things, like having a massage right next to Olivia Newton John at the Westwood Marquis Hotel. She and I were separated only by a thick linen drape hanging between the massage tables. I'll never forget her dainty Aussie giggle and how sweet she was to her masseur, asking him all about his family and whether his hands got tired. That same weekend, I'd also casually waved to Clint Eastwood and Sandra Locke, who were seated just one table away from us at a trendy West Hollywood restaurant. Clint was smoking a cigarette, so I did too, even though I hadn't had one for years. He looked right at me and smiled.

And most importantly, when you worked in advertising, you would occasionally find yourself sitting in a Georgio's swimsuit and fluffy robe next to a heated pool under an umbrella that was perfectly blocking the ferocious midday sun from your face while it tanned your legs. In February no less. And in any other month when the weather is crappy in Chicago, which is generally every month except September and May.

Pretending nonchalance at my immensely good fortune, I ordered a glass of Chardonnay and a spinach salad from a lovely ponytailed waiter, checked my production schedule and casting notes, then picked up the *LA Times*. There he was again, on the front page. Bucky's big crazy eyes were smiling this time as he shook hands with President Reagan.

What the…? Why was he shaking hands with Ronald Wilson Reagan, whose very name spelled out 6-6-6 and thus conjured the devil, and who had by now practically dismantled the EPA and shut down both the air traffic controllers union and Carter's clean energy plan?

In the photo, Reagan was bestowing upon Bucky America's highest civilian honor, the Presidential Medal of Freedom. I laughed to think it was like a cat singing the praises of a mouse he was fully intending to swallow whole. The photo reeked of hypocrisy. How did the conservatives think they could get away with such garbage?

Here's what Reagan said about Bucky: "A true Renaissance man and one of the greatest minds of our times, Richard Buckminster Fuller's contributions as a geometrician, educator, and architect-designer are benchmarks of accomplishment in their fields. Among his most notable inventions and discoveries are synergetic geometry, geodesic structures, and tensegrity structures. Mr. Fuller reminds us all that America is a land of pioneers and a haven for innovative thinking and the free expression of ideas."

I laughed. The irony of Ronald Reagan heaping accolades on Bucky. What a crazy dance our government played to distract us from what was really going on.

The waiter approached with my wine. He seemed the friendly sort, so I held up the newspaper and let myself rant a little. I told him how Reagan, who had openly mocked Jimmy Carter's solar panels on the White House and thwarted his million-billion-dollar plan to transfer us to clean energy, and had famously proclaimed "a tree is just a tree," had now inexplicably bestowed America's most coveted civilian award on the one man who staunchly advocated every idea he was determined to plunder.

The waiter smiled and shook his head. "Tell me about it. Bucky's a brilliant guy, but you know what Michael Corleone said in *The Godfather*: Keep your friends close and your enemies closer."

▽▽▽

Later that spring, I was excited to be sent to Orlando to attend some focus groups for Kraft Singles, not only because it potentially meant another trip to LA, but because Orlando was the location of a new Disney theme park, EPCOT Center, where one of Bucky's huge geodesic domes graced the entrance.

I told everybody who would listen about Bucky's dome—a miraculous marriage of nature and technology, a gleaming bubble in the sky I'd dreamed of seeing my whole life. A coworker in the elevator gave me a sideways look and said, "You sound like some crazed hippie chick," so I told her that Walt Disney himself had created the idea for EPCOT, which stands for Experimental Prototype Community of Tomorrow, and that Walt Disney was not exactly a hippie. (By 1983, "hippie" had become one of the nastiest insults you could hurl at a person, at least in the Chicago advertising world.)

When I climbed out of my rental car at EPCOT Center on that warm spring morning, I was engulfed by intoxicating fragrances of lemon trees in full bloom. Men in futuristic orange suits hosed down wide smooth sidewalks that were already clean. Towering topiary dinosaurs lined the walkways to welcome visitors. This made no sense to me. Why welcome people to the future using prehistoric creatures who hadn't even made it to the present?

As I strolled past an enormous hedge of morning glories in full bloom, Bucky's dome arose before me like a towering alien spaceship, but a friendly one. Golden morning light bounced off its thousands of sixty-degree triangles, which covered the massive sphere like so many diamonds. The vision of it brought to mind one of Bucky's most famous quotes: "When I am working on a problem, I never think about beauty, but when I have finished, if the solution is not beautiful, I know it is wrong."

A family came racing up behind me, three young children shrieking with delight, their parents speeding up to catch up with them, all of them anxious to get a closer look at the astonishingly perfect structure. Its very existence seemed to promise a brighter future. Everyone I saw along the pathway was visibly moved by it.

There's a story about how Bucky loved to eavesdrop on people as they set eyes on a geodesic dome for the first time. At the international unveiling of his two-hundred-foot-high dome at the Montreal World Expo in 1967, nobody noticed the stocky older man in the brown suit listening to visitors gasp with pleasure at the sight of the dome. Their reactions filled him with hope that people were awakening to understand that it wasn't just beautiful, but that the dome was based on thinking that was essential to the future.

"Finally," I breathed as I arrived directly underneath the dome, which somehow felt anything but threatening, no matter how high it towered above me.

I spent the morning soaking up exhibits about better ways to grow and produce food to feed a fast-growing world population, which was already over four and a half billion people. I learned that with the help of innovative companies like Monsanto, vegetables could be produced more abundantly and reliably through genetic modification. The goal was to provide a good life for everyone, just as Bucky had said his design science revolution was all about.

At lunchtime, I sat and looked out over Bucky's dome while nibbling cautiously at my first-ever veggie burger, an invention for the future made with chunks of corn and peas. It was gratifying to eavesdrop on others who were sitting nearby to hear their reverence for the beauty of the dome, which had turned many shades of purple and pink under the midday sun.

I saved the most important exhibit for last. The Universe of Energy featured a futuristic Jetsons-like sign at the entry promising "a thrilling look into tomorrow's clean and beautiful energy world."

But just past the entry, I slammed to a halt so abruptly that the woman pushing a stroller behind me banged into me, nearly launching her baby right out into space. There, on the brightly lit sign in front of us all were the words: Proudly Sponsored by Exxon.

Exxon. I couldn't believe it. Big Oil. The ones we needed to replace.

I turned and apologized to the family, whose baby was now crying. I too felt almost reduced to tears to learn that whoever had designed "the community of tomorrow" had decided that the future was going to be pretty much like the present.

Bucky had predicted that the foxes would soon be guarding the henhouse, and here they were. The oil industry had neutralized the clean energy argument by pretending to embrace it, just as he said they would.

My first-ever veggie burger wasn't sitting so well. I wandered outside and found a bench in the sun and let its heat pound down on me while I thought about its vast, wasted potential. I was catching fire from the inside out. I sat and gathered myself for a time, then returned to the scene of the crime one more time to make sure I hadn't imagined it. But it was true. The great visionary plan for the future of energy was oil. People were being fooled into following the dinosaurs, giving new meaning to those topiary greeters at the park's entrance. The irony was unnerving. I wanted to stand there on the pathway and inform passers-by of the crimes being committed against them. I wanted to do or say something about what Bucky had called the greatest crime ever waged against humanity and the need to speak out against it. Surely this was sign. I had promised I would do something. But instead I just sat on the bench under the shade of a Brontosaurus. Big Oil was in control. Selfish greed was still ruling the planet.

By time I met up with my team that evening for the focus groups, I had changed into an all-black outfit that matched my mood. I twitched an unlit cigarette nervously between my fingers, a renewed post-Bucky habit that helped keep my mind off Big Oil, and focused instead on bloody "cheese food slices" that had made possible my escape from a prolonged winter. (We were legally required to call Kraft Singles "cheese food slices" since they weren't actually real cheese, a typical corporate sleight of hand that advertising copywriters regularly passed on to an unsuspecting public.)

On the other side of the one-way mirror, our moderator, a slim middle-aged blond woman in a red pantsuit, was setting up the room. Carefully selected consumers would look at storyboards for several proposed TV commercials, sample the cheese food slices, and say what they thought of both. My boss, a creative director named Wayne, had insisted on coming, even though it was no secret to anybody that his primary interest was escaping the snow.

While we waited for the consumers to arrive, I lit my cigarette and then Wayne's Marlboro, and told him about my visit to EPCOT Center. "So you'll never guess who sponsored the entire energy-of-the-future show."

"I dunno, Coca-Cola?"

"Exxon."

"Duh," said Wayne, who was never without a cigarette in his mouth, as if to prove why he thought it okay to design ads for them. Even though I too struggled with nicotine addiction, or maybe because I did, I had repeatedly refused to work on cigarettes, even though generous bonuses were offered to the creatives who did. Too many smokers were getting cancer for cigarettes not to be the cause, no matter what the testimony in Congress or the news reports said. A copywriter had to draw the line somewhere.

"Don't you find it ridiculous that we keep letting it happen?" I said. "I mean, we should be transferring to clean energy before it's too late. Bucky says we have ten, maybe twenty years max."

Wayne blew smoke out of his mouth in little rings. "You sound naïve as hell sometimes, girl. You just gotta know the fix is in. Big brother's in charge. Let it go. No way is some airy-fairy utopian world going to pop up. Duh." He wiped imaginary crumbs off his mustache and took another drag off his cigarette.

"But why not? Why do we always have to let the bad guys win?"

"Come on, you're a smart girl. What good does it do to sweat it? You've heard the serenity prayer: 'Grant me the power to change the things I can, the power to accept the things I can't, and the wisdom to know the difference.' Right? American capitalism is king of the world, and Big Oil is the king of American capitalism. And there is nothing you can do about it, kiddo."

I winced. I hated it when he called me kiddo. "I can't accept that."

"You have to."

"I can't."

"Look, hon, nothing's going to change because of what a copywriter thinks—a copywriter who, by the way, carries the worst fake Gucci handbag I have ever seen."

"This is Chanel." I clutched my bag defensively. "And it's real." I'd bought it out of the back of a station wagon at a flea market in Lincoln Park from an older woman selling off her last treasures to make rent. We had hugged and I had thanked her, and she wished me luck. I thought of her every day I carried that purse.

"But seriously, Wayne," I said, "tell me why everybody is so willing to sit back rather than taking on the bastards. Are we really that chickenshit?"

"At least chickenshits survive. Look, it's just the way things are. And here's the main reason to forget all that crap: if you don't get this cheese spot just right, there will be no production trip to California coming up."

He had a point. There was work to do on many fronts. I had long dreamed of writing for TV in Hollywood, commuting by snappy red helicopter, maybe from the rooftop of my Malibu mansion. A girl could dream.

"Save this commercial, kiddo. Let the planet take care of itself."

"Right. I guess I do get a little carried away sometimes."

"Sometimes? Love your passion, kiddo. Love your passion."

For the rest of the night, I stayed glued to the increasingly slimy unrefrigerated orange cheese food slices. Afterwards, back in my hotel room, which stank of cigarettes and mold, I threw open the windows to let in the night air and caught my own eyes in the mirror above the dressing table. Wayne was right.

"Are you nuts?" I said to my reflection. "There is nothing you can do. Wayne is right. Jan is right. Mummy is right. Relax. Fall in love. Get married. Pop out a kid or two. Do what happy, well-adjusted people do, and maybe you will become one of them."

I sneered at myself in the mirror, fell into bed, and slept fitfully.

▽▽▽

The news of Bucky's death came one Friday night that July. After a long week at work, I had kicked off my shoes and mindlessly turned on CBS, where Dan Rather was reporting that the planet had suffered the loss of a great genius, and then he cut away to a commercial.

I was infuriated to be left hanging. I poured myself a glass of wine and suffered through an interminable string of inane sixty-second ads for Coca-Cola, Purina dog food, and my own Pledge commercial, which usually would have thrilled me to see on the air. Rather returned with tears in his eyes saying that the great American genius Buckminster Fuller had been a friend of his and of every being on the planet. He showed old footage of Bucky speaking to packed auditoriums, hundreds of faces turned upward in rapture to hear his profound ideas.

"Despite his remarkable achievements in a wide range of fields," Rather said, "Buckminster Fuller insisted again and again that he was only an average human being."

It was a heartfelt tribute to Bucky, but there was no mention of his views about fossil fuels. Nothing about his urgent warnings regarding the need to switch to clean energy while there was still time. Nothing about how the clock now read four minutes to midnight at best.

I took a long deep swallow of wine.

Bucky was gone. It felt like he had taken the future with him. I had been watching the news pretty closely lately and had seen zero evidence that anybody was even trying to steer the great Spaceship Earth on the course Bucky had suggested. His sudden death filled me with a sinking feeling that humanity was headed in the entirely wrong direction.

I had to do something to mark the death of the future and the beginning of the end, so later that night I got dressed up and went out dancing at my favorite club, PS Chicago on Rush Street.

"The American dream is dead," I drunkenly told a random good-looking guy on the dance floor. I spun around him, playfully flipping my long, freshly highlighted hair for greater effect. I was feeling like crap about Bucky dying, but my tight jeans, tan suede dancing boots, and hundred-dollar haircut was making up for it.

"What exactly are you talking about?" He asked politely. He had perfect teeth.

The music was loud, so I leaned in and tried not to shout. "A great genius has died, Buckminster Fuller, and now, instead of his brilliant geodesic dome, we witness the rise of a great fake." I pointed up at the spinning disco ball. "A rhinestone cowboy. A false ideology based on greed and corruption." I opened my hands to catch the ripples of sparkling light. "We have gone from dome to disco. The American dream now shatters before our eyes — "

"WHAT THE HELL ARE YOU TALKING ABOUT?" he shouted.

I gave him a big fake grin.

He brushed his dark bangs from his blue eyes and said, "You're pretty when you're mad," so I let him buy me a drink. We sat together on a white leather couch in the back of the bar, away from all the noise, and we had a conversation I would not soon forget.

Matthew Martin from Manhattan (MMM, in my mind) was a Harvard Business School graduate, an MBA, and a stockbroker. He said he owned a condo in Greenwich Village and drove a BMW, and he agreed that Bucky had been spot on about the conservatives changing everything by deregulating the financial markets. MMM said that we were now all part of a great experiment in institutionalized greed. After a second drink—martini for him, double vodka cranberry for me—he told me that he and some of his colleagues were intentionally gaming the system. They knew how to make buckets of money and were about to become very wealthy.

"I will take you out on my future yacht," he said.

"Very generous of you, but what makes you so sure—"

"They taught us in ethics class how the system is vulnerable and exploitable. I looked around the packed auditorium and knew somebody was going to make a shit ton of money, and decided it might as well be me."

I let this sink in. He had learned in an ethics class at Harvard that the deregulated financial system was susceptible to corruption and how to capitalize on that weakness. Which he was about to do.

I thought I might throw up. He seemed like a decent enough guy. His smile was genuine.

"That is disgusting. Are you talking about intentionally bringing about the collapse of the American economy?"

His eyes, sharp as tacks, shot defiantly at me as if from a gun. "Maybe. It's going to happen with or without me."

"What about individual integrity?"

"Whose integrity? Mine?" He snorted.

"So you're saying that you and your buddies are going to intentionally rape and plunder the American economy and Harvard taught you how to do it?"

"You make it sound so evil and planned. It happened inadvertently." He rattled the ice in his empty glass. "You can't really teach ethics, you know."

"Apparently not." I knocked back the last of my drink.

"Look, pretty lady who really should learn how to relax and smile, it's happening one way or another. I'm just going to get my fair share. What's wrong with that?"

"Everything."

"So let's try this your way. Let's say I get all self-righteous and decide not to take advantage of the situation. The result will be that I'll end up feeling angelic but eating canned soup while my friends step onto their private yachts with their supermodel wives."

"You're a stockbroker. Living in Manhattan. I don't think you're exactly destitute."

"It's all relative, my dear. The ceiling keeps getting higher. Right now, it's going through the roof."

"But that wealth being sucked to the top is taking money away from everyone else, just like Bucky wrote in *Grunch of Giants*."

"Look, I don't know much about this Bucky guy. All I know is the system has been deregulated to produce a huge fucking lot of cash, and I am not missing out." He looked me in the eyes defiantly. "I am going to buy myself the best life possible."

"You can't buy things that really matter. You can't buy a good wife."

"Watch me. Women aren't that complicated. The most beautiful ones want luxury and comfort and someone to take care of them. The more money I have, the more women I'll have to choose from. I've watched it happen time and again. Finding a gorgeous sexy woman when you're rich is a simple science. Money equals beauty plus youth plus happiness. Money is everything."

One more thing my mother was wrong about: It is much harder to fall in love with a rich man, since they are much more likely to be jerks. My stomach heaved, and it occurred to me that I could intentionally throw up in his lap. I'd never considered vomiting as a weapon before.

Instead I pointed up at the disco ball and shook my head. "We've gone from dome to disco. It's over." Then I stood and walked away to the first notes of Donna Summer's song "Last Dance" — and that's exactly what it was, a sad final song to eulogize Bucky — and probably all of humanity.

That same night, a few hours later, my mouth dry as dust, I awakened to the sound of voices from somewhere above me. At first I thought someone must be in the hallway or outside my window. Then I wondered if the voices were merely a product of too many vodkas.

I sat up to listen. I was wide awake and sober as the dawn.

"Do you want to know?" A clear hollow voice drifted through the air. It seemed real but disembodied. I could feel the energy of its voice as it asked again, "Do you?"

I reached out and waved a hand through the air in front of me. There was an energy there, as real as anything I'd ever felt.

"Who are you?" I asked.

No answer.

To know that spirits actually existed was something of a relief. I'd always sensed them floating around as if they were playing hide-and-seek, waiting to be discovered. But whenever I turned toward them, they disappeared, dancing mockingly just outside my perception.

My father had told me many stories about his great-uncle Leslie, who he said was a well-known psychic in Plymouth, England, in the early 1900s. I had been afraid of ghosts, but Daddy told me not to worry, that I didn't seem to have received the gift of perception. Being an Aries on the cusp of Pieces made me too young of a soul, he said. I had cried myself to sleep that night, believing I had not been chosen to be part of the all-knowing crowd.

"If you are ready, we can tell you everything," said a youthful voice.

"Do you want to know? Do you want to know?" chanted another.

The voices wove together, blending like a choir.

I blew out a long sigh. My chest pounded madly. "Tell me who you are? Tell me."

"We are the ones watching out for you. We can tell you everything about everything, if you want to know. Are you ready?"

Something snapped. The answer was no. It wasn't that I didn't believe them, but that I didn't want to know.

I'd spent my whole life wanting to know, trying to be open to new ideas. I'd studied my dreams at every chance, capturing them upon waking, which I'd learned was the trick to remembering, to send it all back through your brain again, carving the neural pathways deeper. The Technicolor nightmare about plucking the damn flower that ended the world became a nauseating rerun during my teenage years, after Daddy's troubles began. The dream played every time my period was late, and whenever I forgot important homework or heard my parents argue at night.

Up until that minute, bravery had always won out. I'd lived with my eyes wide open. But there's a saying that fools rush in where angels fear to tread. I knew how irresponsible it felt to bite off more than I could chew. What good was knowing when there was nothing you could do about it?

"No, please go," I said politely but firmly. "I just want to lead a normal life. I want to fall in love, get married, and have children. I want to be done with all this crazy stuff. Please leave me alone."

"But—"

"No. Please go. All of you."

The spirits whimpered, and I felt bad and nearly called them back to say I was sorry and try to explain it all, but it was too late. They were already gone.

And then a few weeks later, I got exactly what I'd wished for.

In some bizarre, momentous overlapping of energy events, a tall and handsome man rolled up on a bicycle to the Old Town Art Fair ticket booth where I was volunteering on June 4, 1984. Something about his face evoked Caravaggio's painting of Bacchus. I laughed at the thought of him serving me grapes. The sun hit my eyes. We were introduced by a mutual friend, and by time his full pink lips said, "Hi, I'm Rob," I understood for the first time what Bucky had meant when he said, "Love is metaphysical gravity, omni-inclusive and compassionately attuned to other than self."

The magnetic pull of this Bacchus-like human was so strong that I discarded all notions of doom and gloom at that moment. I stopped fretting. The world stopped ending.

Metaphysical gravity made anything possible.

Rob and I on our wedding day, May 9, 1987.
The world no longer needed saving.
But enough about us...

No small thinker, American genius Richard Buckminster Fuller (1895–1983) was determined to solve the global issues of housing, transportation, energy, resource management, and humanity's state of mind. To accomplish this, he worked to unearth and apply nature's design principles, proclaiming nature the finest and most efficient designer of all, in part because she had been at it so long. "I'm not trying to imitate nature," he said. "I'm trying to understand the principles she's using."

Courtesy, The Estate of R. Buckminster Fuller

Fuller witnesses the first Marine Corps test lift of his thirty-foot plastic and wood geodesic structure in 1954. This test led to the dome's eventual adoption for a variety of military purposes. Geodesic domes are still widely used for scientific exploration and camping, but Fuller's idea for them as modular, prefabricated, energy-efficient, affordable housing never got very far, thanks to a change-averse building industry. Climate change is bringing domes back in vogue today as cities like Dubai build domes over retail areas to keep shoppers cool. Bucky's dome over Manhattan (Google it) will give you an idea of what might one day be. (Don't forget Bucky's ideas were generally fifty years ahead of his time. For many of his ideas from the 1950s and 60s, the time is now.)

Courtesy, The Estate of R. Buckminster Fuller

Bucky's three-wheeled Dymaxion car of 1933 carried eleven passengers, went fifty miles on a gallon of gas, and could turn on a dime. The term Dymaxion was coined by an advertising copywriter at Macy's and is a portmanteau of the words dynamic, maximum, and tension. An accident caused by another car killed the driver and eventually the whole idea, even though the design itself was exonerated in the crash. As to the whole idea of a three-wheel car, if you have ever tipped over in one of Frank Lloyd Wright's three-legged chairs at SC Johnson Headquarters in Wisconsin, you might agree with its critics in questioning its practicality.

Courtesy, The Estate of R. Buckminster Fuller

Fuller's first large dome, some 50 feet in diameter, was erected in Montreal in 1950 by his Institute of Design students, and geodesic structures began to catch on all over the world. More than 300,000 were eventually said to have been built, mostly for housing. But even though Bucky penned a song called "Home in the Dome" and lived in a dome structure in Carbondale, he designed the dome not as housing but as a metaphor.

A geodesic dome encloses the maximum amount of space using a minimum of resources and surface area, exemplifying Fuller's concept of ephemeralization or doing more and more with less and less — another of nature's design principles. For another example of ephemeralization, look no further than the iPhone in your hand.

Courtesy, The Estate of R. Buckminster Fuller

Calvin Tompkins wrote in a 1966 New Yorker *article that the geodesic dome had been widely accepted as the strongest, lightest, and most efficient means of enclosing space yet devised by man. A year later, Bucky's magnificent 250-foot (78-meter) Montreal dome went up over the 1967 World Expo, said to be the most successful event of its kind in the twentieth century.*

The nondescript older man in a brown suit and thick glasses eavesdropping on the delighted gasps of attendees was Bucky himself. While he never set out to create beauty, he believed that unless something was beautiful when it was completed, it wasn't right. The plastic shell of the Montreal Dome burned during a remodel in 1976, and then stood barren for decades as an eerie, pyrrhic testimony that revolutions were not going to happen after all. Today, the Montreal Biosphere is a museum devoted to the environment.

Courtesy, The Estate of R. Buckminster Fuller

Delivering on Fuller's Amazon-like promise of quick and easy delivery, his 15,000-square-foot Kaiser Auditorium in Waikiki was erected in only twenty hours using aircraft structural and construction techniques and unskilled labor. This instant auditorium seated two thousand people and could withstand winds twice the strength of hurricane force. Until demolished for a new resort in 1999, it was a popular tourist attraction.

Courtesy, The Estate of R. Buckminster Fuller

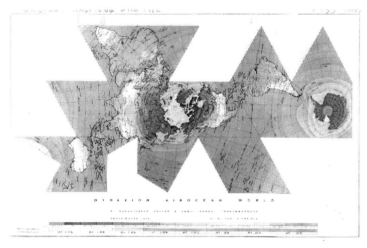

Fuller's 1954 Dymaxion Map remains the most accurate depiction of earth's land and water masses on a flat surface. This map, like all his inventions, was designed to help humanity better harness the resources of the world, or as he put it, "the effective application of the principles of science to the conscious design of our total environment to help make the Earth's finite resources meet the needs of all humanity without disrupting the ecological processes of the planet."

Other Bucky inventions include a Dymaxion house that hangs on a pole, an all-in-one bathroom, a fog gun shower, and an energy-generating seawall that protects against rising ocean levels. He also had ideas for underwater communities and even cities in the air. Since domes get lighter and stronger the bigger they are, they eventually float. Maybe one day, we will live together in domes high above a sea-covered earth, waiting for land to reappear once again.

Courtesy, The Estate of R. Buckminster Fuller

The crown jewel of Buckminster Fuller's geodesic domes is found at Walt Disney's Epcot Center in Orlando, Florida. Strolling up to this immense structural master-piece for the first time is a jaw-dropping experience. If you look closely, you will see the very heart of Bucky's best thinking. Nature builds with triangles, not squares, because they are stronger. His dome is a marriage of nature and technology that has inspired humanity to get its collective head in the game and make a conscious choice for utopia instead of oblivion. For livingry over weaponry. For making the world work for everyone, without harm to the environment. We can do this.

BUCKY CALLED IT

2001

My ideas have undergone a process of emergence by emergency.
When they are needed badly enough, they are accepted.
— Buckminster Fuller

Our three girls were almost ready for school, dressed in their matching plaid Catholic school uniforms. An unusually quiet breakfast was underway at the kitchen counter when Michaela, the youngest, screeched from the top of the stairs in her trademark high-pitched wail.

"Mommy! I can't find my shoes-ons!"

Squeals of laughter exploded from the other two.

Michaela had heard "get your shoes on" so often that she'd come to think that's what they were called, and nobody in this family was about to ruin the fun by setting her straight. I looked up at my fiery little angel on the staircase. Her hair was lit by the morning sun and stuck out like a dandelion pod, a golden halo. Her hands defiantly on her hips and with SpongeBob bandages on both knees, she stared down at me with a fury that made me wonder where it all came from.

Our oldest daughter, Alyssa, at thirteen, had her nose in a book as always. This habit often resulted in book pages eternally stuck together with sugary cereal milk or scrambled eggs. Olivia, at almost eight, had imprisoned her much despised curly hair in tightly braided pigtails secured with matching green bows. She was one put-together kid, the kind who tackled her homework the moment she got home from school and made her bed by slipping out of it.

Michaela bounded down the stairs shouting frantically. "Mommy!"

I looked around, hoping to find her shoes and diffuse her temper before it blew sky high.

Of course Alyssa had to taunt her. "Get your shoes-ons, Michaela! Michaela, get your shoes-ons!"

"Here are your shoes-ons, dear Michaela," Olivia called out with the false sweetness of a big sister, the small white tennis shoes dangling from her fingers.

Michaela stomped over to Olivia, eyeing us all suspiciously. Her eyebrows arched up onto her forehead.

"You mean my *shoes?*"

The gig was up.

The telephone rang. It was Rob's mother calling from Pittsburgh, telling us to turn on the TV, that America was under attack.

I clicked on the remote. They were showing the second airplane flying into the World Trade towers. The anchorman's voice crackled with adrenaline: "This removes any doubt about whether the first was an accident."

Then one of the tallest and most colossal symbols of America went down in a cloud of dust like it was a planned demolition. A sharp acid taste rose in my throat. My gut clenched. I lunged past the dirty breakfast dishes and out the door to the patio, where I threw up into the ivy, roaring out my terror at the evil of it all, not caring who might hear.

Rob came outside, followed by Heidi, our devoted golden retriever. They both eyed me anxiously.

"Hey, hey, honey—are you okay?" He reached out and touched my arm.

I flinched, wanting to blame him for everything; for living with his head in the sand. Realizing the ridiculousness of that, I let myself drop in a blathering heap. He caught me. I wasn't the type to fall so completely apart, but it felt good to sob into his soft wool suit jacket, which seemed so solid and safe to my touch.

He pulled back to look me in the eye, maybe in part to save his jacket from my pukey mouth and waterfall of tears. His eyes darted back and forth as he tried to connect with me.

"Look, honey, I know this is all really terrible, but you really need to hold it together for the kids, okay?"

I searched his eyes for answers. They were calm, as flat as slate.

"So, you do know that our idiotic government brought this on itself, right?" I demanded.

"Look, we don't know anything yet—"

"Are you kidding? For decades, we've been attacking countries all over the world, and now we're surprised when it comes home to roost? This is exactly what we've been asking for, ever since Vietnam. Ever since Hiroshima, actually. What about the Gulf War? Bosnia? Kosovo? Did we really think we'd get away with all our warmongering?"

"Look, honey, everything is going to be okay. Life will go on. Just get the kids to school, and then you can come home and fall apart. Okay?"

Rob's faith was beyond comprehension to me. He's the type who could be sitting on an airplane headed straight for the ground and still be able to put a reassuring hand on his wife's knee and say that everything would be fine. And he would mean it. He was a real Catholic. His faith was bottomless.

Olivia called from inside. "Mommy, where are you? We'll be late. Meet you at the car?"

I managed a smile. She sounded okay. I could fake it for now. "Sure, I'm ready. Your lunch is on the counter."

Rob kissed me on the forehead. I had not only married Mr. Right, but his middle name was Always. Of course, he was right again. Obviously, I had to keep it together — for the kids.

I watched my hand turn the keys in the ignition, thinking how quickly the world could change. The beautiful hanging flower baskets along the winding road through town seemed suddenly superfluous. What good were hanging flower baskets in a world where people hated one another enough to fly full passenger jets into buildings?

As mothers tend to do, I had honed my ability to imagine the worst possible outcome of any situation. This was a defensive move. I figured that by envisioning it, I would be able to see how to prevent it. In my mind, trucks regularly careened onto crowded sidewalks and flattened unsuspecting pedestrians. Kitchen knives plucked innocent eyeballs out of tiny faces. Children regularly fell head first out of trees. All so I could stop anything bad from happening.

It was a relief to see other faces at school looking as shocked and gray as mine felt. I wondered how many of them had also thrown up. With a hollow pit in my stomach, I reached for the hands of my friends Linda and Maureen, whose eyes were also wide with fear and rimmed in tears. The flag was raised half-staff as we gathered with a larger than normal group of parents for morning assembly and prayers.

The usually perky but now grave and stoic principal, a trim blond woman in her fifties stepped to the microphone in front of the kindergarten through eighth grade students, who were lined up and fidgeting as always. Her hair looked like a golden helmet, and the belt buckle on her black slacks caught the morning sun, glinting like some ancient warrior princess about to lead us into meaningful action.

She started in a low somber voice, thanking the teachers, students, and parents for showing up on "this horrific day" but then she said, "Staying the course and living our lives freely in this beautiful country is all that matters. To do anything else, to change how we live, well, that would be to concede defeat to the forces of evil. We will not and we cannot. We must continue to live our blessed lives."

So we should pretend like nothing had happened? Just like Rob had said? Who was writing these stupid scripts? What sense did they make? How would ignoring reality make it go away?

Father Shanahan stepped to the microphone. The stooped gray-haired priest seldom rose to anger for anything other than a Cal Bears loss to Stanford. His robes hung as still as if in an airless room and the words shot out of his mouth like a canon: "We pray. That one day. God will let us know. How something so evil... could ever be part... of His plan."

So now it was all God's fault? God had let this happen? What good did that kind of thinking do? Shouldn't he instead be talking about the real reasons why it happened?

Shouldn't he say something about how our government was bringing this hatred upon itself, thanks to its own bullheaded behavior throughout the world?

Nothing made sense. I felt lightheaded. I gripped Maureen's hand to steady myself. Had the falling of the towers created a new Tower of Babel?

Some of the parents were going to Java for coffee, but I declined. Somehow it felt wrong to go off and enjoy the comforting normalcy of caring friends and a latte when thousands of innocent people had died that very day. Surely there was something else, something more important that I ought to be doing.

I drove home listening to amped-up radio news reporters fretting over whether the Golden Gate Bridge might be next. I envisioned its giant orange metal arms collapsing into the ocean, cars tumbling into the sea, the world disintegrating into itself.

I found myself praying for the first time. Please don't let Rob be on that bridge if it comes down. Please don't let me go crazy. Maybe the Catholic religion had gotten through to me at long last. I counted my blessings that I had given up journalism. For so many years I'd kicked myself for abandoning one of the most noble professions to join one of the most notorious. Advertising had turned out to be not only soulless, but a major cause of America's problem with excessive material consumption. No matter how successful I might have been at writing ads, they were still just ads. Enticements to buy stuff nobody really needed, stuff that was killing the planet. Not to mention that writing ads was a complete waste of whatever meager ration of God-given creative talent I had been given.

Had I succeeded in journalism, I might have been right there in New York, at ground zero, when I couldn't even stomach watching it on TV from three thousand miles away. We were lucky to have escaped to the other side of the country, to be raising children in a lush green paradise where every single day, up until this one, had been a live streaming miracle.

Sunlight hit my windshield as I turned the minivan onto our tree-lined street. I felt full of gratitude. Momentarily blinded, I pulled the car over and smiled at the warmth on my face, and that's when Bucky's voice burst back into my head.

America is likely to fail. Future wars will not be fought by nations, but by rogue groups who will come to see America as the bully.

My hands gripped the steering wheel. Had he made a reservation in my mind all those years ago and now had come back to sit down with me again, on this horrific day?

America thinks it is too big to fail, which is why that is the likely outcome. Our intense sense of nationalism could be our undoing. We are proving ourselves incapable of integrating with the world.

My mind raced. It was bloody unnerving, his voice rambling inside me. Was this what insanity felt like? I tried to snap myself out of it, drove the rest of the way home, pulled into the driveway and spotted two forgotten lunch boxes on the back seat. Oh well, I would take them back to school at lunchtime, when I could check to make sure the girls were okay.

Heidi tail-whipped a dance of greeting when I stepped inside the front door. It was time for her daily walk up the mountain, down into the canyon, or out onto the beach. Heidi and I hiked everywhere together. I looked through the family room window and let my eyes come to rest on our beautiful mountain. Mount Tamalpais, affectionately known as the sleeping lady because of her seductive slumbering shape, relaxed along the horizon as if to offer up proof that not everything had changed. Green and alive, sleeping under the brilliant morning sun, her profile created a picture-perfect postcard. Not a wisp of fog. Not a cloud. A defiantly perfect day.

The world had changed in ways we could not yet comprehend. All I knew for sure was that our children's lives would not be as we had dreamed they would be. They already knew more ugliness in their lives than we had ever dreamed possible when we were their age.

"Not today, Heidi." I flopped down onto the couch. She dropped to the floor with a thud, staying close by like she always did. Heidi had been a willing receptacle for my worries from the time the girls were babies. How often had I looked up from nursing one of them in the middle of the night to see her there at my side, alert, watching on, in case there was something she might do to help.

The phone on the wall screeched. I jumped up to answer it. It was Rob saying another plane had flown into the Pentagon and yet another had crashed in a field in rural Pennsylvania. Authorities were telling everybody to go home and shelter in place in case more attacks were planned. His office was closing for the day.

"I love you," he said.

"Me, too—but this is scary, honey. Everything feels super wobbly. Heidi's chewing on her leg again, and I'm hearing voices."

"What? Look, hey, I know it's awful, but don't panic, okay? I'm on my way."

"Okay. Hurry—no, don't. Drive carefully."

I dropped back down onto the couch, rubbing Heidi's head to stop her from gnawing on her leg. How uncanny it seemed that Bucky had called it so precisely, saying America would be attacked, not by a country but by a rogue group, people we had oppressed.

My hand hit my forehead. My notes! Of course. I would dig them out and see what else he had predicted. I dashed upstairs to the hallway outside the bedroom, pulled down the ladder, climbed up into the hot attic and made my way back to the corner where the file boxes were stacked. I swept away the dust and cobwebs with a tattered pink fairy princess costume, a ruffled taffeta number which had begun as a flower girl's dress for a long-ago wedding. I wrestled opened a window and shook the dust and spiders off the dress before opening the boxes one by one. I found my copywriting files, my television sample reels, some old sketch books, tax returns going back God knows how many years, Rob's college papers, my father's stacks of *National Geographic* magazines, Rob's massive record collection, and some old text books. But no writing box. No Bucky.

I was stumped.

The only things I wrote these days were baby book entries and birthday party invitations. Staying home with the children had been a no-brainer for me, in more ways than one. First, it was a no-brainer because parenting was obviously the most important job ever, but also because if you spend all your days and nights caring for small children you ended up with exactly that: no brain. Motherhood sucked a vast yet undetermined number of cerebral cells right out of you. I had thought of little else other than shopping and homework and dinner in, well, forever.

Now where the hell were those notes?

Maybe I'd put them somewhere for safekeeping. I looked through everything again, all throughout the attic, digging through Mummy's old hope chest and an entire chest of drawers, but all I found were more stupid advertising sample reels and storyboards.

The only thing missing was the only thing that really mattered.

I slumped down into the same cushioned glider I had used to nurse all three babies, releasing a cloud of dust that made me cough. Maybe Rob had tossed the box out during one of his cleaning fits. We never did see eye on eye on political things. His defense of the trickle-down free market remained as passionate as my distain of it. All through the 1980s and 90s I had railed against the corporations' blank check to do whatever they wanted. Rob always reassured me the wealth was trickling down, a theory that Bucky had called a planned indoctrination. It hadn't taken me long to learn that men don't like to hear from their wives that they think they have been indoctrinated.

Rob had been dubious from the start. On that sweet summer day when I first told him about Bucky, I was sure I was falling in love. Rob was smart, caring, funny, and most of all, he had integrity. He was not the type to ever cheat on either his wife or his taxes, and he would certainly never plot to take down Wall Street just to afford himself a yacht. We were on a picnic in Lincoln Park, near the zoo. I tried to casual about it.

"Did I tell you I got to interview the Buckminster Fuller?"

"Really? The geodesic dome guy?"

"That's him. He was so cool, Rob, really brilliant—his synergetic geometry might be the secret to a successful future for us all."

"Huh?" He was preoccupied, carefully slicing a ball of fresh mozzarella with his Swiss army knife. He placed the cheese atop some thick crusty Italian bread, then sliced a fat red tomato he had grown on his fire escape and added it to the creation. A small bottle of balsamic vinegar appeared from his backpack, and I watched his gorgeous masculine hands put together two identical works of art. He handed me one and smiled.

My mouth watering, I asked, "What, no basil?"

He laughed and pretended to take it back from me.

My first impression of him as Bacchus had been prescient. All four of his grandparents were immigrants from northern Italy; one from a small town near Milan, called Suisio, the other from Montecatini Terme, a Tuscan town prized for its mud baths. He had been taught how to cook by his two Italian grandmothers, who were no doubt mired in ruthless competition for the culinary soul of their first-born American grandchild.

He loved to cook. I loved to eat. We were a great match. Biting into his most recent creation was like tasting food for the first time.

"You did this interview as part of your job?" he asked.

"No, I did it on my own. I had been writing these dumb Happy Meal boxes and felt like a sell-out for leaving journalism. I read he was in town so I looked him up. I thought I would do some freelance writing. You know, save the world."

"And he agreed to an interview, just like that?"

"Yeah, pretty much. Bucky liked to talk, and I told him I was a freelance journalist."

His laugh was almost a snort. "Ha! You do have gumption, I'll give you that."

"Guilty as charged, but is that such a bad thing? Anyway, how or why I interviewed him isn't what's important. It's his ideas, Rob. They're brilliant, even miraculous, all about how, if we can let go of negative conditioning and shift our thinking just a scooch, we can improve the world for all of humanity. I promised him I would carry his ideas forward in time and share them with the world when it was ready."

"Go for it, save the world, somebody's got to do it." He wiped his mouth with one of the linen napkins he'd brought along, kissed my cheek, then leaned back on one elbow to scrutinize me. He was always sizing me up. I pretended not to notice even though it was unnerving. What was he thinking? His brow furrowed deeply. The last thing I wanted to do was scare him off, so I decided to cool it on the whole Bucky thing. I would not even bring up politics, unless he mentioned Adam Smith again. The mere mention of Adam Smith's invisible goddam hand in defense of the free market was like a punch to my gut, a reminder to only go along with the truth, even if it means calling out the nonsense of someone you love. By now, surely almost everyone knew that Adam Smith's invisible hand was pummeling the crap out of the little guy.

The bottom line was that there is more to life than politics. I simply could not deny the gravitational pull of this human being. He was perfect in almost every way, and he seemed to be falling in love with me too, although in part I think he must have needed a project because he started inviting me to church on Sundays. Eventually he steered me into the whole Catholic religious training program, and I was baptized, confirmed, and tasted my first communion wafer all on the same day.

Talk about indoctrination! Did I believe the whole Jesus miracle story? Honestly, I don't think so, but it felt good to belong to something bigger than myself. I was open to anything that would help me make sense of the world.

When I met his extended family, I saw a picture of what a happy life could be. They were a big noisy clan, in many ways the opposite of my stiff-upper-lip English brood. Close knit and loving, they seemed to trust one another fully. They would duke it out in fiery arguments over dinners lasting into the wee hours, but then would be laughing and hugging each other by the time we left for mass the following morning.

With Rob and Jesus at my side, life was full.

I had been wanting to tell them both about my past, in part to be honest with Rob, but also to make sure it wasn't a deal breaker, so I worked up my courage one Friday evening as we walked together to a friend's birthday party in Old Town. It wasn't until my hand landed on front door knob that I turned to him, took a deep breath, and said, "What I've been trying to tell you is that I didn't graduate from college."

"Oh. Is that all? I thought you were going to say you'd been married before."

I turned the door knob. "That too," I said, and slipped into the crowded party. Moments later, he smiled at me from across the room and shook his head in wonder with an expression that said he loved me, no matter what, that nothing I could do or say would shake him off.

Bucky had said it best: "Love is omni-inclusive, progressively exquisite, understanding, and compassionately attuned to other than self."

Any lingering fears I had about humanity's impending doom vaporized later that same night in the steam rising off a boiling pot of Rob's homemade fettucine. You do not know what you are missing in this life until it rolls up on a bicycle.

LOST GENIUS

2001

If humanity does not opt for integrity we are through complete-ly. It is absolutely touch and go. Each one of us could make the difference. — Buckminster Fuller

Heidi barked from down below.

The front door slammed.

"Honey, are you okay?" Rob called out.

"I'm up here."

"What are you doing in the attic?"

The ladder creaked under his weight. He ducked his head so as not to hit his head. My tall and handsome husband was still wearing his trench coat, the same one he owned when I met him fifteen years ago.

I raised my head from my hands. "Rob? Rob, where are my notes?"

"Are you okay, honey? What are you looking for?"

"My Bucky notes. I can't find them."

He looked puzzled. "You mean Buckminster Fuller?"

"Yes, you know, *the* Buckminster Fuller? The brilliant genius who predicted this mess? He knew this was going to happen, Rob. I need those notes."

"He knew what was going to happen? This attack on America? I'm sure plenty of people predicted it. The terrorists are pretty determined, you know."

I tried not to roll my eyes. "Fine, whatever, I need those notes."

He dug his hands into his pockets. "Honey, all that was so many years ago. How could it have anything to do with what happened today?" He came closer and reached out to me. "What's this really all about? Are you okay?"

I rocked in the chair, sizing him up, wondering if he'd tossed out my notes on purpose.

His face paled. "Wait—honey, don't you remember? Your files were in the basement when it flooded. In Chicago. You made me throw them out. Don't you remember?"

Shit.

The putrid water at the bottom of the basement stairs. We had just moved in. My mother suggested we store everything in the basement so as not to clutter the upstairs. There were torrential rains all night, and that Monday morning, I took a silk blouse downstairs to iron, only to be greeted by several feet of water creeping up the stairs. My file boxes were entombed in a watery grave, the ink of the words Bucky Files dissolving before me. My wedding dress floated by, its lacy sleeves waving to mock my distress. I screamed out to Rob. He came running downstairs and hoisted the box out the water, saying we should try to dry it out to see if anything could be saved, but I had flipped out. "It's ruined! It's all ruined! Throw it out. Nobody's ever going to care about some dead genius named Bucky!"

Before I'd left for work, I also demanded that he toss out my wedding dress, which I had bought off the rack on sale anyway, so it didn't matter either. None of it mattered.

So there it was. My notes were gone. I could scarcely breath. Sunlight streamed in through the attic window, lighting up the dust I'd disturbed. The twirling golden particles danced to mock both me and this most tragic day. I stared at it and tried to focus on my breathing, but the tears came anyway.

Rob took off his coat and sat on a box in front of me. "It doesn't matter, honey. None of it matters. We're going to be okay."

I was still staring at the dancing dust lit by the sun. I let my tears fall. "It does matter, Rob. It absolutely does matter. You don't understand. I made a promise."

"Hey, hey, honey, don't cry." He shifted uncomfortably. "Look, I know it's unfathomable what has happened. Driving away from you this morning made me realize how much I love you. You are the most important thing in my life. Nothing bad is going to happen. We are going to be okay."

His once comforting blind faith now infuriated me. "Surely you can see that humanity is in decline, and I—"

"Whoa, whoa. Humanity in decline? Are you kidding? Things are going great. The GDP is at an all-time high. The economy is booming. Turn off NPR, Pat. The world is going to be fine."

I shook my head in disbelief. How could two people in love, living in the same world, reading and hearing the same news, see things so differently?

"Look, honey," he said, "bottom line is you really need to hold it together for the kids. They are smart, happy, and well-adjusted. We need to keep them that way."

Of course, he was right. The children were the most important thing.

"But that is exactly my point," I said. "It's their future on the line. One day, the girls will look back and wonder why the hell we didn't do something while we still could."

"Okay, there will be plenty of time for all that later, but for now, unless they see you losing it, they'll be fine. You heard Alyssa this morning. She said it seemed like a movie or something on TV, like it wasn't real."

"But honesty matters. Reality matters!" I had let my voice raise since the girls weren't home. I heard Heidi's leg thumping on the floor below us as she scratched herself. Bucky had said it a thousand times. *Whether or not humanity makes it will be up to the individual, and whether we have the courage to only go along with the truth.*

Rob rubbed my back. "If we let this derail our lives, honey, the terrorists will have won. Things will be fine. You watch."

I stood. I had heard enough. Is there any greater proof that things are going horribly wrong than when everyone struggles to pretend that it's not? I sidestepped his attempt at another hug and climbed down the ladder, grabbed the kids' furry blanket and the remote control, and flopped down onto the couch like a toddler. The blanket smelled like dog.

Even though the state of the world wasn't entirely Rob's fault, he was partly to blame. He and everyone else who had looked the other way for too long, and too often, with too little thought, were at fault. Einstein was right. Ignoring evil was the worst evil of all.

Deny, deny, deny. Don't worry, be happy. Everything will be fine.

Bullshit.

Heidi sat my feet, gnawing at one of the girls' expensive ski socks. A dog's lifelong assignment was apparently to soak up everyone's stress and then chew it to death. I extracted the soggy sock from her mouth just as she was about to swallow it whole. She yipped at me, pleading for a walk. Heidi never yipped, but even a dog's love had its limits.

Rob went outside to cut back the blackberry bushes. How like him to use a day off work due to the coming end of the world as an opportunity to get a few more things done around the house.

The whole story made no sense. I switched channels all around. Every single reporter on every station said the same words. The commercial jet fuel—running down through the elevator shafts—had spread the fire and brought down the buildings. This struck me as utterly absurd. The planes had exploded on impact. Surely the jet fuel had burned up then. I had seen those towering structures first hand. Even a fully loaded 747 was like a toy compared to their massiveness. Each time I watched the towers collapse upon themselves, the reporters' explanations seemed more canned and more ludicrous. At one point, a shaky-voiced journalist called out the tiny puffs exploding out of the windows, one floor after another, saying it looked like a controlled demolition. Her voice wasn't heard again. When the camera zoomed in on the miniscule human figures leaping from the windows, I thought I might throw up again.

Rob came inside from the garden and was rattling around in the kitchen, making lunch.

I called out to him. "Every single reporter on every network is reporting the same absolutely ridiculous story as if there is no other plausible explanation."

"Maybe it's obvious what happened. Maybe it is exactly as they say. Has that occur to you?"

"Rob, think about it. Normally inquisitive reporters aren't even speculating about obvious things. Who is telling them what to say?"

"Their editors. Their managers. Come on, you worked in journalism. You know lowly reporters don't have much freedom."

"I have a hard time believing this massive destruction was pulled off by some bearded man in an Afghani cave. I smell a rat."

"You should come and eat something, and maybe take a nap. I've made a panini for you."

I staggered into the kitchen and drizzled some balsamic glaze onto the fresh melted mozzarella and tomatoes from the garden, ate in silence, then returned to the couch and drifted off to sleep, thinking about my father. What would he have thought of all this? Maybe it was a blessing he hadn't lived long enough to see it. He'd died suddenly of a brain aneurysm the weekend after Rob and I announced our engagement some fifteen years ago. Even though he called us all "bloody stupid Americans," he had cared more than he let on. After he died, I'd found some of my childhood drawings among his keepsakes in a cigar box, which helped me to forgive him a little and made me wonder whether I had ever known him at all.

CNN was still blasting when I woke up on the couch feeling numb and disoriented. Heidi yawned at me mournfully. When I finally arose to get some water, my eyes came to rest on the bookcase, landing on Bucky's *Utopia or Oblivion – The Prospects for Humanity*. Still bleary from sleep, I dusted off the smallish book and flipped to the final paragraph.

"Within decades we will know whether man is going to be a physical success on earth…or whether he is going to frustrate his success with negatively conditioned reflexes of yesterday which will bring about his own extinction from planet earth. My intuitions foresee his success, despite his negative inertias. This means things are going to move fast."

Time moved so fast for me as I began to reread Bucky that I was late to pick the girls up from school. Not at all happy with me, they hungrily gobbled up their forgotten lunches, still abandoned in the back seat. Mother of the year I was not.

On the way home, we learned that a third building had collapsed to the ground, World Trade Tower Seven. "The fire and heat from the other two buildings must have jumped over," a radio reporter said.

I couldn't believe what I was hearing. Jumping fire had taken down another massive high rise. It was like some unbelievably stupid disaster movie had turned into real life. But after an exhausting day of crying and grieving, the truth no longer held its ground. It didn't matter. The only thing that mattered was that I held it together. The world had turned upside down in less than twelve hours, but the job of being a mother went on. I faked it. Fake it till you make it, as the saying goes.

Less than a month later, we were making dinner in the kitchen when we heard the news that President Bush had won the support of an almost unanimous Congress to go to war in Afghanistan against the Taliban. The brilliant men and women now running America's government had decided to "win hearts and minds" by bombing a country to smithereens, with "shock and awe" they promised.

"Brilliant!" I shouted at the television. "Our idiot president is going to kill people to win us more friends, and he also wants us to climb back into those airplanes and go to Disney World!"

Alyssa looked up from her homework. "I would like to go to Disney World."

Rob was chopping onions for his Bolognese sauce. "I think it's a good idea for us to fight them over there. That way they won't have the resources to come here and attack us."

"War is not the answer, Dad," said Alyssa.

"I couldn't agree with you more," I said to her. "Do you realize, Rob, that America has started more than twenty wars since World War II? More than any other country? I know you can't bear to face it — you want to think America is good — but we have become the world's biggest bully."

He looked up and pressed his invisible mute button by blinking his eyes, then asked Alyssa if she needed help with her homework. She did not. She was brilliant. Maybe she would be the one to save the world. I couldn't even get through to my own husband.

I tried to stay calm, but had to finish my thought. "No matter how wonderful you think this country is, our extreme sense of nationalism will be our undoing, just like Bucky said. America has been the world's biggest swinging dick of a bully, and we are getting our comeuppance."

"Nice mouth. Why not think about your children once in a while?"

I lowered my voice. "You are the one enabling a hellish future for them and our future grandchildren, not me."

Alyssa pushed her homework aside. "How is Dad doing that?"

"Well, honey, I would say he is being like an ostrich with his head in the sand. This war is all about oil, which we should be leaving in the ground if we want humanity to survive."

Rob shook his head. "Is this about climate change again? Look, honey, the very idea that after hundreds of thousands of years of relative stability, our climate is suddenly going to go out of whack, it sounds crazy to me. Highly unlikely. And I hate it when you trash America. We are the country that always comes to the rescue in a disaster. We are so generous. We are the greatest nation on earth. Do you realize how well the economy is doing? People are living better and living longer than ever before in history. World hunger is way down. Why can't you ever relax?"

"Yeah, Mom. Don't worry. My speech contest is tomorrow. Come practice with me."

I wanted to scream and throw myself crying onto the kitchen floor, maybe hold my breath the way Michaela did, until I turned blue and passed out, anything to get my family to understand how dumb this new war was. But instead, Heidi and I followed Alyssa obediently into her room and sat on her bed to listen to her speech about an achy, achy bellyache. Ten times.

Don't worry, be happy.

God dammit.

THE
HACKTIVIST

2004

Whenever I draw a circle, I immediately want to step out of it.
—Buckminster Fuller

The sunlit ferry to San Francisco from Larkspur was packed with protesters of all ages, carrying signs reading *Peace is Not a Pejorative*, *Regime Change Begins at Home*, and *Put Down That Crack Pipe, Mr. President*. I had never been much for protests, but I was desperately seeking some semblance of sanity on this whole new war thing, and none of my friends were with me. They all thought bombing the terrorists was the only thing that made sense, so I'd dropped the kids off at school wearing an old tie-dyed T-shirt under my favorite jean jacket, which still sported my *Jimmy Carter for President* button from 1977.

When the ferry docked at the terminal, our all white, mostly middle-aged Marin contingent walked together across the Embarcadero to Justin Herman Plaza, joining a huge and diverse crowd of lively protesters, many pounding on drums or holding up signs. Some had even taken their children out of school for the day. Regretting I hadn't done the same, I joined people of all colors and creeds, some in elaborate native dress, and we chanted, "No more war for oil" and "Mission not accomplished." This referred to President Bush's recent big-headed premature declaration of victory on an aircraft carrier.

A voice from a megaphone announced that the march to City Hall was starting. I followed along as the crowd began to move up Market Street toward the Civic Center. The streets were closed to automobiles. Hundreds, even thousands of people filled the street ahead and behind me. A flock of lovely young women wearing diaphanous white dresses came dancing up from behind. They carried homemade torches of burning sage and a sign proclaiming they were *Angels Dancing Peace.* They pirouetted through the crowd, flowing gracefully through us, singing about love and nonviolence. I wished I was one of them.

My reporter's instincts come out at times like this. I wanted to understand fully what was going on and share it with others, but when you're swallowed up in a large, slow-moving crowd, you know nothing about the big picture. I looked around for reporters but there were no news trucks, no television cameras. Did it matter how many millions of people marched for peace if the only witnesses were the marchers themselves? Weren't we just like trees falling in an empty forest? What did it matter if nobody was watching?

When we arrived back at the plaza, a woman who had introduced herself to me earlier as one of the "Raging Grannies of Oakland" held out a shiny glass pipe.

"You look worried," she said. "Would you like a tiny puff? It's medical, clean and nice."

I hadn't tasted reefer since I'd learned I was pregnant for the first time, which was a lifetime ago. But hey, Hunter S. Thompson had called it a staple of life, along with beer, ice, and grapefruits, and millions of Americans agreed. (Just not about the grapefruits.)

And besides, desperate times called for a relaxing of old self-imposed rules, so I took a long slow hit. The raging granny and I sat back under the shade of a tree and let our ideas bounce around like cotton balls. We saw eye to eye on everything. We both feared that Bush's war would create a whole new generation of enemies for America, and we wondered how anyone could be so shortsighted as to not see this.

Other raging grannies joined us, and I sat back to savor the old familiar feeling of being in touch with another dimension, a place located just outside my own head. Looking around at the earnest and intelligent women around me, women who had given up their time to protest, my heart filled to know how many good, caring people of all colors, ages, and walks of life surrounded me and agreed with me. I had found my tribe.

The pipe got passed around again. I told the women about Bucky's ideas regarding the role of women in the world, about how our leadership was critical. Bucky had spoken at length about the value of women at a national convention on leadership in 1982. "It is men that got up the false story that they are superior," he said. "Men should realize that only women are continuous, and only women are hard-wired for compassion."

In a 1968 cover story for *McCall's* magazine, Bucky wrote that that women, the original industrialists, had always been "more than equal" to men: "Woman was domesticator, manufacturer, and industrialist. Men only hunted. When prehistoric man brought home a strange new creature, it was the woman who decided whether to kill it, skin it, and eat it, or whether to keep it alive to carry or pull loads, to crop its hair for wool, or to milk it. Women organized the home crew to pound the corn, thresh grain, comb wool, and dry the skins. Women invented pottery and weaving and food storage. Women intuitively knew that Nature impounded the sun's energy through vegetation, and gradually they domesticated fruits, nuts, and seeds."

He wasn't alone in his feminism. Futurists and philosophers back in the 1800s had also sensed it was time for a new feminine paradigm of governance. One such visionary was Bucky's great-aunt, Margaret Fuller, who was widely known as an outspoken feminist before the word even existed. She was friends with Ralph Waldo Emerson and Henry David Thoreau, and she was also the first female foreign correspondent for a major city newspaper. She had inspired Bucky greatly.

The grannies loved being reminded about Bucky, especially his ideas about how our society was built on fallacies, such as the accepted mandate that everyone needed to "earn a living." Bucky had known that automation and ephemeralization would soon make traditional jobs obsolete.

"We should give up the specious notion that everyone must earn a living," I said, quoting Bucky, who had explained that one in ten thousand of us could make a technological breakthrough capable of supporting all the rest. He said the youth of today were right in recognizing the nonsense of earning a living, that the false idea everybody must be employed at some kind of drudgery stemmed from Malthusian Darwinian theory that man must justify his right to exist. The true business of people, Bucky said, should be to go back to school and think about whatever it was they were thinking about before somebody came along and told them they had to earn a living.

Some of the grannies knew Bucky's ideas as well as I did. "Grass doesn't pay for sunshine," the lady with the pipe quoted him. "Fish don't pay for water. How did nature's most sophisticated species get roped into thinking they had to work so hard to earn the right to live?"

We stood together and held hands for a closing prayer led by a Native American tribal chief, and for the first time in years, I didn't feel alone.

On the ferry ride back to Larkspur, I stood outside on the bow to feel the cool breeze and misty spray coming off the waves and thought about Rob and how his inherent goodness made him more susceptible to propaganda. Because he had so much integrity, he assumed others did too. Scofflaws like me knew better. I was feeling a little sorry for him, and thinking maybe it wasn't his fault he was so clueless to the reality of things, when I walked off the ferry without my wallet and keys.

I pounded back to fetch them, feeling like an idiot. The unnerving downsides of smoking pot returned to me. Your mind floats off onto another plane, which feels utterly delicious, but then just when you start to relax and enjoy your new-found brilliance, something happens to let you know that the totally clueless one is you.

It wasn't until I saw Heidi's wagging tail at the front door that I remembered the girls. I grabbed a breath mint and raced to school, where I greeted them with a big fake smile.

Alyssa was fuming. "Where were you, Mom? We tried to call."

Olivia's hands were clenched, on her hips. "The principal even tried to call you, Mom. How embarrassing can you get?"

"Sorry, guys. I was running errands and got held up."

Alyssa smiled and hugged me. "It's okay."

"Are you all right, Mommy?" asked Michaela. "There is sad in your eyes."

"Oh, sweetheart, yes, thank you, I'm okay."

I drove home feeling like one twisted, screwed-up human being. Brooding women do not make good mothers or wives, or even friends. Smoking weed with raging grannies was simply not the answer. Going to protest marches was a waste of time. Talking to Rob was like pounding my head against a wall. Nothing was working.

Bucky's words were now on my mind every day, like this passage from *Critical Path*:

"Humanity has to qualify to survive...we're designed to live by trial and error. Don't worry about making mistakes. Study your mistakes; admit them, study them again, and be terribly excited about them too...it is all part of living up to the miraculous human being you can be."

I'm trying, Bucky. I'm trying.

WATERFALLS
OF DENIAL

2008

Tension is the great integrity.
— Buckminster Fuller

The air in Baltimore Canyon had that heavenly quality that comes after a rain, overflowing with the negative ions that reportedly help human brains fire more efficiently. Long hikes under the redwoods with Heidi had become a necessity now that all three girls were teenagers and life was an eternally unfolding roller coaster ride.

Rob and I were getting used to all the drama. We handled teary-eyed arguments about curfews and unsupervised parties, even shouts of "I hate you" as bedroom doors slammed. What kept things in perspective for me was the simple fact that humanity was still racing toward extinction. Somehow, pilfered mascara and missed curfews paled in comparison to the big ugly picture of all that was not happening in the world.

Al Gore's 2006 movie *An Inconvenient Truth* had shaken me to the core. The few climate scientists brave enough to speak out were even more alarmed, some saying New York would be underwater soon and that the tipping point was near or had already passed.

The good news was that Barack Obama had been elected president, and Rob and I had voted the same way for the first time. I'd been thinking it was time to apply myself fully to the job of bringing Bucky's ideas back in some serious way, so I mustered the courage to break the peaceful mood of our hike with something Rob probably didn't want to think about.

"So I want to talk to you about something." I fell in behind him on the narrow stony path. Heidi bounded up ahead, thrilled to be let off her leash.

"What's up? Something with the girls?"

"No, the girls are fine, getting along better."

"They've been fighting like cats and dogs from what I can see."

"They're fine. They're learning how to get along. It's not about them. It's about climate change. And Bucky."

He exhaled a deep sigh. "What? Bucky again? What is your deal with this?"

That didn't seem fair. I was sure I hadn't mentioned him for years. Or at least weeks. "Don't you see? He was right. In 1982 Bucky said we were entering a dark age, and that's exactly what happened. Compared to what we knew back then, America is in a dark place, Rob. Surely you can see that."

He tossed a stick for Heidi with an irritated grunt. "What are you talking about?"

"Bucky worried that Americans were becoming oblivious, that we would let pride and nationalism get in the way of the truth. And true to his predictions, we have done nothing for decades. We've accepted the wall of denial intentionally built to block the truth."

"Dark age? Here? In America? Are you crazy? We're so much more informed now, thanks to the Internet. There's more information available than ever before in history. You can Google anything now."

"I'm not talking so much about information as insight. People don't understand the harm our government is doing. It is screwing things up for all of humanity by creating enemies the world over and by allowing earth-destroying carbon pollution to go unchecked."

He said nothing, just kept trudging up the trail.

"Can't you see, honey? Don't you think it makes at least a little sense?"

He stopped walking and turned to face me. "You know, I hate it when you get all high and mighty like this. Your view of what's happening is just that: your view. Who are you to claim to know the truth about what is really going on?"

"I don't know. But I just do. I've been paying attention for a long time."

I stepped aside to let a young bearded man with a black Labrador retriever pass us on the trail and lowered my voice. "I'm not saying it's anybody's fault or some big conspiracy, honey. Our denial has grown organically. Our day-to-day lives distract us just enough so that we never get around to thinking about big-picture things. We've let corporations run unchecked for thirty years and a lot of damage has been done. From chemicals to big pharma and especially fossil fuels, they run our government now, with no concern for their impacts on people or the environment. You get that, right? Isn't that the very definition of fascism?"

"Fascism? Are you crazy? Here's what you need to get. People are living better than ever before. World hunger and poverty are declining. And climate change is a slow-moving problem. It's never going to be an urgent crisis. Okay? Can you please just stop worrying so much?"

"Einstein said it best. There is greater peril from those who tolerate evil than from those who actually commit it."

He glared at me. "Wow."

"What? It's true."

He threw the stick for Heidi and gathered his thoughts. When you have been married to someone for twenty years, you can sense when thoughts are being gathered, even when his back is turned. There was a certain hunch of his shoulders, a stillness to his head. Heidi made a big fuss returning with the stick to distract us. Rob rubbed her neck and ears, then turned and looked me right in the eye. "Look, honey, can't you please just look around at this amazing place? These trees have been here hundreds of years, and they will still be here long after we're gone. Climate change is a glacial thing. It will happen glacially... which means very, very slowly..." He said the words at a snail's pace to annoy me, but I didn't bite.

"I know," I said. "I know. But the problem goes beyond climate, Rob. What about the massive transfer of wealth going on? America's poor are getting so much poorer, you know."

He shot me a flat look. "Poverty is way down."

"Bucky spelled it all out in *The GRUNCH of Giants*. GRUNCH stands for 'gross universal cash heist.' He said the ultra-rich were sucking up all the wealth while getting everyone to look the other way at a constant stream of manufactured crises."

"Both sides are guilty of spreading propaganda. Al Gore sounds ridiculous sometimes, like when he warns that things are going to suddenly go wildly out of control."

"But we *do* know we only went to war in Iraq because America wanted easier and cheaper access to oil. The WMDs were faked. We know that now, remember? As a result, thousands — some say hundreds of thousands — of innocent people died. Maybe even a million. That blood is on America's hands. Honey, think about it, a bogus war was waged under false pretenses. If that's not a crime against humanity, I don't know what is."

He stopped to pick up Heidi's stick. "Can you please keep your voice down? Even Heidi looks worried."

I took a deep breath. "Even dogs know things aren't right. She can probably feel the excessive carbon in the air."

He snorted. "You're nuts."

"I'm sorry, Rob, but the only crime committed against humanity greater than the Iraq War is the fossil fuel industry's deliberate obstruction of clean energy. The ever-rising carbon numbers indicate it's an increasingly urgent situation. Something has to be done."

"What about the Holocaust?"

"What about it?"

"Surely it was a greater crime than Iraq?"

"Well sure, but even that pales in comparison to what the fossil fuel industry is doing."

He threw the stick for Heidi. "Can't we ever talk about anything else? Ever? Can't we talk about this amazing place we're so lucky to live in? Or our wonderful kids? Or our friends, of which we used to have plenty?"

It wasn't the first time he blamed me for the recent deficit of invitations from friends. I knew he was still angry over the incident at the neighborhood Christmas party when I'd accidentally poked one of our favorite neighbors in his red plaid holiday vest while attempting to make a point about the deceptions of the fossil fools. Rob had watched me do it from across the room. His eyes had grown wide as saucers, and he spilled some of his martini to witness me breach my promise to stop haranguing people.

We kept walking. It was awhile before either of us spoke again. Heidi pranced up the trail toward us with a huge tree branch in her mouth. We both laughed, which felt good. I waited until we reached the top of the waterfall where we always stopped before I took a deep breath and circled back around one more time. "Honey, I'm telling you from the bottom of my heart and from ninety-nine percent of climate scientists, that it is time to shout, time to do something big and dramatic about carbon levels now — or this fabulous life you love will be gone, maybe sooner than you think. Who are we to deny scientists who would be screaming in the streets if they were permitted by their society and culture to do so?"

"I'm not denying science."

"But by not demanding that anything happen, you actually are."

He stood up and stared at me. "It doesn't help to obsess over it like some crazy person."

I scrambled up onto a boulder overlooking the small waterfall. As if I were Mufasa in *The Lion King*, I thrust an imaginary baby out in front of me, threw my head to the sky and gave a silent scream. It was the soundtrack of my life ever since 9/11, a muted and mournful scream.

▽▽▽

In the dead of that night Rob bolted upright in bed.

"I can't do this anymore."

It wasn't like him to cry out. I figured he was having a bad dream.

"What's the matter, honey? Are you okay?"

He sighed and dropped back onto his pillow.

"I think you were talking in your sleep." I checked my phone. 3:19 a.m.

"No, I'm wide awake. Can't sleep. I've been thinking. Our friends think you are crazy. I think you need help."

My eyes opened fully. Long shadows of birch trees swayed on walls I had just had painted a beautiful new color called Skipping Stone, a subtle brownish gray. Moonlight washed over the walls. This was my life. Beautiful, but damaged. My husband thinks I am crazy.

I rolled over to see if he was awake. He looked up at the ceiling then said it again. "I can't do this anymore."

I sat up. "Who says I'm crazy, Rob? And what do you say when they say your wife is crazy? Do you say you agree with them?"

"No, of course I don't."

"Then what do you say?"

"I tell them the truth."

"Which is what, oh, Obi-Wan Kenobi?"

"I tell them that you're really smart, but you're obsessed with complicated ideas of some dead genius nobody understands or cares about. You've gotta admit, it sounds a little crazy."

I watched the shadows dance like ghosts on the wall, feeling as thin as moonlight. "Why can't you ever just believe in me?"

"I do, honey, I really do. But do I think Buckminster Fuller gave you urgent messages to pass on that will secure the survival of the human species? Uh, no."

"I never said that."

"Yes, you did. You first said it forever ago in Lincoln Park."

"I did? Like that?"

"I'll never forget it," he said, rolling over to face me. "We were lying together on a blanket outside the zoo. It was a nice warm summer day. You looked right into my eyes and told me that you had been chosen to pass on great secrets to help secure the future of humanity."

I laughed. "I did? I said that?"

"You did. Those were your exact words. I thought you were kidding at first. Then I got a little worried. Then I realized I loved you."

"You did? Right then?"

"Your passion was amazing. I knew I needed to watch over you. And you were highly entertaining."

I turned my back to him. "That's nice. That's really nice."

"What?"

"You married someone you thought was crazy for the entertainment value? What kind of sicko does that?"

"It wasn't like that, and you know it. You were a fiercely happy nut back then. Now you're just fierce."

I tried again. "I'm sorry. But I'm tired of playing perky in a world that feels like it's going to hell."

"In case you haven't noticed, I've been working my ass off so we'll be able to put the kids through college. Therefore, I do not have the luxury to sit around all day on Facebook." He threw back the covers, got out of bed, and cracked opened a window.

"I do not spend all day on Facebook."

Heidi banged her tail on the floor, keeping time with Rob's footsteps as he trudged to the bathroom. I took a long drink of water, dehydrated from last night's wine. Heidi came over to my side of the bed so I could rub her head. She always seemed to know when I needed her.

"Look, okay," he said when he returned. "I always knew you were something of a piece of work, what with your screwed-up childhood and all, but I knew you were the person I wanted to be with. You were hilarious, and nice, and you still have more passion for life than anyone else I have ever met."

This kind of outpouring was rare for him. I didn't realize it was a setup until he climbed back into bed, looked at me sympathetically, and said, "But honey, I gotta say—and you are not going to like this—despite all your passion and all your talent, you have less ability to actually manifest anything with it than anyone I've ever known. For all your hand-wringing, what have you actually accomplished?"

I turned away again so he couldn't see my face. He was right, of course. I had been studying both Bucky and climate change for years now, but had nothing to show for it. I'd read several of his books and almost everything written about him and still didn't fully understand what his ideas were about, but I was convinced of two things: Bucky's math and science somehow added up to a philosophy that could save humanity but for some reason, people tuned it out.

The 1986 discovery of a molecule Bucky predicted back in 1929 was turning out to be a big deal. Fullerene molecules are a class of closed hollow carbon compounds that comprise only the third form of pure carbon ever discovered on Earth. The most remarkable of these is a sixty-carbon molecule which scientists named the buckminster-fullerene because of its structural resemblance to the geodesic dome. For this same reason, it became known as a buckyball.

Bucky had predicted the existence of this molecule long before the advent of high-powered electron microscopes proved him right. When a researcher wrote to him in 1962 that his design was discovered in certain viruses, Bucky was delighted but not surprised. He knew the spherical structure was everywhere in nature. It follows the geometry of the icosahedron, creates what Bucky called a tension integrity, and encompasses the maximum amount of space using the minimal amount of materials.

Nature, Bucky said, always designs in the most efficient way possible, and humans needed to take note and start doing the same. It was all spelled out in Bucky's fourteen-hundred-page magnum opus *Synergetics*.

It was obvious to me that fullerenes were nothing short of miraculous. Their hollow structure made it possible to trap atoms inside them like a molecular cage. This strange capability caught the attention of the medical community, where researchers believe they will one day use buckyballs to deliver medicines to specific tissues and cells, like tiny delivery drones working inside your body. The buckyballs are remarkably rugged and capable of surviving collisions with metals and other materials at speeds in excess of twenty thousand miles per hour, a pace that would tear most organic molecules apart.

The most amazing thing of all is that despite their rather recent discovery in a laboratory, these molecules have been naturally present on Earth all along. They'd recently been identified in meteorites, impact craters, and materials struck by lightning, leading some scientists to speculate that fullerenes may have played a role in the onset of life on Earth, just as Bucky had speculated. Was it possible that buckyballs are what brought to Earth, from their stellar origin, the essential ingredient to kick-start all of life?

It occurred to my ordinary nonmathematical brain that these little molecules just might be the stem cells of the universe, since everything on earth is made of carbon and since buckyballs behave differently depending on what is inside them, just like a stem cell.

Maybe that means they might also hold the secret to creating energy right out of thin air, or at least storing it more effectively. Shouldn't energy researchers at places like Stanford be all over this? Bucky's ideas about energy had great resonance during the oil shortages of the 1970s, but since then they'd seem to have been forgotten. Why?

Rob was staring up at the ceiling. He turned his head my way. I could tell he'd been thinking long and hard about what to say next.

"Honey," he said, the lines forming like waves on his forehead. "You mean more to me than anything in the world. I just want us to be happy. I really think you need to talk to someone."

"You mean a therapist?" I searched for his eyes in the dark.

"Yes, I think you need to figure out how to be happy. I need you to be happy. The girls need you to be happy."

"So I should just turn off part of my brain?"

"It might help. I mean, do you ever go back and read the stuff you write?" He picked up his iPad, clicked to my Facebook profile, and scrolled through some of my postings.

"'Systemic ecosystem collapse?'"

"That's a link to a peer-reviewed science report—from respected professors at Stanford, no less, Paul and Anne Ehrlich, a married couple who have done exhaustive research in conservation biology and have concluded that we absolutely cannot continue in our current direction and still survive as a species."

"Okay, then the next post about one hundred percent clean energy?"

"Yes, this has been proven possible. Look up *The Solutions Project*, also from Stanford. It details exactly how to make the transition to one hundred percent clean energy, state by state."

"What about this one, 'unlocking the secrets of free energy'? You sound a little nutty sometimes, like you think you are some kind of genius."

He had me there. The free energy stuff was all my speculation about the potential of electromagnetic radiation and buckminsterfullerenes as potentially infinite energy resources. But it wasn't true I thought of myself as a genius, except by contagion from Bucky. Rob waited, but I didn't answer.

"You know, honey, you are a great mom and a smart woman, but come on. You're not a scientist, or an engineer, or have any of the credentials necessary to be an expert on this stuff."

Damn if he wasn't right again. Who the heck did I think I was, going on about things I didn't really understand? Just because our species was in big trouble didn't mean it was my job.

Even though I had heard it with my own two ears, on good authority, from a great and respected genius, I would catch myself wondering about the origin of the fierce maniacal voice of doom emanating from my own mouth. Was it possible Bucky spoke through me? Or is that just what all schizophrenics said right before they got leveled into conformity by the latest medications?

Was this whole Bucky thing not just about finishing an assignment, but about facing up to something cracked and broken inside me that needed fixing?

My obsession had turned out to be every bit as worthless as Rob's obliviousness. Neither of us were accomplishing anything.

"Okay, I'll find a therapist. You're right. I need help."

"Promise?"

"Promise."

He kissed me on the forehead and patted my leg as if I were a puppy.

Rob's snoring resumed immediately, but I was wide awake. My eyes had fully adjusted to the dark. I looked over at one of my favorite photographs on the bookshelf, the girls on a camping trip to Trinity Lake long ago. They stood in a line on the pebbly beach at sunset in their brightly colored swimsuits, all three grinning triumphantly at me, proudly holding up snakes of varying sizes they had caught themselves.

The girls were growing up aligned with nature, cherishing the natural world and all its miraculous inhabitants, which Bucky had said was essential to the future of our species. Even as teenagers, they still marveled at the rhythms of the stars and the moon, listened raptly to choirs of frogs and crickets, and gasped with delight at the murmuration of starlings.

I had raised three brilliant and sensitive Bucky girls. Maybe that would have to be enough.

DIAGNOSIS

2008

Dare to be naïve. — Buckminster Fuller

I immediately began living up to my new self-imposed gag order on the subjects of Bucky, climate change, and the end of humanity, but since seeing a therapist felt like an admission of defeat, it took me awhile to seek out a recommendation from a neighbor, and then another few weeks before I phoned him up for an appointment.

Dr. Henry Austin was roundish, fifty-something, and had a trim salt-and-pepper beard. I liked him immediately. His handshake was firm but warm, and his eyes said he could handle anything I might throw his way. I took my place on his worn red leather couch and began to fill him in on everything, talking quickly, knowing that time was money. I had exactly fifty-five minutes to explain my entire life and get a response to help me make sense of it all.

He immediately recognized Buckminster Fuller's name, which was a relief.

"Ah, Bucky," he said. "A true captain of the social revolution of the 1960s, which unfortunately never got off the ground."

"Exactly, thanks to the fossil fuel industry." I sat forward, excited to vent about my verboten but favorite subject.

"What's that?" He wrote something in his notebook.

I told him I was angry that oil companies had known for decades about the harm carbon was doing to the climate and yet had still intentionally derailed clean energy, apparently concluding that their profits were more important than humanity's future. I told him I felt an overwhelming need to do something other than rant and rave at my family. I told him that doing nothing was no longer okay, that I had to figure out what to do, and soon, because time was running out."

It wasn't until the words spilled out of my mouth that I knew I'd been thinking them.

He asked about my childhood.

"Huh? Oh."

Shifting gears wasn't easy. Where to start?

I told him how I'd grown up on a magical lake in a small Indiana town, but that my brilliant English architect father, who was probably an alcoholic, had become bored and ended up running off with his secretary. It all sounded like a cheesy daytime soap opera.

"After everything fell apart, my parents came back together like a silent wall and dragged us kicking and screaming to a new town. I flew off the rails over being forced to leave my friends in my junior year of high school. I stayed out late drinking and smoking pot and demonstrated my own unique brand of wisdom by keeping my English teacher's son out until three o'clock on a school night, which earned me my first D."

I shot him a glance to make sure he was still cued in. "You see, I had all these notions as a kid about how humanity could rise up and become something better, and then my father showed me how despicable we really were, and I guess I was just living down to my own expectations when I got thrown out of the house the same day I graduated from high school. I stormed out with my whole life in a duffle bag to words from my mother's mouth I would never forget: 'You're smart enough. You don't need college. We can't afford it anyway.'"

I stopped to draw a breath. He was still listening. "Three years later, I had pulled myself together and was working as a reporter, but I knew I needed a degree if I was going to be the next Barbara Walters. I got accepted at Michigan State but was denied financial aid because my parents had been writing me off as a dependent on their tax returns all those years. I should have ratted them out to the IRS, but who does that to their own parents? So I let it go and went looking for love in all the wrong places. I found it in the laundry room of my apartment building. He made sparkling drinks and told funny stories, and it wasn't until our wedding night that I realized neither of us had a clue about the person we'd married."

Dr. Austin cleared his throat, and I realized I'd wandered off course. Time was running out.

"The bottom line is I got even. I eventually fell in love with and married the right person, and now we are raising three miraculous human beings. Life turned out to be pretty damn great."

"Really? That's good to hear. Go on."

"My daughters are strong and confident. Rob is as trustworthy and loving as a man can be. I have good friends and a close family..."

He was writing steadily now. Lines of concern swept across his face. Did he know something I didn't?

"So you say everything is going great, other than this Bucky thing?"

"This Bucky thing. That's good. Yes, this Bucky thing is the elephant squatting ponderously on the carpet in the middle of every room I occupy."

He laughed, and I joined him. I had no idea why we were laughing. I was livid with myself, always making excuses. I'd accomplished nothing.

"So which is it? Are you satisfied and grateful, or going crazy with unrequited worry?"

"Both."

"Do you feel out of control at times?"

"Like a boat about to flip over."

An alarm on his desk beeped gently. My fifty-five minutes was up.

His flipped through his notes and scratched at his beard. It was a lot to process, he said. He needed more information and some time for serious thought before making a diagnosis "if indeed one was necessary."

I was relieved to have vented. A person could get used to being listened to.

He pulled something from a file folder and handed me a sixteen-page questionnaire of multiple-choice and essay questions I was to answer and drop in his mail slot before I left. He encouraged me to take my time and answer honestly, and in as much detail as I could, promising that only he would see what I wrote.

I spent the better part of the next hour trying to be fully honest. This was difficult. For each question, I could guess what sane people would say, but I also knew what my real answer would be. How much did I want to reveal? Did I want him to conclude that I was sane or not?

The questions were intense:

Have you ever thought about committing suicide? *Not really. But I do think it might be a good idea for someone like me to become a martyr for the environment. I've dreamed of doing that, of doing something to match my crazy, outsized passion. But others might follow, and that would not be good, although a certain amount of human pain and suffering will be necessary...*

Do you ever hurt yourself? *I do. I pick at my cuticles and obsess over scabs. I think the little nips of pain make me feel more alive, but then I'll look down at a bleeding cuticle and wonder what is wrong with me. Friends say I am hard on myself, so yes, I probably hurt myself in a hundred ways I don't understand.*

I read the whole thing over when I finished and became pretty sure I had created more questions than I'd answered, so I jotted down a note to the doctor on the back of the test.

Dear Dr. Austin:

It probably makes me certifiably crazy that I believe I was born into this life with a great mission. I also believe there is a deadline I may have already missed — but either way, the clock is ticking louder and the fuse has been lit, and it's my job to be some kind of Paul Revere for climate change.

"The fossil fools are lying! The fossil fools are lying!"

I am determined to do something. I have started writing a blog, which has gotten me a few hundred followers, but I need a million. The problem is nobody wants to read bad news. I must find an upbeat and positive way to say that the world could be ending. I don't blame my family and friends for not wanting to face all this, but their unwillingness to get involved leaves me with no idea about how to be in my own world or even in my own family. Things feel genuinely wobbly for the first time. I have al-

ways thought of myself as a survivor. But the darkness is closing in and sometimes I cannot bear to think of what we are doing to our grandchildren. I need to know what I'm meant to do. And then I need to do it.

Or maybe I should turn it all off. You know, "don't worry, be happy" and all that.

Thanks for your help. I know it's a big job.
Pat

▽▽▽

For our follow-up the next Wednesday, I arrived fifteen minutes early so I wouldn't be late and waited in the overly warm, stuffy lobby. I couldn't stop fidgeting. I flipped through some magazines, played Tetris on my new phone, picked at my cuticles—anything to stop myself from obsessing over what the doctor was going to tell me.

Was I crazy? Or just depressed?

By now I was often losing my cool, as I did one night at a trendy restaurant while on vacation with the family in Santa Cruz. Dinner in the artsy converted barn began with ridiculously expensive foam appetizers, which I found outlandishly extravagant and a perfect illustration of spoiled and mindless American consumerism.

The girls chatted happily about events at school, friends, dates, plans for trips, all the stuff I once loved to hear about. My mind wandered. The day's news had not been good. The United Nations Panel on Climate Change had issued urgent warnings saying excessive greenhouse gases were already causing critical problems on every continent. Climate change was disrupting economies and communities, and happening faster than even the direst predictions. I'd seen a report on NPR while everyone else was napping, but then flipped around to all the channels and not a single major network had covered the story.

Eventually there came a lull in the conversation. I momentarily forgot my Bucky embargo. "Did you see the news today?" I asked generally to the table. "From the United Nations on climate change? Not a single network touched it."

"Huh?" said Olivia, who had still not taken a bite of the precious architectural food structure on her plate.

I thought she hadn't heard me, so I repeated it. "The United Nations released a report today saying it's urgent for us to act now to control greenhouse emissions or we're toast."

Michaela dropped her fork. "What?"

Frown lines rolled across Rob's forehead. "Really, Pat?"

Olivia rolled her eyes. "Thanks for the great news, Mom. As always."

Everyone looked down at their plates.

I took a long deep swallow of my margarita. My eyes stung from holding back tears. I wanted to bite my tongue and shut up, but I loved them too much. "All while we sit here like ostriches, our heads in the sand, enjoying fancy foam appetizers."

Rob pushed back his plate. "Not anymore, we're not."

Alyssa put down her fork. "Weird analogy, Mom. Ostriches eating appetizers? What the heck are you talking about?"

Even I wasn't sure. I felt bad for upsetting everyone, and I wanted to explain why it had been important enough to drop a turd in the punchbowl, as Rob would put it.

"The thing is, it's from the United Nations and even the Pentagon, and there was still absolutely no media coverage." I looked at Rob. "Don't you realize how strange that is? Nobody except NPR carried the story. And nobody watches NPR except people like me. Our mainstream media is apparently now a wholly-owned subsidiary of the oil industry."

"Wow," he said.

Michaela reached out her hand and patted my arm. "Mommy's right. We've been reading all about climate change in environmental science. But Mom, what are we supposed to do about it? What good does it do to keep bringing it up?"

I felt like I'd been punched. Michaela was the one who almost always took my side. She agreed awareness was critical. But I got what she was saying. What good could five sunburned people sitting at a funky table in a Santa Cruz restaurant do? And if the answer was indeed nothing, then why drag everybody down by bringing it up?

The table fell silent until one of my daughters said something under her breath I would never forget—and I won't say which daughter because I love her madly and hope she will continue to tolerate me and love me back—but she said it. "Mom, can't you just relax about this stuff? Don't you know climate change is a hoax?"

I almost shot out of my chair like a rocket ship to Mars. A hoax? Had she learned this at school? At one of the great liberal progressive campuses of the University of California, no less? Surely she was just being contrary. Or joking. I looked at her face for a read. She was defiant. Her arms were crossed. Her food still untouched.

Was it possible for a human being to burst into flames? I was at the age when hot flashes were supposed to start, but this felt like I was turning into a nuclear missile. The heat rising up my spine was unbearable. I leaned across the table toward her, knowing I was losing my composure.

"Is this what we are paying for you to learn at college, that climate change is a hoax?"

She didn't answer. Other diners turned to look at us, making me realize I'd raised my voice.

Rob stepped in, in Dad mode, where remaining calm and collected were all that mattered.

"You know, honey, we're on vacation to enjoy ourselves, not to fret about the end of the world." He dropped his voice to a near whisper. "Of course, we are all concerned. But that doesn't mean we want to talk about it every time we get together. We're trying to enjoy a vacation. Is that so hard to understand?"

"But I haven't mentioned it—for weeks."

"Not true, Mom, not true," said Alyssa.

Rob nodded in agreement.

I pushed back my chair, stood up and excused myself to the restroom. I was so livid I didn't care who saw me take a wild swing at the pair of deer antlers hanging over the bathroom door, which I whiffed completely. I tried to slam the door shut, but it was the soft-closing kind. Damn. Was the whole world mocking me?

I bent down to look under the stalls to make sure they were empty, then turned to face myself in the mirror. I touched my face. My skin felt clammy. Was I coming down with something? What a complete catastrophe that my own family had shut me down. Surely this moment was the very definition of failure.

Of course, it was partly my fault for acquiescing to Rob's requests for nearly a decade that I keep the peace and the kids' sanity by staying mum about things that bothered me. It occurred to me that I was one of thousands, even millions of people who were at this very moment looking at themselves in bathroom mirrors all over the world, realizing that their complicit silence had been a crime—an ongoing thirty-to-forty-year crime against humanity. The gag orders imposed on us and accepted by us were destroying humanity's chance for a future.

I snarled at my reflection and wiped the mascara from under my eyes with a paper towel.

Was I really obsessed like they said I was?

Obsessions, according to peer-reviewed articles in Google Scholar, are caused by catastrophic misinterpretations of the significance of one's own thoughts. Was it possible the whole thing about Bucky and climate change was just a "catastrophic misinterpretation?"

Wasn't grappling with the end of humanity always on everyone's mind? Who was I to be the one to insist on speaking about the unspeakable?

But then the pendulum in my mind swung back and I knew Bucky was right, that this had all gone on for too long, and it was time for action. I gave myself a final disgusted look in the mirror and went back to the table. I calmly said I wasn't feeling well, that I had a headache, and wanted to walk back to the cottage alone. They let me go with hugs and wishes that I felt better. It was only a few blocks away. They all seemed to get that I needed a time out.

The walk back to the beach filled me with the darkest gloom I'd ever known. It was now obvious that humanity was not going to wake up unless and until something or someone shocked them into it. As I reached the cottage, I knew it was time to make the ultimate sacrifice for what I believed, for the future of my grandchildren, and the planet.

I would become the first environmental martyr for all of humanity's sake. One life in exchange for seven billion seemed like a fair trade.

The night was warm with a nearly full moon when my tanned French-pedicured toes dug into the cool sand. I slid off my long woven skirt and tucked the bird feather I'd found on the beach into my journal to mark the page where I'd written to Rob and the girls. I wrapped the skirt around the journal and my glasses before placing the bundle carefully at the top of the wooden stairs where they would find it.

I tiptoed down to the water's edge, wanting to feel every last grain of sand between my toes. The normally ferocious Pacific Ocean was almost smooth, as if the moon had flattened it out. Dozens of baby turtles scampered by, racing in the shadows to reach the water's edge before something snatched them from out of the sky. The powerful instinct to live was so awe-inspiring to me at that moment, I had to stop and think.

It wasn't that I had no will to live. It was that my will to accomplish my mission was worth more than this individual life. I knew my family would edit and publish the manuscript I'd left behind. I'd told them to do so in the letter I left in my journal. This would result in helping to bring Bucky's realistic utopian ideas back into the world, which could help save humanity. Or, at the very least, I would know I lived up to my promise.

While it will be heartbreaking to miss out on the chance to hold and cherish my grandchildren, in exchange the world would get a story it so desperately needs, the story of one human willing to sacrifice her life for her species. She so loves the world that she takes her own life to help save it. Before she goes, she writes her Bucky manifesto for humanity's future and leaves it behind. It is a quiet mindful act of hari-kari that changes the world. The perfect plan, and the ocean was a beautiful place to do it.

I forced myself to step into the freezing water. I drew circles in the water with my fingertips to distract myself, causing the moonlight to splinter into millions of glittery crescents all around me. I gritted my teeth and stepped in up to my waist, wishing I'd thought to put on a wet suit. This is the one big downside to the Pacific Ocean. The water is freezing, always, even in LA, even in San Diego. Even in August.

Plunging myself in fully, I pushed off the sandy bottom and breaststroked forward. It was a stroke I'd learned clinging to my mother's back in the warm summer lake in Riley. "Like a frog, my lovely," she had said. "Just use your legs like a frog." I was a strong swimmer, and my body warmed up as I kept stroking farther and farther out, past the break into an area of almost glass-like calm. Wispy clouds parted to reveal the naked full moon. The sky brightened. I turned to see the shoreline lit up like midday, an endless line of meandering beach houses snoozing happily with tiny porch lights burning. Humanity was fast asleep.

I stopped and began to tread water, using the old egg-beater kick Alyssa had taught me during her water polo days. I lifted my face up to the perfect full moon, so bright and clear I could make out its craters and mountains. I took a long deep breath then spoke to the sky with a calm I hadn't felt in years.

"I hereby make this sacrifice on behalf of all humanity, to help us all awaken to a new understanding about our individual responsibility for this beautiful little spaceship we call Earth." My voice echoed over the water. I waited for a moment, wondering if there might be an answer, like the voice Bucky had heard back in 1927, but there was only silence. This made perfect sense, of course. Bucky had been a young man, his whole life ahead of him. But for me, well, my children were raised, time was marching on, and the highest value of my life could only be achieved by ending it. It was the perfect sacrifice.

One life for seven billion. A fair trade.

I took one last deep breath and let myself sink into the blackness, opening my eyes wide to take in the fuzzy moonlight dancing above me. I exhaled slowly through my mouth, watching tiny bubbles rise in front of me, and when I had finally run out of air and was about to fill my lungs with water, something hard pressed against my lower back. The hand of God? The curvature of the earth? Whatever it was pushed me upward, toward the moon, carrying me so fast I outpaced my own still rising bubbles. I twisted around to get a look and found myself staring straight into a single eye of a massive sea turtle. He was paddling furiously to save me, using all four of its massive legs to push me upward until I exploded through the surface of water.

I burst out laughing at its crazy eyes and savage determination to keep me alive.

And then I woke up, next to Rob, who was spooning me from behind.

My heart thumped so hard I thought it would wake him. I breathed as quietly as I could and lay there for a long time thinking. Any world magical enough to send that dream my way was surely worth sticking around for. Something cracked open in me as I lay there with Rob's warm legs resting against mine. A light came on in my mind. I saw myself as part of something bigger. I was intricately connected to a vast invisible universe of love and light. Life was an overlapping series of energy events. Love was progressively exquisite. Something good was going to happen.

▽ ▽ ▽

Dr. Austin finally appeared in the lobby. He gestured toward his couch and placed a box of Kleenex on the coffee table, which I took as not a good sign.

In his festive red plaid vest over a white shirt, he looked through his reading glasses at his pad of paper and began thoughtfully. "Well, Pat, after reviewing my notes, including the transcript of our session and your written input, I have determined that you are most likely bipolar — bipolar one, to be exact. It appears to a mild case, but it does often worsen with age. And in your case, it clearly presents with a side of ADHD."

A side of ADHD? Was he making a fast-food joke about mental illness? I could barely take it in. I was, or had, not just ADD but ADHD. Hyperactive. And bipolar. I had an actual, diagnosable mental illness. Two of them.

I twisted a bit of cuticle until it bled. "Bipolar?"

"Yes, that's —"

"I know, I think — but wait, it's not just ADD but ADHD too? I'm hyperactive?"

"Surely you've noticed your inability to sit for any length of time or focus on one thing. I noticed you tend to be always moving or fidgeting or picking at your nails."

"My cuticles."

"What?"

"I don't pick my nails. I pick my cuticles. I'm not sure why I do it." I pressed my thumb against my finger to stop the bleeding. "But holy crap, you're right about the impatience. Back in college, I couldn't stand waiting in line to register for classes. I always knew that was the real reason I'd dropped out. I was too impatient to get life going I guess."

I sat back to consider this version of myself. It was as though he had placed a new kind of mirror in front of me, one that showed my insides, and it was not pretty. How I must drive my family crazy, not only with my constant impulsive and alarming remarks about the state of the planet but also with my fidgeting. How awful for them.

"I don't think of myself as someone who fidgets," I said. "No wonder why my family can barely put up with me sometimes."

Dr. Austin leaned forward. "I'm sure your family loves you more than you know. Your daughters sound happy and healthy, and you deserve credit for that." His voice had softened in a sympathetic way, grasping at the silver linings on my behalf. "These things often spring from painful incidents, like the traumas in your childhood. They create patterns."

Tears sprang to my eyes. I knew exactly what he was talking about: Being abandoned by the only person who believed in me. The pain of seeing my mother's heart break in two, night after night, for all those weeks and months. The murder of the turtles. Evidence was piling up that human beings were anything but a miraculous ascendant species. Human beings were pretty damn disappointing. At least if me and my family were any example.

He was watching my face for clues. I tried to smile.

"Those experiences will always be part of you," he said. "But that doesn't mean they have to control you. If you can come to love and understand that younger you, the one who suffered all that heartache, you may be able to find some healing without taking meds."

Tears ran down my face. I reached for a Kleenex.

"It's time to let it go," he said, scanning my face again. "Time to let go of all the guilt and forgive yourself for whatever you are blaming yourself for."

I had no idea where to start.

When I arrived home, Rob was setting the table to serve the rotisserie chicken he'd just pulled off the grill. His trademark Caesar salad with homemade croutons was waiting on the table, along with a peach crumble for dessert. He looked up at me and smiled, obviously having forgotten where I'd been.

Dinner was peaceful now with only one daughter at home. I waited until Michaela left the kitchen to do her homework before I told him.

"I saw the psychiatrist today."

"Oh, I forgot. How did it go?"

My plan was to keep things light. "Well, okay, this may not be as bad as it sounds, but he says I'm bipolar—just bipolar one, a mild case—and, along with it—are you ready for this—it comes with a side order of ADHD."

He looked up and frowned at my dumb joke then closed his iPad with a click.

"Oh, wow. Oh, honey, I'm so sorry."

He stood and approached, but I slipped off the bar stool and turned away, not ready for pity even though it was an unambiguously pitiful diagnosis. I wiped down the counter with a sponge, refusing to face him. I washed and put away the pots and pans. He followed me around the island like a puppy. I flipped on the garbage disposal and wiped out the sink. There was nothing else to do. He was still waiting for me to talk.

"The doctor says there are medications that will help, but he needs time to evaluate things more fully before he knows what to prescribe."

"Okay. So how are you feeling about all this? I mean, does this make sense to you?"

I dried my hands and replaced the towel on the hook. "Well, I've been saying for years it would be good to find an "off" button. Maybe popping a pill will help me throw the switch once and for all."

I went online after dinner and was dismayed to find myself looking back at me from page after page. Bipolar people had savage mood swings. Huge highs followed by lasting lows. Unexplained anxiety attacks. And just like the doctor said, often it was due to psychological traits created in childhood that were hard to break.

It was me in a nutshell.

There was a report about megalomaniacs' fantastic imaginations and grandiose delusions, typically with a science fiction or religious theme. An example, wrote one doctor, was someone who believed they'd been chosen for a great mission to save the world or even to destroy it. It apparently didn't matter which it was; both were manifestations of the same illness.

I also read about obsessive-compulsive disorder, which sounded familiar. An article explained that the "inflated responsibility" of an obsession can lead to debilitating anger and guilt, inability to control thoughts, fusion of impulsive thoughts and action, procrastination and unfinished tasks, even hypochondria. I was able to check every box.

There were also some mental conditions that made me think of Rob. Normopathy is when someone is obsessed with fitting in and remaining invisible so as not to cause controversy. Repressive desublimation is when you use escape valves such as drinking, sex, or football to help you forget how bad things are. It occurred to me that these two conditions together explained why America's social revolution had never come to pass. Everybody just wanted to be normal and not think too much about the ugliness of the world.

One thing was certain. Whether Bucky's ideas were right and worthwhile or not was no longer the most relevant question to me. What mattered now was that I might be mentally ill and getting worse. And since, as the old saying goes, you need to save yourself before you save the world, I picked up my journal and began to write.

To hell with saving humanity. I am sick. I will save myself. I will let myself be medicated, even though it all sounds a little too much like Brave New World or 1984. I will stop being a Debbie Downer or Negative Nancy – or a Pity Pat, as a neighbor has taken to calling me. To hell with my carbon footprint. I will enjoy traveling on airplanes once again. I will even eat a damn cheeseburger once in a while, no matter how many cow farts may have been released in their making. I will be perky, positive Pat. This means accepting the fact that Bucky may have wasted some sixty-three thousand words on me back in 1982 because the empty vessel he chose to fill was cracked.

I heard Rob's gentle snoring upstairs. Heidi still needed to go out, so we slipped quietly out onto the deck. I dropped off my robe and climbed into the hot tub, sinking down into steaming hot water up to my neck. One more thing to feel guilty about. I was a hot-tub environmentalist.

The jets pounded at me and I willed the hot water to pummel and pulverize the crazy right out of my system. I was determined not to let myself go insane. I would focus totally on me and my own well-being. I would eat healthier food, get more exercise, drink less wine, enjoy longer sleep, and stop worrying myself sick. I was determined to be okay, which is surely half the battle.

▽▽▽

Two eternal weeks later, I returned to Dr. Austin to discuss treatment options. He smiled broadly as I settled onto the couch, which seemed entirely inappropriate. He rubbed his hands together as if he were washing them, and then he spilled the news.

"Well, I've reviewed everything carefully, and I have come to the conclusion, of which I am at least ninety-five percent certain, that you are not bipolar after all."

"Ha!" I said. "You have cured me."

"Well, it's not that easy. You still are clearly ADHD."

"But don't you see? It's perfect. You gave me the diagnosis two weeks ago, and I, of course, being also at least somewhat obsessive-compulsive, read everything I could find. I came here prepared to deal with it. Now you've taken it away. It's a miracle. Do you do this on purpose?"

He laughed. "No, but I realized your behavior was actually pretty normal, considering the hand you've been dealt. You appear to be functioning remarkably well in a stable marriage. You also seem to be a good and responsible parent. So, while I've concluded you're somewhere on the spectrum, your symptoms aren't serious enough to warrant the bipolar label."

I sat back to let it sink in. I was not crazy after all?

"As to the ADHD, I do think Adderall might help you," he said. "Just a baby dose — ten milligrams a day. It should help you focus on your work."

"My work?" I thought he meant housework, which I had come to hate. The house had gone to hell in the past two weeks. There was now a whole litter of small puppies made entirely of Heidi's fur in every corner of the house. Every time a door opened, they would come floating out to play. But how often in a lifetime can any person actually enjoy vacuuming up dog hair or unloading a dishwasher or folding laundry? Whatever the number, I had surpassed it long ago.

"Your Bucky work, of course."

"My Bucky work?"

"Absolutely. Your passion is impressive, Pat. It's the main reason I concluded you were not mentally ill, simply driven. If you were ranting on about nothing, we would have something to worry about. But informed passion based on something as real as the teachings of a famous genius like Bucky, well, that is truly rare. You are lucky to have had such a profound experience. Not everybody gets that kind of opportunity."

My world flipped upright. I had thrown the outsized yoke off my shoulders just two weeks ago, and now he was telling me to put it right back on. I could go back to Bucky.

"You know," he said, "if you promised him you would do something with what he told you, well, you pretty much drew your own line in the sand at that moment."

"So now you are saying I'm not crazy, but I might go crazy if I don't do something?"

"Well, we don't like to use the word 'crazy,' but I think your peace of mind will be greatly helped if you accomplish something you can feel good about."

He reached for his prescription pad, wrote something on it, then looked up and said something I wouldn't soon forget. "You know, bringing Bucky back into the world would be a huge deal. His ideas are really needed right now, more than ever."

I walked out into blinding sunlight and had that overwhelming sense again, of love and light and that I was one with everything. Something good was going to happen.

STANFORD

2010

The youth of Earth are moving intuitively toward an utterly classless, raceless, omnicooperative, omniworld humanity.
— Buckminster Fuller

Not long after my un-diagnosis I was gobsmacked by yet another Bucky prediction coming true, that he would be rendered invisible.

The messenger was a friend of Alyssa's. Lisa, a tall blond collegiate swimmer-turned-CEO of an Internet startup, had come to dinner on Sunday. Over Rob's fresh porcini risotto and glazed salmon, she looked right at me through her chlorinated bangs and said her passion was to use her excellent education from Stanford, in science and history, to save the world.

I raised my wine glass to her in a salute. "Cheers to that, Lisa. You fill me with hope. Our generation kind of blew it for you guys. I hope you'll be able to undo some of the damage."

"Uh yeah, there is a lot to do," she said, half laughing, half grimacing. "By the way, Rob, the salmon is amazing. I'd love to have the recipe."

"Thank you," he said. "The ginger glaze is from *Bon Appetit.*"

She turned back to me. "So, like, you're the first person I've met from your generation who accepts responsibility for the mess we're in. Usually people want to blame it on anybody else."

I let out a long slow breath. My gut had long churned with guilt—plain old wow-we-sure-screwed-that-up guilt. "I'm thinking we baby boomers owe the world a major mea culpa for falling for so much nonsense during the last couple of decades," I said. "President Reagan accused the Democrats of voodoo economics, but it was his trickle-down theories, whipped up out of thin air that justified all the profit-taking by the super wealthy."

I looked over at Rob's skeptical face. Lisa sat chewing her risotto and listening to me thoughtfully, something I wasn't used to.

I softened my tone. "The baby boomers were also bam-boozled about climate change. We didn't know the oil guys knew the seriousness of greenhouse gases all along, while pretending the opposite."

"Maybe you guys should be renamed the bamboozled generation," Alyssa said.

I laughed.

Rob raised his glass. "Okay, take a drink everybody, then duck and cover. Time to prepare for the end of the world."

Lisa looked confused.

Alyssa explained. "Dad has created a new drinking game. Every time Mom mentions climate change, everyone over twenty-one has to take a drink."

This was sadly true, and his taunting infuriated me. He seemed intent on undermining me, not to mention the ninety-nine percent of scientists who were on my side. He'd been a lot nicer to me back when he thought I might be just a little bit mentally ill.

"Wait," said Lisa, "I don't know what this drinking game is all about, but Pat is right. The foxes moved into the henhouse when Ronald Reagan was elected president. He was the worst president ever when it came to the environment. He tried to demolish the EPA and rolled back all kinds of environmental regulations. He turned the job of writing these regulations over to the very corporations that needed regulating. Now, thirty-five years later, we're still paying for the side effects of his trickle-down nonsense, including poverty, endless wars, and lowered life expectancies. Not to mention the climate situation, which is, of course, happening even faster than scientists thought it would."

I wanted to kiss her feet for the look on Rob's face. A Stanford grad was putting old Adam Smith in his place. It was pure redemption to know there was a person at the table who saw things exactly as I did, which made me remember Bucky's archives. They were at Stanford.

"Wait, Lisa, I almost forgot you went to Stanford. While you were there, what did you learn about Buckminster Fuller?"

Her face went blank. She frowned and shook her head. "*What* is a buckminster fuller?"

I couldn't move. I glanced at Rob. His eyebrows shot up his forehead and he shrugged as if to say I told you so.

How was this possible? Bucky's massive archives had been at Stanford since 1999. He had predicted he would become invisible, and now here was a bright Stanford graduate sincerely asking me, "*What* is a buckminster fuller?"

She was still waiting for an answer. When my clenched jawbone finally released itself, cracking like an old lady's knees, I stammered like an idiot. "Well, he's, um, a genius, um, a comprehensivist, and a great social philosopher. He, um, invented a new kind of math called synergetic geometry..."

"Okay, so — "

I tried to pull myself together. "Okay, for starters, Steve Jobs called him the Leonardo da Vinci of the twentieth century. And his archives are right there at Stanford."

"Huh? How could that be?" She was obviously not used to being stumped. "Why wouldn't I even know his name?"

"I don't know. I can't imagine. Bucky created a new math called synergetic geometry. It basically deciphers nature's own design principles, with which he said we must realign ourselves — which means, among other things, transferring to clean energy as soon as possible."

"Renewable energy? At Stanford? Ha! Then I'm not at all surprised." Future wrinkles lined her brow. "Stanford is fossil fuels all the way. They don't believe much in solar or wind."

We both took long sips of our wine, giving me time to think. "Bucky said that fossil fuels' obstruction of clean energy was a crime against humanity. The greatest crime ever. Are you sure you never heard of him?"

"No, not ever. Buckminster Fuller? I would remember a name like that."

Feeling thunderstruck, I rose from the table, took my plate to the kitchen, dropped it into the sink, and kept walking. Heidi padded behind me and flopped down heavily next to me on the garden steps. We took some long deep breaths together.

It wasn't just that Bucky had disappeared; his ideas had, too. The deliberate, orchestrated denial of the conservatives—or more specifically the corporatists—had been a success. Fracking was booming all over the globe. Big oil had convinced the world that fracking was necessary because solar and wind were futile. The accompanying methane leaks, poisoned water supplies, and earthquakes were not just rare accidents; they were an expected part of the process. What big oil should have explained to us all was that solar and wind were indeed futile, as investments, for energy companies.

Heidi placed her paw in my lap. I thanked her and rubbed her greying head. I looked down into the ivy, the very spot where I'd lost my breakfast on 9/11. A decade had passed. I had accomplished exactly nothing.

I returned to the kitchen to find Alyssa and Lisa loading the dishwasher, laughing and talking as if nothing had happened. Later, over Rob's homemade strawberry shortcakes topped with fresh whipped cream (I added a generous shot of Grand Marnier to mine), Lisa asked me again about Bucky. She shook her head in disbelief while I gave her a quick Bucky 101. She said she'd taken several classes on energy and the environment, but the focus was always on how to extract natural gas and oil more efficiently and safely. The only good-paying jobs for environmental science majors were with the oil companies, which was why she had gone another way and become a software engineer instead.

"The oil companies genuinely were looking for engineers who would help make drilling safer and more environmentally responsible, you know," she said.

"Well, sure. But there's really no such thing, you know, as safe fracking."

Alyssa chimed in. "But Mom, at least the oil companies are trying to do the right thing."

I put down my fork, failing to understand why people were always making excuses for the fossil fuel industry. "Are they really? For decades, they've successfully lobbied in favor of their own subsidies. They've almost always gotten what they wanted, especially since their campaign contributions have by now purchased both parties of our government."

"What we are seeing is collusion against the people," Lisa said.

Rob's eyes were open, but I couldn't tell if he was listening.

"Exactly," I said. "Consider that Dick Cheney's company, Haliburton, actually won the right to keep secret the ingredients it pumps into the ground, to protect trademarks, which means they can pump any damn chemical they want into the aquifers."

Alyssa sighed. She had heard it all a million times.

"Maybe you're right," Lisa said, "but like I said, that's why I didn't go that way. I don't want to be part of the oil industry. I switched from environmental and went into computer science. What more could I have done?"

"Nothing, I guess. The playing field is so comically slanted that unless you chain yourself to an oil rig, there isn't much else you can do."

"That's one of Mom's goals, to get arrested." Alyssa said and rolled her eyes.

She'd heard me threaten that to Rob. I'd recently attended a meeting of 350.org and learned how to go about getting arrested and still live to tell about it: Carry $100 cash. Stay calm. Do it intentionally, as a group. Do not be provoked into violence. That is what they want you to do. Numbers count. Recruit your friends, the older the better. The older you are the less your resume matters, and police officers are utterly disarmed when hosts of gray-haired white people calmly say they would prefer to be arrested rather than enable further denial about climate change.

When I drove the two girls to catch the last ferry back to the city, Lisa promised me she would write some of her old professors at Stanford and ask why they had never talked about Bucky, and she would let me know what she found out.

Falling asleep that night, I struggled to recall his exact words.

They are already calling me a crackpot and a hippie, and when I am gone, the same conservative voices will be hard at work to make sure all is forgotten.

Humanity is entering a dark age.

BACK TO
SCHOOL

2010

*The minute you choose to do what you really want to do, it's a
different kind of life.* —Buckminster Fuller

The following Monday, I woke up early, swallowed an
Adderall with my toast and coffee, and told Rob I was going to spend the day digging into some of Bucky's files at
Stanford. He looked at me as if I'd said I was going to
drink some bleach, but said not a word, so I packed up one
of Alyssa's old high school backpacks with some note-
books and pens and took the ninety-minute drive down to
Palo Alto.

Stanford's massive campus was a tree-lined labyrinth
with several roads under construction, others permanently
blocked to cars. Google Maps didn't know any of this, so I
got terribly lost but finally ended up in a massive underground parking garage close to the Green Library, where
Bucky's archives were kept.

A young male security guard in a white shirt and red tie asked me to register on a nearby computer, then ran my driver's license through a scanner, and gave me a day pass. He directed me through another labyrinth, this time a series of hallways, to the Special Collections Department in the Bing Wing. All this rigmarole made me wonder if Stanford purposefully made itself complicated so it would seem more scholarly and unattainable.

In the Special Collections Department, a ponytailed librarian in tortoiseshell glasses and a name tag that read Albert checked my driver's license against my visitor's badge, then welcomed me with a warm smile. I had previously requested materials online, as was required. Albert looked over my long list. There was so much I wanted to see, such as Bucky's original writings about the World Game, so I could better remember what I'd heard back in 1969. I'd also requested the contents of his desk from the day he died, in part to learn if he had died as intentionally as he lived, as some of his acolytes had claimed. He had promised his wife of sixty-seven years they would go together and that Bucky would go first, which is exactly what he did.

I also wanted to read everything he said or wrote from about 1981 to 1983, when we met. And of course, I was hoping to glean why a very bright Stanford science and history student had never even heard his name.

Albert pulled a large brown cardboard file box off a metal cart and hoisted it onto the counter. He dusted off the lid with a cloth and opened the box, releasing a musty odor that made me realize how much time had passed. He flipped through the manila envelopes and pulled out three or four of them. Then he looked again at my long list, shrugged his shoulders, and slid the whole box toward me.

"Might as well take it all, but be sure to get everything back in the right envelopes. Order is important. Do not mix things up."

"Okay. Yes. Thank you. I will be very careful. Thank you."

I walked away from the desk not quite believing what I held in my hands. It felt like Christmas morning. A boxful of wisdom, and maybe the answers I was looking for.

Time melted away as I pored over the contents of that first box. Thick brown envelopes were filled with so many mysterious treasures of history I couldn't believe I was allowed to touch them, let alone hold them in my hands for as long as I wanted to.

A handwritten letter from India's Prime Minister Indira Gandhi was dated July 10, 1975. It was written in tiny, sharp cursive letters and the ink was fading, but not her feisty spirit.

People like me are called corrupt, whereas the really corrupt politicians and businessmen who have misappropriated money and indulged in reprehensible activities are shielded. In the name of democracy, all kinds of undemocratic and unconstitutional acts were being indulged in. Suddenly it seemed as if the country were disintegrating before our very eyes. This is why I had to act to declare an emergency. With good wishes.
Yours sincerely,
Indira

Gandhi was the first and only female prime minister of India and an ideological and political twin of Bucky's. They had both spoken openly about the need to end the use of fossil fuels. She and Bucky had become friends on his many travels to India. He had traveled the globe more widely than perhaps any human ever, early on at his own initiative, then later in response to his many invitations to lecture. She was assassinated in 1984.

There was another handwritten card from Walter Cronkite, the famous newscaster who had been named America's most respected man for many years. He wrote to thank Bucky for dinner. Cronkite had hosted a television special about Bucky's ideas and inventions back when Bucky was still alive. (I'd watched it on YouTube some years ago. It focused on his inventions but barely touched on the idea of clean energy, except for a general statement about the potential of solar and biofuels.)

There was something so magical about actually holding these personal handwritten notes and cards in my hands that I didn't want to put them down. I arranged them around me on the big wooden table, to let their spirits breathe and the wisdom rub off on me, so I would be able to piece it all together.

From an envelope labeled "Contents of Desk," I found a fourteen-page typewritten document held together by a rubber band entitled *A Proposal for a World Livingry Services Industry.* This document outlined Bucky's strategy for transforming the military's war machines into a massive, global, life-sustaining enterprise. The manpower resources for this would be made possible by clean energy, because with clean energy, we would no longer need to labor for our daily energy supply and would therefore have a great deal of free time to do all sorts of good things for the world. It was such a brilliant idea it seemed destined to happen.

This document represented the America I thought I was growing up in. I thought we were the good guys. But how unrealistic his altriistic notions seemed all these years later.

He was right about the dark age. I was sure we were right in the middle of it.

In his proposal, Bucky articulated his idea about weaponry versus livingry in some detail. He used artifacts such as his house, car, a bathroom, a wave barrier, a fog gun and even floating cities as examples of how a livingry services industry could manifest itself to serve the basic needs of all of humanity.

Was this the big idea? Had he wrapped this report up and left it on his desk hoping someone would see the genius of it? Was this my job? Would *A Proposal for a Livingry Services Industry* make people wake up and pay attention to him again?

Maybe I should focus on the even wilder ideas, like the vast two-mile invisible dome he proposed from east to West Manhattan at Forty-Second Street. The dome would be like a greenhouse, creating a lush, climate-controlled environment year-round. It would protect against air pollution and moderate the temperature and humidity for ideal human conditions. It would also generate solar power and collect rainwater, and, because domes became stronger and cheaper to build the bigger they were, something of this scale might be feasible.

But even though Bucky had patiently explained how the savings in snow removal costs alone could pay for the dome in about ten years, people thought he was nuts, and the idea had remained as invisible as the dome would have been. People just couldn't wrap their brains around something that seemed fantastic, even if it was entirely plausible.

Another magical idea was his proposal for a floating city in Tokyo Bay. He had been commissioned by Japanese royalty to design a tetrahedral structure to house a million people and be totally self-sustaining, providing for food cultivation, energy generation, and rainwater collection. It featured vast community spaces to bring people together and provide housing for the multitudes right on top of the open waters, which Bucky knew would begin rising soon.

His Old Man River proposal for East St. Louis astounded me. This massive plan for a new community, constructed out of the earth like a great donut-shaped spaceship, was intentionally designed to provide the ideal dwelling environment for humans. Each living unit had a spacious private garden on the outer side of the earth mound, for food production and connecting with nature, while the interior featured shared community spaces providing all the resources and entertainments of a city. It looked a little like a space-age version of Machu Picchu. The idea was to fully cater to humanity's instincts, desires, and needs, because, as Bucky often said, it is much easier to reform man's environment than it is to reform man.

It is not that humans wish to despoil their environment, only that we have allowed our life support systems to mutate into weapons of mass ecological destruction, such as forestry and industrial agriculture. An example is the palm oil industry, which wreaks havoc on forests, causes steep declines in animal populations, creates more child labor, and contributes to climate change. More than half of all consumer products contain palm oil, including healthy vegan and organic products and everything from soaps and cleaning products to dog food and margarine. It will continue to lead us toward environmental, social, and long-term economic disaster until people wake up and realize they choose either utopia or oblivion with every dollar they spend.

Stanford's files included so many big-thinking ideas that I floated home feeling high as a kite. Was it possible there could really be cities under the sea and others that floated in midair? According to Bucky, if you built a geodesic dome big enough it would eventually weigh less than the air around it, and thus would float. Anything is possible, as Bucky said.

I got stuck in traffic in San Francisco for over two hours that night, so I turned off the radio to give some thought to what I'd learned so far. Feeling hungry and tired, and far short of anything miraculous, I realized the only thing I knew for sure was that understanding Bucky was somewhere above my pay grade.

Even scientists and mathematicians didn't claim to fully understand Bucky's synergetic geometry. I knew better than to even try. I could read forever in awe at his ideas and inventions, yet I had no understanding of the math or science behind them.

One of Bucky's promises kept turning in my mind: *You will know exactly what you need to know when you need to know it.* So I returned to Stanford day after day for the next couple of weeks. I was determined to wade through the entire contents of Bucky's Chronofile, until Albert observed it would take a lifetime to go through it all. It didn't help that after so many long days of searching, I still didn't know what I was looking for. But the good news was I was now up to the task. The Adderall was working. I could sit and read and take notes for hours on end, and since I was learning so much, I decided not to worry that I had no clue where it was going.

I spent the better part of two days reading through stacks of press clippings, yellowed and fragile newsprint cut out of newspapers from all over the world, all featuring Bucky's ideas and inventions. The reverence with which he was written about back in the 1960s and 1970s starkly contrasted his current invisibility. Even icons like Frank Lloyd Wright had called Bucky "a man with more absolute integrity than any man I have ever known."

I came across ideas that whacked me upside the head, like the one about how human beings needed to give up "the specious notion that we must work to earn a living." Even these ideas made perfect sense to me. "It is mistakenly assumed that employment is the only means by which humans can earn a right to live," he was quoted in an interview. "This is total fallacy. It is eminently feasible for our environment to provide full life support for all humans, but also to permit all humans' individual enjoyment of Earth, without anyone profiting at the expense of another."

Bucky warned about the pitfalls of overspecialization. "Advancing science has now discovered that all the known cases of biological extinction were caused by overspecialization. Specialization breeds feelings of isolation, futility, and confusion in individuals. It also results in individuals leaving the responsibility for thinking and social action to others."

In other articles, he discussed how to set things on a better course. "Only a comprehensive switch away from specialization can bring about reorientation of the extinction-bound human in the critical time remaining before we pass the point of irretrievability. We must each take responsibility for this outcome."

Surely this was America's Achilles' heel in a nutshell. So few of us believed the big picture was our responsibility. We thought it was someone else's job. Leave it up to the smart people to solve things, we thought, closing our minds to the possibility that we were the smart people. Too many of us had looked the other way for too long.

The day came when I got my hands on Bucky's appointment calendar. It had occurred to me that I might be able to find myself in it. I'm not sure why that was important; nobody had ever challenged me. But for nearly an hour, I flipped through pages and pages of typewritten schedules. It seemed hopeless at first. I had narrowed the meeting date down to 1982, because that's when I was at Frankel & Company working on the McDonald's account, but I couldn't even recall what time of year we'd met, let alone the month or day.

Then just as I was about to give up, I saw my name in faded, typewritten letters on a graying sheet of mimeograph paper:

May 18, 1982. 2 pm: Pat Field — Sky deck
And then again, on the next day:
May 19, 1982. 7 pm: Pat Field — dinner — Conrad Hilton
May 19 was Rob's birthday. Another irony.

I practically floated out of my chair to show Albert, goose bumps twinkling like stars on the backs of my legs. He was leaning over the counter, reading the *San Francisco Chronicle*. I approached him like a kid with all A's on my report card.

"I found myself," I whispered.

"Aha, always a good thing to do," he said with a crooked smile. "Let's have a look. Well, check it out — there you are, two days in a row. And the very next night, he had dinner with Walter Cronkite and his wife. You were in good company."

I celebrated in the plaza with a slice of chocolate cake and came up with a plan to recreate my interviews with Bucky. I would read everything he had written and spoke about around that time and reconstruct it all. The cosmic surfing atop the John Hancock Center. The tea afterwards, the elevator ride, and the crazy beautiful sunshower when we stepped outside.

The next day, I raced back to the campus. To help me understand the math, I thought maybe I could take some classes about Bucky at Stanford, at least audit them. Why hadn't I thought of it sooner? I took the stairs two at a time to the Special Collections Department and raced through the door get Albert's help logging into the current course catalog.

I looked through the entire online catalog in every department—earth sciences, engineering, every other academic area. In every instance, I was dumbfounded. The results for my search for Buckminster Fuller numbered exactly zero. 0 results for your search. Even when I searched in the interdisciplinary Earth Systems program, which had been created to promulgate and share earth-saving ideas, the result was the same. Zero.

I typed out the permutations carefully: "Buckminster Fuller" and "R. Buckminster Fuller," "Bucky Fuller," "geodesic dome guy," "Leonardo da Vinci of the twentieth century," "planet's friendly genius." It didn't matter how I entered it, the results were the same. 0 *results for your search*. It made no sense.

I approached the desk where Albert held a large stack of books to his chest as if it were a fragile child. He smiled patiently and lowered the books gently to the counter to listen. I had come to adore this sweet guy with his tidy sweaters, neat ponytail, and calm demeanor. I brought him some chamomile tea one day, somehow knowing it would be a hit.

"Albert, I'm sorry to trouble you again, but I must be doing something wrong. I've been trying to search online for classes at Stanford that cover Buckminster Fuller's thinking and inventions, but I can't find anything. I don't get a single hit."

His eyebrows shot up playfully. He shrugged his shoulders and smiled broadly.

"I don't get it," I said. "Why would there be no courses about Buckminster Fuller? I mean, this man was known as the Leonardo da Vinci of the twentieth century. What happened?"

His eyes narrowed, and his eyebrows danced as he lowered his voice and spoke in a pretend conspiratorial whisper, play-acting he was some nefarious spy. "Aha, so you are asking me the eternal question?"

"What is the eternal question?" I honestly didn't know.

"Why has Buckminster Fuller become virtually invisible right here at Stanford, the very institution which owns his archives?"

"Exactly." I held my hands out, ready to receive whatever information he might have to throw at me.

He shook his head gently, checked back over his shoulder again to make sure the other librarian was out of range, and spoke even more softly. "You hereby join the quiet army of brave souls who have demanded to know over the last couple of decades why Stanford has done so little to share Richard Buckminster Fuller with its students."

I was getting frustrated. "But why? What's the story?"

He sobered. "In all honesty, I don't know. I have my opinions. I think it's a shame — or worse, a crime against humanity — that Bucky's ideas aren't being carried forward to today's students. The kids in architecture might know about him, but engineering and sciences put Bucky in history's dustbin. Don't forget the conservatives and oil guys hated him. Still do, I'm sure."

"So why did Stanford even buy his archives?" The answer hit me the moment I asked. "Was it like the old Mafia ploy, keep your friends close and your enemies closer? Like in *The Godfather?*"

Albert nodded. "Big Oil is more like the Mafia than the Mafia could ever hope to be. Whenever they're challenged, they retrench, then come bullying back together *en masse* to spread the news that environmentalists are impractical quacks. Again and again over the years, they convinced the government to withdraw its support of solar and other renewable energies. If it couldn't be metered and its distribution controlled, it wasn't of value. It wasn't of value to them, as investors, is what they should have said. Instead they made it everybody's problem."

I blew more air out of my lungs than I knew they could hold. The back of my ears burned. Albert gave me a minute to get hold of myself.

"It was in 1999 when they bought the archives," he said. "Remember Y2K?"

I did. I had refused to put my family on an airplane that holiday season because of fears about Y2K. People went crazy, thinking computers were going to crash when the calendar rolled over from ninety-nine to zero because the computers had only used two digits for dates.

"While all that fear was getting whipped up," he continued, "a lot of other crazy things were happening. It was like a magician's trick. They made us all look one way while they did diabolical things elsewhere. Corporations took control over our government by spending millions to 'lobby' elected representatives. Alternative energies got the shaft again.

"New Year's Eve 2000 came and went without a hitch. Then one day soon after that, Bucky's files showed up here. Stanford made a big deal about it at first, like they were preserving something essential for all of prosperity, saying they were excited to share Bucky's wisdom with Stanford's students."

Albert shook his head with disapproval and waited for me to catch up. I got it, but I still couldn't understand why Bucky had been silenced. Unless it was because humans were so despicably greedy they would intentionally disregard the future of their own species if it took money out of their pockets. And that just didn't seem possible.

Albert was still watching my face. "Here's what you might want to think about. Bucky ardently opposed free market capitalism, calling out the corporations and government for their 'gross universal cash heist,' which started when Reagan and his cronies took over in '81. Bucky predicted the GRUNCH would bring about great inequality and serious instability in our society — "

I gripped the counter with both hands. "And so here we are. So let me get this straight. Some of the world's brightest students come to Stanford hoping to learn how to save the planet, and instead of hearing about the miraculous transformative possibilities of clean energy and other astonishing ideas about humanity's potential, they're taught that better fracking is the future?"

"That, and hydrocarbons. As long as distribution can be controlled and they can turn it on and off like a spigot, Big Oil will play along. Exxon has put millions into algae harvesting, for example, because they think they can own the technology. They absolutely hate solar energy, which could make all the difference since no organic matter at all is used to create it once the panels are up and running."

I wondered what Rob would think of all this. He'd probably call the entire conversation insane, say we were conspiracy theorists, that Bucky's thinking was just obsolete.

Albert must have read my mind. "Not everyone is born with the vision to be able see the truth, you know. Some very good people have become so entrenched with the status quo it will take time to awaken them. So, when it comes to Bucky and Stanford, don't worry too much. Stanford is a dinosaur in the tar pits on this issue, desperately clinging to their oil derricks and pipelines. I'm even sure they know it. The writing's been on the wall for a long time that oil is over."

He wrapped his arms around the precious stack of books. "Check out classes at Cal in Berkeley. Their design and architecture program has carried Bucky's ideas forward."

I went back to the computer. The results were uncanny. At the University of California in liberal, progressive Berkeley, catalog mentions of Buckminster Fuller totaled 117 hits. I clicked on many of the course links. Each description made some reference to Bucky's inventions, his nature-based design principles, his synergetic geometry, or his social philosophies.

My searching continued and soon I was no longer surprised at the uncanny correlation between a school's politics and the number of mentions of Bucky in its course catalog.

The University of Washington: 109

Harvard: 100

Brown: 96

Yale: 51

Princeton: 44

Columbia: 10

Pepperdine: 2

Even Pepperdine, once home to professor Ken Starr, the arch-conservative special prosecutor who had tailed Bill Clinton for years until finally turning up some sexual peccadillos with an intern named Monica Lewinsky, had two Bucky mentions.

But as for Stanford: ZERO

Feeling disgusted as I realized how great a role politics played in the universities' decisions about what to teach and not teach, I started digging around to understand more about what was going on in 1999, when Stanford bought the archives.

As the new millennium approached, there had been renewed interest in the environment and in renewable energy, and a great deal of press about Bucky's proposal for a
global energy grid, called GENI. A report in the highly-
respected journal *World Citizen Update* quoted Bucky on the
value to humanity of switching to clean energy:

"The immense benefits of unlimited energy for all is
immediately apparent. First, you protect the environment.
No need to cut down the rainforests or pollute the ground
and oceans with oil, coal, and radioactivity from nuclear
plants. Then when everyone has sufficient energy, living
standards rise as population declines, especially in the de-
veloping countries... With everyone sufficient in energy
needs, poverty disappears, greed, crime, strife is reduced
to zero. Wars become unnecessary and therefore obsolete.
Peace can reign on Earth."

As you might expect, there was a bit of a backlash against
this kind of thinking from the corporate establishment.

A 1999 report from Harvard entitled "Bringing the Environment Back Down to Earth" captured the capitalist
mood of the time: "Companies aren't in business to solve
the world's problems, nor should they be. After all, they
have shareholders who want to see a return on their investments. That's why managers need to bring the environment back into the fold of business problems and
determine when it really pays to be green."

This is one of the great understatements of the decade.
In the 2000s, environmentalists became the enemy. Conservative media continued to discredit anything that
threatened to get in the way of economic interests. That
included Bucky. An article in the 2006 issue of the *Weekly
Standard* said, "The ghost of Buckminster Fuller (1895–
1983) had been thankfully dormant for the past quarter-
century, but now, not only is Manhattan's trendy Whitney

Museum putting on a retrospective in his honor, but *Newsweek* resurrects, for a few minutes' duration, the reputation of one of the arch cranks of the sixties."

Bucky's brief return to notoriety that year included dozens of stories about the Whitney show, and others speculating about the lost wisdom of his ideas. It seemed he was making something of a comeback. In 2009, Stanford's Board of Trustees published a book called *New Views on R. Buckminster Fuller,* a collection of scholarly essays about Bucky on the tenth anniversary of the archive's acquisition.

When it arrived in the mail, I immediately flipped to the index to check the references to fossil fuels. There was one. Only one reference to fossil fuels in an entire 187-page book about the genius who had been adamant about the need to do away with them. The singular mention was in an essay by Professor David E. Nye of Warwick University. Nye wrote about Bucky's call to wean ourselves off fossil fuels, saying that this idea had found resonance during the oil shortages of the 1970s, but it was "characteristic optimism" when Bucky declared it possible to produce enough renewable energy for the world while phasing out fossil fuels and atomic energy. Nye wrote at length about Bucky's idea for a Global Energy Network International or GENI, saying that access to electricity for everyone was a primary measure of a modern society. This was another idea the oil industry hated, since it required cooperation instead of competition. Nye repeated Bucky's words again and again. "There is no energy shortage. There is no energy crisis. There is a crisis of ignorance."

Yet Nye apparently did not have the courage to explain the source of that ignorance. Nowhere in this allegedly scholarly new book about Bucky from Stanford was there anything about climate change or the fossil fuel industry's role in it, but I had reached the point where nothing about the fossil fuel industry surprised me. Their behavior had been uniformly despicable. For decades.

It eventually occurred to me I should spend some time talking to Stanford students about Bucky. What did they know and think about him? The school had promised Bucky's family they would share his ideas with its students. But had they?

Mimicking filmmaker Michael Moore's interview style, I situated myself at the Coupa Café outside the Green Library and approached students while they stood in line waiting for their lunches. I had a small clipboard in my hand to make me look official.

Since I knew talking to hungry people can produce less than great results, I kept my survey to four quick questions. After asking their major and school year, my first question was, "Do you know who Buckminster Fuller was?"

The answer was an immediate no, from nine out of ten students.

"Are you sure?" my regular follow-up.

"Of course. I would remember a name like that."

Next question, "Do you know who Steve Jobs was?"

Duh. Every single Stanford student knew everything there was to know about Steve Jobs. He was and is the unofficial god of Stanford, the genius who'd lived right down the road while single-handedly changing the world. His 2005 commencement address admonished Stanford's students to "Stay hungry. Stay foolish." It was legendary, as was everything about the recently passed creator of Apple.

It was my third question that got them hooked. "Did you know that Steve Jobs called Buckminster Fuller the Leonardo da Vinci of the twentieth century?"

At this point, many students opened their iPhones and typed in Bucky's name, asking for the correct spelling. After giving it to them, I pointed at the library building next to us and asked my final question. "And so, you probably also do not know that the massive archives of this modern-day Leonardo da Vinci are housed right there, in the Special Collections Department of this very library, right here in the center of Stanford's campus?"

Most of them looked at me dumbfounded and promised to check it out.

Over the next couple of days, I talked to over a hundred students. Only one in ten had heard of Bucky. The only students familiar with him were art majors (some were studying his ideas for sustainable communal living developed at Black Mountain College) or postgrad engineering students who had learned about the buckminsterfullerene, which some of them knew were nicknamed the buckyball. But even they were under the false impression that the carbon molecules were so named because someone named Bucky had discovered them. They knew nothing about the math that predicted their existence or what that math might mean in the development of sustainable solutions. The extent of their ignorance was mind blowing.

It took a while for the significance of this to sink in.

Almost none of the brilliant students who come from all over the world to learn how to save it are even taught about the ideas of the man still regularly credited as the grandfather of sustainability. Instead they learned how to frack more cleanly.

How was it possible that they were so in the dark? Some of the engineering and science students explained that Stanford was working hard to create solutions for problems in the extraction of oil and gas, maybe even coal, so there was very little bandwidth remaining for solar or wind, which were seen as minor niche solutions.

Awareness of Bucky's archives at Stanford was so low that even one gray-haired professor waiting in line for a bowl of soup, a self-described Buckminster Fuller fan, was visibly flabbergasted, mindlessly taking off his glasses to clean them so he could take another look at me. He said he'd been teaching at Stanford for eleven years, and had been a huge fan of Bucky in his hippie days.

"What? Are you sure? Here at Stanford?" he said, jotting down a note on his tablet. "I will have to look into that."

I would not soon forget the look on his face. Stanford professors did not like learning things they should have known all along from random women carrying clipboards.

Driving home that night, on the now familiar rolling ribbon of green-forested open lands along I-280 at twilight, it occurred to me that Bucky had been wrong about one huge thing. He had always insisted that politics was going to become irrelevant, that by the year 2000, political affairs would fade away and we would no longer have or need political parties.

Politics was doing just fine.

It was Bucky who had faded away.

EMERGENCE

2011

The thing to do is to look around and see what needs to be done that nobody else is doing. — Buckminster Fuller

With no idea of what to do with what I'd learned about Bucky at Stanford, I thrashed around night after night like a trapped animal, haunted by Bucky's words in a letter he wrote to a ten-year-old boy. "The thing to do is to look around and see what needs doing that is not being done, and then do it."

By now, news was out that Exxon and other oil companies had lied for decades about their understanding of the science of climate change. They knew fossil fuels were killing the planet, but had apparently decided their profits were more important. For help with communications, they had hired the same charlatans who had long ago convinced Congress and the world that cigarettes were not addictive and did not cause cancer.

Like many people, I was livid, but what difference did that make? What could anyone do?

Years ago, in my determination to walk the walk and not just talk the talk, I had started a folder on my computer called *Our Big-Ass Carbon Footprint*. Even though our family had blown our carbon budget for life by bringing three children into the world, there were ways we could make amends, and doing them made it much easier to forgive myself for all I wasn't doing.

For years we had recycled and reused whatever we could. Our progressive Northern California county's recycling program made this easy, since we could toss all our glass, aluminum, and paper into one big can without even sorting it. They also collected and composted our food waste.

I stopped buying plastic whenever possible, especially single-use containers that were toxic anyway — likely yet another cause of all the cancers popping up among our friends and in our neighborhood. I shopped at second-hand clothing stores whenever possible, which also reduced the amount of cancer-causing chemicals I brought into my house and the world. We graduated from CFLs to LED lightbulbs, and I reduced the ridiculous volume of junk mail we received by unsubscribing from offending companies. When Restoration Hardware finally stopped sending its massive color catalog to everyone who had ever shopped there, I felt the whole planet breathe a sigh of relief.

But the biggest step of all was to give up eating meat. You had to be living under a rock not to know that giving up meat was one of the most powerful things an individual could do to reduce their carbon footprint. The girls led the way on this. One of them told me vegetarians vibrate at a higher frequency than meat eaters do, which I found entirely compelling since I was now aiming to consciously evolve myself as Bucky had directed. If a plant-based diet aided in human evolution, sign me up. I wasn't sure what the whole vibration idea was all about, only that it felt right.

Soon after becoming vegetarian, the sight of raw meat would make me feel nauseous. I now saw it for what it was: the murdered flesh of a sentient being. Thinking, feeling animals, precious creatures with mothers, sisters and brothers, were killed thoughtlessly and even torturously, sometimes after witnessing the murders of their friends and family members. How good it felt to know that was no longer happening in my name, or for my plate.

Eating fish wasn't the answer either. Ocean sciences professors at UC Santa Barbara were known to break down into tears about the growing acidity and temperature of the oceans, as they begged auditoriums full of students to refrain from eating ocean fish.

And because by now everyone knew that repairing the world first required that you fix yourself, I also started meditating. Monday evenings at Spirit Rock in West Marin and occasional Sunday mornings at Green Gulch Farms in Mill Valley helped me feel more centered and in control. Meditating with ADHD isn't easy, but if you can force yourself to sit and breathe, even for a few minutes, it can feel miraculous, like you have tamed a fire-breathing dragon and discovered some lovely new real estate like a sunlit meadow between your ears. And it's easier to do in a group, where you have no choice but to sit motionless, torture though it may be.

While doing these things helped sooth my eco-guilt, it wasn't enough. News of a warming climate and a world tipping toward catastrophe was now the daily backdrop of my life, mournfully mocking the too-perfect bubble of a world around me. Countless nights I snapped awake, my heart thumping, my mouth tasting like death, waves of fear gripping my gut. This nighttime monster was nothing like the vague ones of childhood nightmares. It was nothing less than articulate, rational, complete awareness of our horrific global situation as a planet.

Night after night I would slip out of bed and tiptoe down to the hot tub (I know, not exactly a tiny carbon footprint), descend silently into perfect 104-degree water, and think. For over a decade I had let walls of silence build up around me, a way to hide my growing desperation, to protect my children from my obsessive and hyped-up worries. But suppressed desperation turns into depression, and eventually there came days when I couldn't get out of bed.

I would tell Rob I had a headache, that I hadn't slept. Neither were a lie, but the real reason I couldn't get out of bed was the sadness descending over me, pressing me down into a deep black hole of my mind's own making. But it felt justified. Surely there is no greater legitimate cause for sadness than knowing that all the human energy given to loving and raising of children, in every corner of every continent, was a waste. A complete waste of time and love. I couldn't stop reading and rereading my stack of books about the coming end of times. *The Sixth Extinction* by Elizabeth Kolbert. *Eaarth* by Bill McKibben. The realization that so many brilliant women and men were frighteningly unanimous. Spaceship Earth was in trouble. Yet when I flipped on the television evening news, it was still all about the Kardashians and Kanye West. Nobody was talking about climate change or the stubborn, decades-long problem with fossil fuels.

I did what any self-respecting depressed Northern Californian would do. I started writing poetry. At first this felt like vomiting onto paper. Definitely a relief to get it out, but how would I know if it was any good? I had never been a big poetry lover. To me most poetry was either in-

comprehensible or painfully obvious and overly senti-
mental. But the more I wrote, the more the angst flowed
right out of me.

I also started to write a blog about Bucky's ideas related
to climate change. The facts were now so familiar they had
become banal. Oceans warming and acidifying, aquifers
drying up, ice caps melting, the sixth great extinction underway. Reading and writing made me more and more
confident I knew what I was talking about. And equally
confident that worried scientists were dead right.

But then came the day when my blog caught the attention of another climate blogger named Anthony Watts,
whose site *whatsupwiththat.com* is reported to be the
world's most popular climate change website. He's a major
climate denier, or skeptic as they prefer to be called, and is
reportedly supported by the Heartland Institute, a fossil-
fuel-funded conservative think tank. Watts attacked me on
both my blog and his, saying my clean energy ideas were
"unicorn dreams" and "fairy dust." His attention immediately got me thousands of new visitors and followers. This
was great at first, but then he got nasty, and since I was
never much of a shrinking violet, he and I really got into it.
Then one evening an infuriated Rob strode into the house
after a long day at work waving his cell phone at me.

"Who the hell is Anthony Watts?"

"Who? Oh! He's a climate change denier, probably the
most powerful in the world. Why?"

"He called me."

"What?"

"He phoned me up. Said you were harassing him. That
I should make you stop."

"Oh my god, are you kidding me? He called my husband? Does he think it's 1950?"

Rob put down his briefcase and walked over to where I was sitting at the computer. I thought he was going to peak over my shoulder to see what I was writing as he often did, but instead he just said, "You must be getting through to them."

"So you're not worried?"

"I didn't say that. Don't get sued or anything."

"Okay, I'll go easy."

It felt good to watch my list of followers grow, but blogging was still akin to burrowing yourself into a dark hole. I had become an angry and depressed warrior in a bathrobe, and I knew Rob was tiring of the permanent scowl I wore. I knew I had to actually do something, so one evening after finishing up the dishes, I told Rob I was going out to see a movie with a friend. Instead, I drove across the Golden Gate Bridge to an open-mic night at a San Francisco bar. I had no idea what I was getting myself into, but it didn't matter. It was long past time to do something—I had to do anything but nothing.

The twilight air was crisp with fall on the sunset drive across the Golden Gate Bridge, which lifted my spirits as it always did. I parked the car several blocks away from the bar so I could practice reciting my poems as I walked. Using the clacking cadence of my boots to keep rhythm, I mouthed the words to myself, looking around to see if anyone was watching, but they weren't. This was San Francisco, after all, where it was more than okay to be a little bit crazy. I took a deep breath and reminded myself I wasn't setting out to be a performer, but just a reader, which took some of the pressure off.

The place was dark and packed with people drinking mostly coffee and talking loudly. A man at the door took my name and told me I would go fourth. I would have five minutes, no more. There were a few older men sitting at the bar, but mostly the crowd was hipsters (millennials?) dressed in black. Dramatic haircuts dyed various colors vied for attention with some serious tattoos and penny-size ear plugs. I ordered a vodka soda.

The first performer stepped to the microphone and told funny stories in rhyme about romance and the struggles of life in the city. Another older man read a touching poem about the loss of his partner to AIDS in the 1980s. When it finally came my turn, I walked up to the microphone feeling disembodied, glad nobody knew me there. I adjusted the mic for my height and let the spotlight warm my face. My hands trembled, but I gripped the microphone for dear life, and began.

I found myself—
Outside.
As a young girl,
every summer,
in the woods,
by the lake,
in a valley,
beneath the stars,
stars aligned in staircases
thoughts and words in rhyme
messages out of time
about the world,
of what it will take
as a species of nature
to prove our worth,
to pass our test.
In search of secrets,
In search of life
Again and again
I found myself
outside.

Nature held me as I camped, first alone,
then with a lover,
Then with a husband and babies under covers,
loving dogs nearby, and my friends and always and every-
*   where,*
the singing of the crickets and the frogs,
under the light of the moon inside the whisper
of the leaves in the breeze.

I found a better self, in her.
A greater love of life.
In the woods, beside a river,
the gently rolling stream
of my own consciousness
respecting all life,
floating eternally by,
a mystery unfurling
into the ever-present now.
And no matter where I go
Or what the world might bring
I will find trust and love in
those same arms that hold us all up high
when we find ourselves outside.
And once you fall into her powerful arms,
you too will know that you can always, and forever
Find.
Yourself.
Outside.

The audience broke into applause. The warmth of it surprised me. I smiled. It felt a little like a drug, like some new and miraculous substance was coursing through my veins. Unlike in radio, they could see me. And I hadn't melted. It felt amazing. My mind raced. This must be what heroin felt like.

"Thank you," I whispered into the microphone. Was it a good thing to feel this good?

"Very nice," said the man up at the bar. "Keep going."

"Well, I only have one more poem for now." I pulled the paper out of my pocket. "This one is not quite so warm and fuzzy, but it's even more important. It's on the same subject, about the need for humanity to realign with nature before it is too late."

I took another deep breath and willed the tremble in my voice to stop. I had never felt so good. Calm. Together. Wise enough to not care so much what people thought of me, only wanting to get my important messages across.

I started out pretty loudly and dramatically, wanting this one to sound completely different than the sweet inno-cence of the first one.

They scrape and detonate
The very veins of our flesh
in pursuit of a fossil fool's fix,
and Buckminster Fuller
is spinning in his grave.

We lie back and allow it.
In pure cotton we sleep,
dreaming simple dreams,
living simple lives,
while they frack at the flesh
of the only being who matters.
They scrape and detonate
the very veins of our flesh.
Our belly so ravaged,
our blood so poisoned,

our wounds never to heal.
Buckminster Fuller is spinning in his grave.

Scars cover the skin of our heartland.
Death rattles now
as the earth shakes us off.
Killing water, killing life...
For what?
For why?
Of all addict's addictions,
it's the worst kind to kick.
There is nothing as deathly
as the fossil fool's fix.
A binge without hangover,
No pain to be felt.
A high without lows.
Till the bottom reaches up and sucks us down.
Buckminster Fuller is spinning in his grave.

The swamp no longer draining.
The fossil fools are gaining.
Seas to die and rivers run dry,
Storms blow and carbon numbers grow.
They lied and obstructed,
Being planetarily destructive.
Put their profits front and center.
Making a hell for us all to enter.
Buckminster Fuller is spinning in his grave.

We lay back and allowed it.
Cheap gas. Gimme oil.

We lay back. We allow it.
We must now awaken.

We must now speak.
It is time for the revolution
which sputtered fifty years ago.
Clean energy.
Green planet.
A world that works for everyone
without ecological harm.

United
Spaceship
Earth
Rises
Now.
Because Buckminster Fuller is spinning in his grave.

I lifted my face to the applause. It was like some main-line connection of light pulsing right into the pleasure centers of my brain. Who would have thought it would be this good — even better than an orgasm — to know that what came out of my mind, and the words that came out of my mouth, were so appreciated?

I looked around and said thank you. I was out of poems and time. All I could think was where and when would I get my next fix?

Driving home that night in a happy daze, I plotted my new future. Surely that incredible high from being behind a microphone was a sign that this was my path. This was the way I would introduce Bucky's ideas to today's young people, the people who needed to hear them most. Maybe I would even compete in poetry competitions, or create a one-woman show and take it on the road.

Something big was surely going to happen. I could feel it.

My natural high withered the moment I walked in the door and heard Rob's snoring upstairs. No way could I tell him what had happened to me unless I confessed that I had lied about going to the movies. Never had something this big happened that I was going to have to keep to myself. I hated secrets. But I was stuck.

When I slipped into bed, he rolled over and reached out to me.

"Hey, how was the movie?"

I responded with a long kiss right on his mouth. His eyes shot open in surprise and I poured out all the love I had absorbed from that audience right into him. It was the only way I knew how to share what had happened to me without confessing that I had lied.

Afterwards, he rolled over and said, "Wow, that must have been a really good movie."

AWAKENING

2011

When I'm working on a problem, I never think about beauty. I think only how to solve a problem. But when I am finished, if the solution is not beautiful, I know it is wrong.
— Buckminster Fuller

A hundred or so metal folding chairs were lined up like soldiers in an abandoned auto showroom in Berkeley, awaiting attendees of an Awakening Symposium. The car dealership had stood empty for several years, ever since the financial collapse of 2008. Apparently there was still little demand for rugged Ford trucks but plenty of interest in an Awakening Symposium sponsored by the Pachamama Alliance.

It had finally broken through into mainstream consciousness that desperately worried climate scientists were right; that something had to be done, and that it needed to happen soon. For Earth's ecosystem, 2011 was a turbulent year. The United States saw a series of record-busting extremes, from record heat and a devastating tornado season to epic droughts in critical agricultural regions. These extreme events kept global warming in the public conversation even as "climate" became a swear word in Washington.

I stood in a long line to check in, then joined another queue for some Peet's coffee. It was a diverse group for Marin, even though still mostly women, mostly middle-aged, mostly white, and most of them chatting as if they were at a party. It occurred to me that this is what women do. No matter how awful things are getting or how worried they are, they beam their best light at one another. Even when they are desperately worried, they 1) show up and 2) they smile.

An elegant silver-haired woman stepped to the microphone. Her perfectly coiffed hair rested artfully on shoulders covered in soft earth-toned layers, something expensive, probably cashmere. She introduced herself as Eileen, a long-time global marketing consultant who had lost so much sleep for so many years worrying about climate change that she had finally decided to drop her career and work instead with the Pachamama Alliance to help save the Amazon rainforests, which she called the lungs of the planet.

"I stand before you today because I have recently committed my life to making a difference, which I assume is also why you are here."

Eileen told the story of the Pachamama Alliance, about how concerns regarding the clear-cutting of rainforests in South America had brought together a group of women from the Bay Area determined to protect the lands of the indigenous people from oil companies and industrial farmers.

"These dedicated women worked with tribes in South America for several years," she said. "Good things were accomplished and some lands protected, but then one day the elders called for a meeting. They explained that while they appreciated everything the Alliance was doing, they had reached the unanimous conclusion that the problems in the Amazon began with the United States, with the insatiable western demand for material goods. They asked the women to return home, to fix the problem with the western world. They said Americans had become a throwaway people, and that is actually what they were in danger of doing — throwing it all away."

And so the Alliance had created the Awakening Symposium, a day-long program to inform, motivate, and snap us out of our capitalistic stupor.

Eileen explained what many of us already knew, that conservative organizations like the Heartland Institute and the American Enterprise Institute, backed by the big oil companies, were spending fortunes to intentionally confuse the public on the issue of climate. Well-researched investigative journalism in the book *Merchants of Doubt* by Naomi Oreskes and Erik Conway revealed that not a single peer-reviewed environmental science paper disputed the fact that fossil fuels were a serious contributor to the climate problem. Yet almost unbelievably, nearly every major news network in America still reported that the jury was out, that climate change science was still in dispute.

Eileen quoted Oreskes: "'Ever since the Supreme Court ruled that corporations could spend freely to elect candidates they preferred, massive amounts of money flowed in every direction that would keep oil and gas flowing. This same dysfunctional, out-of-control power is playing out in every sector of our lives, creating a variety of crises that are all intertwined. Terrorism. World hunger. Water shortages.'" She looked up from the book on the podium. "The question is what can the ordinary individual do about it?"

Exactly. The question of my life. I was glad I had given up a day of sipping wine with a couple of friends in Sonoma to be here. Maybe I would find some answers.

Eileen divided us up into small groups to brainstorm ideas. The questions: What could we do to contribute? What could we, as individuals, actually accomplish that would help? She asked us to delve into any issue or idea we chose as a group and come up with some "creative and crazy ideas" to report back.

"Keep an open mind," she instructed. "That is the one and only rule for successful brainstorming. No judgments. No editing. Just build on each other's concepts."

I scooted my chair into a circle nearby. Two grandmotherly women from Santa Rosa introduced themselves by stating proudly that they had already been arrested twice for civil disobedience; they were committed partners "in love and crime," which made everyone laugh. A former television producer named Dee said she was determined to get progressive news programs back on the air and was looking for story ideas. The only man in the group, Jeremy from Berkeley, said he was a reformed bank executive feeling terribly guilty about the state of the world and worried about his grandchildren's future.

A middle-aged woman from Fairfax named Fran, wearing Birkenstocks and a flowing tie-dyed dress, said she wanted to learn what she could do other than take sleeping pills and smoke weed.

Next up was a striking blond, a ponytailed twenty-something in yoga pants, one of the youngest people there.

"Rebecca Brooks, reporting for duty!" she began brightly with a mock military salute. "I'm a burlesque dancer, singer, and songwriter. Ditto for me about craving sleep at night. I need to figure out something to do, something to make me feel hope for this crazy world. You know what they say. Raise hell. Sleep well. Have dance shoes, will travel!"

I wasn't sure what to think of her. She was charming and very pretty, but what did she think she was going to do, pole dance to make people think about polar ice? That didn't make any sense, did it?

Then came my turn. I told them I was a worried mother of three nearly grown children and that my hair had first caught fire about climate change way back in 1982 when I sat down to interview a genius named Buckminster Fuller.

"Ah, Bucky," said Fran with the Birkenstocks. "If only we had listened to him back in the 1970s, we wouldn't be in the mess we're in now."

The older people nodded in recognition, but Rebecca's face went blank. "Who the heck is this Bucky dude?"

Fran frowned. "Back when America was smart, everyone knew who Bucky was. The fact that today's younger generation doesn't know of him pretty much indicates, well, that the dumbing down of America is a done deal."

I nearly applauded her. How satisfying to hear someone else sing Bucky's praises who also understood the loss of his brilliance.

Rebecca snapped upright in her chair. "Dark age? I think not. My generation is very enlightened."

"About what?" scoffed Fran.

"Well, for starters, about ourselves and the people all around us." She moved forward in her seat. "We are much more compassionate about those who are less fortunate. Much more inclusive of diversity. We understand how America's consumption habits are using up the planet. Many of us are vegetarians, even vegans. We've also gained the ability to go deeper than your generation, exploring and expanding our own consciousness with meditation and yoga."

She waited for some response. Fran rolled her eyes a little, but nobody spoke.

"Being veg isn't just an environmental or health choice. It's also a psychological one. When you know you are not unnecessarily murdering other beings, it feels a lot better to be a human. And you do know that those terrified animals release all kinds of fear hormones right before they are slaughtered, right? And that you are eating those fear hormones when you eat that meat. It's all pretty simple when you just remember we are all one." Her ponytail flipped back and forth over her tanned shoulders to punctuate her many points. She had a dancer's way of moving, communicating her every emotion with her body.

Everyone jumped in to share what they were doing to reduce their footprints, from flying less to planting trees and basic things like using reusable shopping bags.

Rebecca made me think of Bucky's only regret, that he hadn't been a song and dance man.

As if she had read my mind, Rebecca turned to me and, out of the blue, said, "How about a Bucky Burlesque show?"

We grinned at each other.

"Holy crap," she said. "I get it! It could be political subterfuge. A fun and even funny show with women singing and dancing while they got the message across. We could load up a tour bus and hit the road in time to influence the next presidential election."

"I'm game for anything," I said.

"It could be like *The Full Monty*," said Dee, the TV producer. "I can see it now, a chorus line of beautiful women flashing the audience at the end, baring all for the good of the planet!"

"I'll tell you what this show really could be," said Rebecca, whipping her ponytail back and forth as she made sure she connected with everybody in the circle. "It could be about women the world over rising up and doing something to knock some sense into our misguided species. A vast majority of the world's problems are caused by males — more specifically, alpha males. Whether we're talking ISIS or NFL or bad cops killing black kids at random, it needs to stop. If women come together and put ourselves — our bodies — on the line, maybe people will listen."

It occurred to me that Rebecca was not your average burlesque dancer.

"Do you think we could actually make this happen?" I asked.

"Sure. It could be a great little show. I can see us now, a happy cast and crew eating pancakes together at some crazy truck stop in Alabama."

My mouth watered, but not for pancakes. I wanted the kind of experience where you know you have put it all on the line, and maybe even solved the puzzle of your life, and where you are with people who see the world the same way you do.

Life begins right outside your comfort zone. Effective activism begins somewhere beyond that. The fearless Rebecca broke out in song.

> First we were on oil, we were petrified,
> Kept thinking we could never live without it by our side,
> But now we've put up solar panels, taken down the fossil
>   fools,
> We will survive!

Jeremy grimaced. "Okay, well, so it needs a little work — but hey, maybe you could even take the show on the road to fracking towns, give those poor people some hope."

Rebecca, glowing from her brief performance, grabbed my arm. "Okay, so, seriously, I know at least a dozen kick-ass dancers who would do this. Let's do it. We could do it on the cheap, raise some money, maybe on Kickstarter."

She paused to catch her breath. "You all are looking at me like I'm insane."

"What's crazy," I said, "is that I always dreamed something like this would happen—that the right idea would just pop up and everything would fall into place."

Eileen announced it was time for a break, that we should come back in fifteen minutes to present our ideas. Our group chose Rebecca and me to present our idea, so the two of us headed outside to rehearse.

When the conference reconvened, we held back. Rebecca wanted to go last, so we sat patiently in the back of the room, listening to a long string of ideas for environmental activism. One group was plotting to hang from bridges in swings and hammocks to block oil rigs from passing out to sea. No, this wasn't legal, they said; that was the point. Getting arrested was part of the plan. They wanted the exposure their stunt would bring. It would be a great photo op.

"We are older and wiser now," said a slim gray-haired woman. "And at this age, I'm not exactly worried about my resume, so if I get arrested, who the fuck cares?"

That got a good laugh. There was something about a conservative-looking seventy-something woman saying "fuck" that was very funny.

Other groups presented more conservative ideas such as a letter-writing campaign to the editors of big-city newspapers. Good writing was important, said the well-groomed man in an expensive knit sweater. "The energy issue is so complex," he said. "We must use simple, clear writing to make the facts easy to understand."

Next came a plan to infiltrate conservative organizations like the Heartland Institute. Members would pretend to be insiders so that they could learn how the lies were created.

By the time it was our turn, I was a bundle of nerves. I picked up a long blue-and-green scarf I'd borrowed from Fran and draped it around my neck. Rebecca whipped off her jacket. We approached the makeshift stage in the front of the showroom, which included a huge Styrofoam boulder once used to display trucks.

I started us out. "We know we are up against billions of dollars being spent in thousands of ways to confuse people about climate change, so simply telling the truth isn't enough. The genius Buckminster Fuller once said that his only regret was not being a song and dance man, because then people might have listened more attentively. Our idea is for a traveling road show, something sexy and fun that people will line up to see—something that will change their thinking about nature, energy, and the fossil fuel industry."

Rebecca was perched up high on the boulder like she was a rock star, holding aloft two metal trash can lids like protective shields. People were apparently in the mood to laugh, because they started giggling even before Rebecca smashed the metal lids together and began to sing.

First we were on oil, we were petrified,
Kept thinking we could never live without it by our sides,
But then we spent so many nights reading by our solar lights,
And we grew strong and with the sun we got along,
But now they're back, from fracking space,
We just woke up to learn they lied about the damage we now
* face,*
We should have changed that stupid lock, made them leave it
* in the ground,*

If we had known for just one second they'd come back to drill around,
We will survive!

She bowed to rousing applause then banged her trash can lids together in celebration. I got goosebumps. She truly was a fearless and talented performer. She made anything seem possible. As the conference wrapped up, Rebecca and I promised to get back in touch soon. Dee said she would produce. Jeremy offered to pull together the financing. It felt like the real thing.

FORWARD TO THE PAST

2012

How often I found out where I should be going only by setting out for somewhere else. — Buckminster Fuller

Life shifted into overdrive the next day thanks to an email from the organizers of a festival to honor Buckminster Fuller at Southern Illinois University in Carbondale, where he taught from 1959 to 1970. They were impressed with my blog and invited me to be a presenter — and it would happen in the place where I was first swept away by Bucky's ideas.

I had no idea how I would pull it off. Money was tight, and Rob didn't know I was still even thinking about Bucky, let alone singing and dancing and reading poetry about him in public places. So of course I answered with an immediate yes.

I worked up my courage to tell him over a glass of wine, expecting groans of protest, but he surprised me:

"Great. Whatever you have to do." He barely looked up from his iPad. Maybe he was coming around. While he wasn't thrilled there would be no reimbursement for travel expenses, especially since we were now paying two college tuitions, he nodded approval when I promised to book an inexpensive red-eye flight and eat on the cheap at places like Denny's. Maybe he was learning that a happy wife made for a happy life, or maybe he had seen the latest news about climate change.

Either way, I wasted no time getting to work on my slide presentation. My goal was to capture all of Fuller's most important ideas and share them in a story people could relate to, all inside of thirty minutes.

▽▽▽

A hazy red sun was breaking over Indiana's pancake-flat horizon when the Hertz agent, a slim black woman in a white sundress, gave me a curious look. "You travelin' all by yourself?"

"Yep. I'm back home where I grew up to speak at a conference." I'd slept surprisingly well on the red-eye, and it felt good to be back home in Indiana.

She looked at my driver's license. "All the way from California? You must be rockin' life, girl. I'm upgrading you to somethin' special."

"You can do that?"

"Damn right, I can."

Next thing I knew, I was roaring out of Indianapolis in a red Mustang convertible, feeling as if I'd been crowned queen for a day and trying not to think too much about the extra carbon emissions my muscle car and I were producing. Indiana's spring was in full force, and the thick morning air was so warm I pulled over to put the top down.

When I got out of the car to put my bag and jacket in the trunk, I was bowled over by sights and smells so familiar it was as if they were in my DNA. Rolling green and black ribbons of young corn and soybeans. Faint, musky smells of skunk and recently tilled soil.

How miraculous life was to bring me back where it had all started to speak at the same college where Fuller had taught. I'd left this part of the world so broken. But now I leaned against the car, turned my face up to the sun, and took in several long, deep breaths. Good things were finally happening.

The leafy Southern Illinois University campus felt like home. On a lake much smaller than the one I recalled, ducks still nibbled their way obliviously along the shore.

My speech was only an hour or two away and my nerves were jangling by time I entered the student activity center. The festival organizers welcomed me warmly, set me up with a badge, and gave me a quick tour. The auditorium where I would speak was huge—much bigger than I'd envisioned. A daunting black podium towered over hundreds of empty red velvet seats. I was escorted to the sound room, where a technician checked my laptop for compatibility with the projector. I pretended as if I'd done this sort of thing a hundred times before. Fake it till you make it, the mantra of my life.

My laptop worked fine, so I wandered into the lobby in search of coffee. A huge Styrofoam cup, now banned in California for its multiple environmental sins, was handed to me. The notoriously weak midwestern coffee was a perfect match for the outmoded cup.

I perused a sale of Bucky's books. Festival founders Brent Ritzel and Janet Donoghue had curated an impressive display that included most of Fuller's twenty-six volumes, including two published posthumously. There was also a whole table of books written about Bucky by others, many of which I had never seen.

A few college students thumbed through the stacks casually, and I wondered how much they knew about their famous former professor and whether I could teach them anything. This gave rise to old, familiar doubts — imposter syndrome, it's called, when you secretly think you're about to be revealed as a fraud. My hands shook as I fished for my credit card to buy a book about Fuller I knew nothing about. I loved the title: *American Dreamer.*

I settled into a seat near the stage and willed my brain to slow down. Just as the monks at Green Gulch had taught, I took three long, deep breaths and calmly took my seat in the storm.

The festival organizers welcomed us and introduced the first speaker. I twisted around. Most of the seats behind me were still empty. My heart sunk until I remembered that the organizers had cautioned this was a first annual event and attendance might be light. I told myself it didn't matter. We were all here for the same reason, to bring Bucky's ideas back into the world.

But where were the students? Weren't they the ones we needed to reach?

The speaker was L. Steven Sieden, the author of an excellent biography called *Buckminster Fuller's Universe* as well as an anthology about Bucky called *A Fuller View.* I'd read, annotated, and dog-eared them both. Sieden had known Bucky personally and worked with him for many years. A soft-spoken man, he expressed disappointment over the current lack of awareness of Fuller's ideas. His frustration had turned into depression, he said, until he found Zen Buddhism, through which he had found peace and come to terms with "what the world no longer seemed to understand." He had come from Seattle, hoping this festival would change things, that the world would begin to embrace Bucky's thinking anew.

I glanced back at the empty seats. A few more students had trickled in. But Bucky wasn't exactly the It Guy of the moment, not even at the university where he had taught for more than a decade.

The next presenter was D. W. Jacobs, the charming, twinkly-eyed playwright who had done more than anyone to keep Bucky's ideas alive by writing and directing a popular one-man play called *The History (and Mystery) of the Universe*. I'd already seen it twice, the first time in San Francisco when Rob surprised me with tickets for my birthday. It featured actor Ron Campbell, who expertly dived into synergetic geometry to convey the magic of Bucky's thinking and explain how everything was created by patterns in nature.

Throughout Jacobs's play, I had felt myself merging with the stage lights, feeling a oneness with everything and loving every minute of it. Surely Jacobs was doing exactly what I was trying to do, which meant I was blissfully off the hook. It wasn't until long afterward that I realized there had been an absence of any remarks about the fossil fuel industry, which Bucky had told me was the most important thing. The fossil fools, as he called them, were why he had called me back that second morning. He'd wanted to make sure I knew humanity's crucial examination was about whether we could end our enslavement by big oil.

Here in Carbondale, Jacobs spoke of the need for better storytelling to capture the imaginations of a new generation. Unless new narratives illuminating humanity's potential could capture the world's hearts and minds, he said, we were sunk. "If we have any hoping of waking people up, it is going to have to be a damn good story," he said.

I took copious notes. If storytelling was the answer, what kind of story did we need? What would it take to change the way people think? I zoned out, deep in thought and racing to copy down all his ideas, until the emcee jolted me back to reality.

"We discovered our next presenter in the blogosphere," she began. "Patricia Ravasio hails from Northern California and calls herself a lifelong student of Buckminster Fuller. She has painstakingly combed through Fuller's archives at Stanford, where she has unearthed important writings never before published. She also has some interesting ideas on why nobody seems to know about Bucky today and what we can do to bring him back. Ladies and gentlemen, Patricia Ravasio."

I stood and strode up to the podium, feeling like a total imposter. Thank goodness for my Stuart Weitzman boots. The masculine, almost military bearing and click of well-built heels made me feel empowered.

But thinking about my shoes made me feel trivial. Here I was following in the footsteps of a genius playwright, and I was thinking about my footwear.

I looked out over the mostly empty auditorium and noticed something else to panic about. It wasn't that so many seats still sat empty. What unnerved me was that the occupied seats were filled by the kings of Buckydom, people who no doubt knew way more about him than I did.

With no idea what I was doing or why, I opened my laptop, clicked on the Keynote icon, took another deep breath, and began with a breathtakingly beautiful photo of the Spaceship Earth dome at Epcot Center.

"Something most of us share is that we find ourselves driven just a bit mad by the unrealized possibilities of our time. By now, humans were supposed to be thriving in sustainable colonies, or floating on or under the sea, or blissfully protected from the changing climate under city-wide domes. At the very least, those of us who were here for the last go-round, the last attempt at a clean energy revolution in the 1960s and '70s, thought that surely by now we'd be finished with war and fossil fuels and a government controlled by the interests of a few. This was the American dream of 1969, the year the practical utopian ideas of Buckminster Fuller first swept me away on this very campus. What happened? How did this practical utopian dream disappear? And how do we get it back?"

There was nervous laughter from a man sitting in front. A few others cleared their throats.

I clicked through my colorful slides about Bucky's ideas, revealing what I called The Fuller MIRACLE, Bucky's seven simple guidelines for improving the prospects for humanity.

M for mindfulness.

I for individual integrity, the most important thing.

R for realignment with nature. This is where I lambasted the fossil fools.

A for anticipatory, which is what design science must be.

C for comprehensiveness, since specialization leads to extinction.

L for livingry, the opposite of weaponry.

E for ephemeralization, doing more and more with less and less.

It had taken me months to organize Bucky's thinking into something concise and cohesive, although it still didn't encompass the math the way Jacob's play had. The girls had thought the MIRACLE idea was a little corny. Alyssa, home on break from UCLA, worried that it didn't sound academic enough. I reminded her that my goal was to translate Bucky's ideas for ordinary people.

And it was working. I was getting smiles and nods from the audience — until the question-and-answer period began.

An older man in a flannel shirt stepped up to the mic in the side aisle and challenged whether Bucky had ever called for an end to fossil fuels. "Aren't you interpreting his comments too literally? Surely Fuller would be very impressed by today's fracturing technology, which is freeing up natural gas supplies and securing America's energy independence. This was something he couldn't have known about at the time."

I had heard this objection before, that Bucky would have admired the technological success of the natural gas boom instead of seeing it as proof that we were losing the battle. I tried to stay cool. "I'm quite sure Buckminster Fuller meant it when he said, 'We must stop burning up the house to keep the family warm.' He might be impressed with some of today's technologies — he would have loved the iPhone — but he would be spinning in his grave if he knew we're still driving combustion-engine cars. He would be dismayed to learn that we still haven't fully harnessed the sun, the wind, the waves, geothermal power — "

The man guffawed. "Ha. You know, Ronald Reagan is the one who put this country on track to secure our energy independence from the Middle East."

I swallowed hard and gave myself a minute to think. It was a hard-and-fast rule to never get into a debate with an audience member. I was supposed to thank him for his comments and move on. But I was new at this, and holding back from a debate had never been part of my repertoire. Especially when the human race was at stake.

"Consider this: Bucky estimated the sun gives off enough power to meet the energy needs of the entire earth for a whole year, every single minute." I thumped the podium with my finger for emphasis, accidentally hitting the mic with my elbow. "Think about that. Every single minute, Earth receives enough solar power to run the entire planet for a year. Yet we've been duped into believing it's not possible, that the technology isn't there yet."

He'd been waiting for an opening. "Ridiculous! Solar is only a sliver. Fossil fuels are the future, no way around it. No way is solar and wind ever going to be enough to do the job."

I suggested he check out The Solutions Project from Stanford, which had calculated in detail how to transition to completely clean energy in every state in America.

But the man turned away, yielding to another who asked me about the Livingry Industry plan Bucky had left on his desk the day he died. I explained how Fuller had used his inventions as examples of projects that could be undertaken if livingry were ever to replace weaponry as our national objective. As I spoke, I made a mental note to spend more time with this document. It might be more important than I had thought.

The next questioner took us back to energy, reminding me that Fuller had called pollution just another resource waiting to be put to work.

"While it's true that Bucky said pollution was but a resource waiting to be harvested," I said, "our all-important realignment with nature demands a move away from fossil fuels, especially since we're already seeing clear effects of climate change and especially when an energy evolution is entirely possible. Does that make sense?"

"So you're a warmist, then?" he asked with a defiant glare.

That was putting it mildly. Being in the hot seat was making me think I might catch fire. Despite the sweat pouring down my sides and soaking into my bra, I forced myself to leave my jacket on. Instead, I envisioned the serene, beaming face of the Zen monk at Green Gulch telling my meditation group that "taking your seat in the storm" was the key to effective activism. I raised a hand to my thundering heart and followed his three steps for mindfully grounding oneself when under attack: One, fully acknowledge the pain of the moment. Holding a clenched fist up against your heart can help. Two, consider the impermanence of that pain and the impermanence of everything. No matter what it is, it too shall pass. Three, make a silent vow to serve the universe by responding only with kindness and compassion.

I managed half a smile. "Do you have a question, sir?"

He muttered under his breath and walked away.

Another older man in tortoiseshell eyeglasses stood up and spoke from his seat. "You're obviously quite enamored with Bucky, but you seem a little starry-eyed. Don't you think it's important to keep a sense of balance when you present in an academic setting?"

This accusation hit hard. He was right.

He sat down, and I wished I could do the same. Maybe the girls had been right to be concerned about how the acronym "MIRACLE" would play. Maybe it should have been a "FORMULA" or some kind of "ABSTRACT."

I knew I didn't seem objective. I believed in Bucky's ideas with all of my mind and all of my heart. His thinking had made immediate and obvious sense to me from the beginning.

I had no idea what to say. "Well, I guess to me the most important thing is to live up to my own convictions. It's not rocket science to understand that whatever we believe ourselves capable of is exactly what we are capable of, and nothing more. We must actually work to envision life in a new context, or it will be impossible to achieve. It won't just happen. We have to decide to make it happen. That's all Bucky was really saying, that we can create a cleaner, healthier, and more just world but only if we fully apply ourselves to the task."

He stood up again to speak, but I wasn't finished.

"Sir, I have taken on the task of communicating some important lost ideas, not necessarily accepting responsibility for serving up a complete evaluation of all competing possibilities."

There was a smattering of applause. He didn't speak at first, then stammered a thank-you. This hadn't gone the way I wanted it to. I had wanted to end on a hopeful and positive note.

"Anything is possible. Humanity has miraculous potential, but only if we believe it."

Another trickle of applause. The emcee stepped onto the stage and rescued me by announcing a fifteen-minute break. The lights went down.

My hands were shaking. I felt like an idiot. I took time to gather my things, not trusting myself to walk down the steps or look at anybody. I didn't dare remove my jacket, even though I was still melting. Sweat trickled down my back. I didn't understand what had just happened, only that it wasn't good.

A young, bearded man in a leather jacket was waiting for me below the stage. I motioned for him to come up. He bounded up the stairs and shook my hand vigorously.

"I'm graduating this year," he said, "and I had to come up here and tell you that I felt I was hearing the truth for the first time in my life."

I laughed in relief. "Thank you. Where were you during the Q&A?"

"Oh wow, sorry. I don't know why some people don't get it. It was mind-blowing about Bucky's miracle and the whole conscious evolution thing. And fossil fuels—of course you're right. It seems obvious that this is what we must focus on, doing whatever it takes to control the fossil fuel industry."

A young woman appeared at his side and began shaking my hand equally enthusiastically. "I'm also graduating this June, and what you've just told us is what we most needed to hear — and yet we've never heard a word of it. Why did it take so long for this to happen at the very school where Bucky taught for all those years?"

I felt a spark of hope. The younger generation had been sensing for some time that things were screwed up in the world. They were hungry for ideas that made not just money but sense. Now if only their need for answers ran deep enough to keep them engaged and outspoken over the long haul about issues that mattered.

For the rest of the day, I immersed myself in wall-to-wall Bucky. In session after session, young people seemed to get intuitively what the older ones needed to debate endlessly. Not until a panel discussion about how to reignite interest in Bucky's geodesic domes as dwelling units did the two groups agree. But this was one idea I didn't embrace.

Bucky's dome was originally intended as a metaphor, a real-world demonstration of nature's design/build capabilities. You could think of it as a "megaphor" — the idea is bigger than life. A two-mile dome over Manhattan to control its climate might make sense one day, but using domes as housing wasn't really the point. Yet people the world over had become fascinated by them, and since they were so easy to build, living in them seemed the natural thing to do. But when they leaked in heavy rains, that was reason enough to dismiss them entirely, contributing to Bucky's reputation as a something of a counterculture crackpot.

At the next opportunity, I raised my hand.

"The lady in the back. Do you have a question?"

"What are we going to do about it?" I asked. "We know humanity's progress is being stymied by greedy private interests, but how do we stop it? What can we actually do?"

He thought for a minute, then cleared his throat. "That's the million-dollar question. I'm not sure. All I know is that my small role in the big picture is to keep Bucky's domes out there in the world, not just as houses and playgrounds and aviaries but also as proof that big ideas are still possible. I can't solve the whole thing. I don't know how to get the dinosaurs to give up their fossil fuels before they turn us into Venus. Do you?"

I didn't. I was starting to feel hopeless again. It didn't matter if hundreds of enthusiastic Buckyphiles chatted for centuries; it wasn't going to change anything. The American dream was morphing into a horrific, silent scream.

By five o'clock, my saturated brain was done. I slipped away and drove to the Holiday Inn near the highway to check in and call Rob.

He answered the phone over the clanging of pots and pans, sounding downright cheerful. "Hey, honey, how's it going?"

"I'm doing okay. My talk went okay, I guess. I love being back in the Midwest. The frogs are serenading me right now from the woods outside my hotel room."

"Great. So the presentation went well?"

"Um, mixed reviews. But the young people seem to get it, and that's who matters most, right?"

"Absolutely. I'm sure you were great. But hey, listen, the risotto is at a critical point, so…"

"Oh, okay. Well, I just wanted to say it's going great, everything is going great."

"Okay, super. Congratulations. Is there something else?"

"No, no, I know you need to go, so…"

"Okay. Bye. The kids all say hi. Love you."

"Love you, too."

I don't know what I had expected or needed from that phone call, but whatever it was, I hadn't gotten it. Even if I'd been a huge success, I would've needed something more from my husband. Maybe my call was just bad timing. Risotto was time sensitive after all.

Exhausted, I flopped down on the bed and drifted off to sleep.

I woke with an hour or so later. I'd put my name on a list to perform at a poetry reading. Damn. I'd feel like a total loser if I bailed out after coming all this way. I checked my phone. The poetry reading started in twenty minutes.

I had no idea where the bar was, and I still needed to change and reapply my makeup. I rolled off the bed, considered myself in the mirror, and decided that just as Woody Allen said, eighty percent of life was just showing up.

The dark campus bar smelled of stale beer. An older woman in a woven skirt and wooden beads greeted me at the door. She checked my name off a list and pointed me to a table where she said some of the other Bucky fans were seated.

I recognized one man who had questioned me earlier about fossil fuels. I smiled and said hello, went to the bar, and ordered a glass of chardonnay.

When I returned to the table, a younger man stood up and gallantly pulled back a chair for me. I was the sole woman at the table. Not counting the hostess or the woman playing guitar onstage, I was the only woman in the bar.

The man from earlier spoke. "You know, I gotta say, your enthusiasm for Bucky is refreshing. Never even heard a woman 'round here talk about him before."

"Really? One of the festival organizers is a remarkable woman." I wanted to be nice and not get into it with this man, whose eyes said he was looking for trouble. "But you're right about one thing. I do feel passionately about the value of Bucky's ideas."

"But you don't wanna go around soundin' all overboard like some lovesick pup, right?"

He leaned forward in his chair in a macho way and rested his arms heavily on the table. This boisterous, bearded, manspreading fellow was intentionally trying to take up the maximum amount of space using the minimum amount of brains.

The other men looked away, embarrassed at their somewhat inebriated friend.

Obviously, he was baiting me. But I wouldn't bite. I hadn't spent all those Sunday mornings at Green Gulch and all those Monday nights at Spirit Rock meditating and learning how to ground myself only to be derailed by a beastly Neanderthal.

My hand clenched at my chest, holding my wine glass in front of my heart. I acknowledged my suffering and its impermanence, and I set out to speak with kindness.

"I don't believe I idolize Bucky," I said calmly. "But I do believe his ideas have merit and should make their way back into mainstream thinking. I want people to understand his ideas so they can evaluate their potential for themselves."

He wasn't letting up. "Seems to me like you might have a crush on him. It felt a little weird in your show today, how you said you fell for him when you were a young girl and how you still got some big infatuation still going on."

I put down my wine glass and stood. My hands were clenched so tightly that my fingernails dug into my skin. Apparently, I was not going to be able to respond with kindness to this man. This meant I needed to leave before I lost it completely.

But not without a few parting words.

"One thing Bucky always said was that it's hard to get a man to believe something when his paycheck depends on his believing something else. I know this is coal country and people are worried what solar energy might do to their jobs. But can't you see that it's killing the planet to keep burning so much coal and oil? Technology for clean energy has been ready to go for decades. Why not get on board?" My neck was growing hot.

The man rolled his eyes. "Buncha lefty California malarkey is what you've fallen for with all that global warming nonsense, honey."

It was the "honey" that did it. Spirit Rock was now a boulder I wanted to drop on his head, but I could feel the monk from Green Gulch grinning at my predicament, reminding me to keep my seat.

"I don't think so, sir. Almost every climate scientist agrees: fossil fuels are a big part of the problem. It's only disputed by those with a financial stake. You are either being duped by them, or you are one of them. Which is it?"

So much for kindness and compassion.

He shook his head. "You know, I'm starting to think there is something entirely too personal for you in all this. Come on, spill it, darling. What really went on between you and your beloved Bucky? Did you, you know..." His furry eyebrows rose and fell nastily.

I had never felt such an urge to haul off and clock someone. Surely I was not so stupid as to get into a bar fight. Only hurt people hurt people. I put down my glass and walked out.

The sweet night air rushed over me. I blasted the toxic fumes out of my lungs and slumped, letting my head hang. Had that truly just happened? Had I really gotten into an ugly public argument with a man in a bar? About Bucky? And nearly hit him? What was wrong with me?

Why was this all so entirely, fuckingly impossible to get right?

I threw off my jacket and stretched toward the sky. I needed to go ahead and break down and let myself cry.

"Ms. Ravasio, we came to see you!" cried the young woman I'd met earlier, waving her hand as she and her boyfriend rushed toward me.

"Did we miss it?" asked her companion.

I stood silently, a bit awkward, still in shock.

"I'm Michael, and this is Ashley."

"Oh, hi. Nice to meet you again. Um, no, it's not over, but it really wasn't my scene in there. Some of the old guys…I'm afraid I'm too…"

"Too what? Too smart? Too outspoken?" Michael's eyebrows raised.

"I don't really know. But I sure have a way of ticking people off and a hard time staying cool when they attack."

"Don't let the old geezers get you down," said Ashley. "You were great today. You were courageous to carry the torch for the end of fossil fuels, right here in coal country. You are fearless."

"Ha! What's that old saying, how does it go? 'Fools rush in where wise men fear to tread.'"

"Don't even think that way," Ashley said. "Someone has to speak up, or nothing good is ever going to happen."

Michael nodded. "Today you said exactly what needed to be said—"

"—that nobody else is saying," Ashley finished.

They were right. What did it matter what the old coal geezers thought? These two young people were who mattered. They were empty vessels just like I had been in my twenties, ready to take in the truth about everything.

"You give me hope," I said, looking into their eager eyes. "And your timing is perfect. I was about to get slaughtered in there. They'd be throwing lumps of coal at me about right now."

They laughed.

"The guy actually accused me of having a romantic crush on Bucky. I tried to stay calm, but I thought I might hit him." I looked at my own fist in wonder. Sometimes I did not know myself.

"Forget that old fart," said Michael. "We came to hear you. We want to know more about this magical Bucky dude."

There had never been a time when I didn't want to talk about Bucky, but I could still hear the clean coal fanatics yukking it up inside. "Can we go somewhere quiet?"

"Sure," he said. "Let's go down to Campus Lake."

We walked together to the very spot where my father had shown me his inky sketches of Bucky's fantastic ideas, causing the universe to turn its somersaults for me.

Ashley took off her shoes. Barefoot was her new religion—earthing, she called it, a real thing about reconnecting our physical bodies to the earth's energy. Michael made a joke about her being a feral creature, to which she replied that he was lucky to have lured her out of the woods.

They flirted and played together like puppies, like two halves of a whole. I got the feeling they saw eye to eye on just about everything. I couldn't imagine what that would be like.

I asked about their plans. They were both about to receive undergraduate degrees in environmental sciences. Neither had a job lined up.

"What do you plan to do after graduation?" I asked.

"We want to save the world," Ashley said matter-of-factly.

"But the problem is the only companies hiring in our major are oil and coal," Michael said.

It was the same old story.

"*Clean* coal, don't forget." Ashley's sarcasm was charming.

"So even though the planet isn't hiring, we've decided to work for her anyway," he said.

"Earth needs advocates," she said. "Fracking just feels wrong to me — creating explosions underground to release gas, using undisclosed toxic chemicals that nobody understands. Next to water aquifers? How did America become so gullible?"

"So," he said, "we are going to hit the road and do what we can. We're going to live simply."

"The money will take care of itself," she said.

"Right."

Ashley wasn't the only sarcastic one.

We arrived at the lakefront, where a geodesic dome-like picnic pavilion perched on the grassy bank.

"How long has this been here?" I asked.

"It's called Bucky's Haven," Michael said. "It was built in the early 1960s."

"Wow. I was here in 1969 with my family. I don't remember it."

"Memories aren't always perfect."

But for the most part, they were. With or without the pavilion, I could see myself skipping stones with Roger on the grassy shoreline as clear as day. I stood for a moment listening to the frogs croaking, fighting the crickets for airtime. Their haunting rhythm and the familiar sweet fragrance of a midwestern lake in spring—it all felt eerily perfect.

"Yikes, did you see that shooting star?" Michael pointed to the northern sky.

"I forgot the meteor showers are tonight," Ashley said.

The two of them sprang into action. They dragged the wooden picnic tables out from under the dome and set them up side by side. Michael grinned, climbed up on one of the tables, stretched out his long, angular frame, and clasped his hands behind his head like a pillow.

"The perfect place for a show." A Bucky boy if ever there was one.

Ashley and I climbed up on the other two tables and sprawled on the cool, damp wood.

"So let's hear more about this magical Bucky dude," she said.

"I learned about him in architecture class," Michael said, "but nobody said a word about fossil fuels. Or realigning with nature. Or conscious evolution. Or cosmic surfing. What the hell is cosmic surfing?"

"That is one of my all-time favorite questions." I led them down to the water's edge and had them stand facing west with their eyes closed. They held each other's hands at first, and I separated them so they could focus. "You must first breathe deeply to calm and center yourselves so you will be open to the sensation of knowing."

Just as Bucky had done for me, I connected them to the reality of where they stood: on a spinning, revolving, hurtling-through-the-cosmos planetary spaceship.

"I love this," Michael whispered. An owl hooted from the deep trees on the other side of the lake. The frogs and crickets had fallen silent.

"I don't get it." Ashley dropped her arms.

"Bucky called intuition cosmic fishing," I said. "He said, 'When you feel a little nibble, all you've got to do is hook the fish.'"

"Amazing," said Michael. "Just open your mind, and it's all right there."

"I think I need better bait," Ashley said.

We laughed. Maybe every good couple has one of each—a ready and willing cosmic fisher and a practical, feet-on-the-ground land dweller.

We returned to the picnic tables, and Michael pulled a flask from his pocket. "They're lying bastards, you know. I've been watching for a while. Big Oil has blatantly obstructed development of renewables."

He took a swig and handed the cool metal flask to me.

"You're exactly right," I said. "If we don't get energy right, nothing else will matter."

"So we'll take to the road after graduation."

"To do what?" I took a sip. Whiskey, not my favorite, but the warmth in my throat was nice.

"We're going rogue. We're going to show up to support protesters, help people find a voice. I aced environmental rhetoric. I'm going to be a writer, probably a journalist. We've decided we'll go to jail if necessary to be part of the revolution that must start happening on the streets soon."

These kids got it. "I predict success, because you've done exactly as Bucky recommended. You looked around, you saw what needed to be done that wasn't already being done, and now you're going to do it. You're in alignment with universal energies, so the money should take care of itself."

"Nice theory," Ashley said.

I returned Michael's flask, which he pocketed. I could tell money was a big concern for him, as it was for most young people. So I told them about Robert Kiyosaki, the best-selling author of *Rich Dad, Poor Dad*. Kiyosaki attributed his fortune to harnessing Bucky's ideas about universal energies. If your goals are aligned with the energies of the universe, Kiyosaki wrote, resources will flow naturally to support them.

Michael high-fived me and howled at the sky. "I'd always had a hunch that was the way things worked."

The shooting stars continued their show as we talked about Bucky's predictions and how they had all come true. The 9/11 attacks. Fuller's disappearance at Stanford. The highly effective fossil fuel propaganda, now swinging wildly out of control, with zero mentions in the mainstream media about the climate change.

We talked about Bucky's idea of using computer technology to facilitate a true digital democracy, how an objective and rational computer might be the only way to bring disparate ideologies together. That people all over the world could participate in collaborations to solve problems locally and globally. We agreed that leaps forward in social media would make implementing this new version of the World Game much easier, if only someone set out to do it.

It was all still possible.

A duck squawked a throaty good morning from the shore. The sky was turning pink. I couldn't believe how many hours had glided by. As we pushed back the picnic tables and gathered ourselves for the walk to my car, I felt electrified.

Morning had broken, just like the Cat Stevens song. And I had found a new voice, one older and wiser and somehow more like my father's. It was another Bucky prediction come true: I had come to know everything I needed to know when I needed to know it.

My feet hovered just above the sidewalk. I had done it. For the first time in my life, I had calmly explained Bucky's ideas to people who were interested in hearing them. The once-empty vessel had effectively decanted her well-ventilated contents.

There was just one small problem: it had taken me all night.

At this rate, bringing Bucky's ideas back into the world would take a millennium. And no way was there that much time remaining on humanity's clock.

SHOWTIME

2012

A designer is an emerging synthesis of artist, inventor, mechanic,
objective economist, and evolutionary strategist.
— Buckminster Fuller

I saw myself in a mirror, dabbing blue and green acrylic paint onto my face to make it look like the planet. Unsure this idea of Rebecca's was working, I put on my glasses and stepped back to appraise myself in a full-length mirror. Nope, a human face painted like the earth and wearing glasses looked absolutely ridiculous.

My dress, however, was gorgeous. When I spun around, the long flowing silk in layers of green and blue lifted off the ground, and hundreds of tiny LED lights created a shimmering vision of the earth combined with a geodesic dome. My rib cage featured bright green lungs that looked like lush tropical islands on the blue oceans, symbolizing the lungs of the planet. We stole the idea from a Salvador Dali painting someone had seen at the Pompidou in Paris.

I spotted Rebecca off stage, perched atop a huge Styrofoam boulder. Costumed as the sun, her blond hair was piled high in a halo and her glittering gold dress twinkled with hundreds of tiny lights. On cue to the music, she leapt down onto the stage pounding together two metal garbage can lids. The banging and clanging sounded like thunder. With her muscular suntanned arms she held the lids triumphantly above her head, pounded them together and proclaimed, "It's not nice to fool Mother Nature!"

She got the laughter she was looking for and then spun across the floor like some crazed tribal dancer, hilariously shouting incomprehensible chants while banging the metal lids together in a frantic rage. She dropped them noisily onto the floor, fell to her knees, placed her hands together as if in prayer, then solemnly sang, in the sweetest imaginable voice, the words from Crosby Stills Nash and Young's *Woodstock*:

> *We are stardust.*
> *We are golden.*
> *We are billion-year-old carbon.*
> *And we've got to get ourselves back to the garden.*

The music rose and segued into a rap song we'd written especially for the trash can lids called *Watch Out for Garbage*, which was all about the lies being told by corporations. Rebecca was joined by backup dancers who turned the sketch into something akin to a number in a Broadway musical. I looked out at the audience and saw Rob and the girls transfixed, their faces beaming with pride. At the end of Rebecca's song, the stage grew silent and dark.

A floating geodesic sphere of light elicited an audible gasp from the audience. The dome of light encircled the stage, then grew larger and larger, accompanied by a haunting electronic soundtrack, until the entire auditorium, with every seat filled, was awash in tiny sparkling triangles of light.

A hush fell over the crowd. It was my turn to speak. Softening my tone so I would sound more goddess-like and ethereal, I began, "We have been sent to you today by Mother Nature. We are her children, the sun, the earth, the wind, the plants and animals. We bring you news that your dear mother is ill and losing her patience. She wants so badly for humans to succeed, but we have backed her into a corner with our putrid blanket of invisible gases, and she has no choice but to unleash upon us her great storms, her terrifying floods, and her persistent droughts in an instinctive effort to throw us off like a bad case of fleas."

There was a trickle of nervous laughter.

"What is happening to humanity today is a totally predictable biological occurrence. Mother Nature is having an allergic reaction."

On cue, Rebecca sneezed an uproariously loud sneeze, which got a huge laugh just as she'd predicted it would.

"Mother Nature is desperately hoping we will come to our senses and stop the idiocy of the fossil fools in time to cool things down before it's too late."

The dome of geodesic light faded to black.

In time to sparse new electronic music, stars popped into the pitch-black sky and then began to slowly rearrange themselves into a staircase, a glittering spiral of stars suspended above the stage. At the top, a small hologram image of Buckminster Fuller popped into view. Wearing a tuxedo and a top hat, he rapped his cane on the top stair before tap dancing his way down toward me, accompanied by singing crickets and croaking frogs. His image grew larger the closer he got, and when he touched down lightly on the stage in front me, his eyes shot out in comic surprise.

"Hello Bucky," I said. "So good to see you back on Earth."

His image grounded itself for a moment, then nodded at me and turned to take in the audience. Touching his fingers together as if to divine the energy of the room, he turned all the way around in a circle, then stopped, lifted a pocket watch out of his cummerbund, and looked directly at me. "I am honored to return to Spaceship Earth in this remarkable way. Thank you, Miss Pat. And while I would love to chat with you about the odd space and time continuum of our meeting here today, there are more pressing matters."

He turned to the hushed audience. "It is now one minute until midnight. Time is of the essence. Our political leaders have proven themselves corrupt and therefore of no use. The people of Spaceship Earth must unite and come together to create a world that works for one hundred percent of humanity, in the shortest time possible, without ecological harm or the disadvantage of anyone."

He turned back and looked me right in the eyes.

"You have done it. You have come to know everything you needed to know, exactly when you needed to know it. But now, it is time to *do* something."

"But what?" I asked. "What can we actually do, now that we know?"

Bucky reached out his arms to embrace the whole audience. I looked out into the crowd and caught Rob's awestruck gaze. Olivia grinned. Alyssa shook her head in wonder. Michaela's hands were clenched over her heart as Bucky stood tall and proud and faced them all silently for a moment, then spoke in a decidedly somber tone.

"To all crew members, planners, architects, and engineers, welcome aboard a newly united Spaceship Earth. There are no captains. We are all crew. The future of humanity rests on our individual integrity. We must wean ourselves off war and fossil fuels as soon as possible to make maximum use of our planetary resources. Take the initiative. Go to work, and above all, cooperate. Do not hold back on one another or try to gain at the expense of another. Any success in such lopsidedness will be increasingly short-lived. Universe is governed by synergetic rules and laws of nature. Our evolution depends on us employing these immutable laws and leveraging them for humanity's benefit. They are not man-made laws. They are the infinitely accommodative laws of the intellectual integrity governing Universe. Ordinary humans have miraculous potential to harness these laws, which can set humanity on a new course toward a higher standard of living than ever before imagined."

When he finished, it seemed like nobody was breathing. The girls were leaning so far forward in their seats I thought they might leap up onto the stage.

The hologram of Bucky smiled, then bowed and nonchalantly danced his way back up through the stars, growing ever smaller until he disappeared with a funny "pop" at the top of the staircase. The audience roared to life with applause, giving a standing ovation and shouts of "Bravo!" and "Encore!"

I breathed a sigh of relief. I'd done it. I had even won over my own family, the biggest miracle of all.

Rob mouthed "I love you" as I took a final bow. The heavy curtain came down with an awkward thunk and I awoke on the grassy bank of the lake in Riley, where I had stopped on my way back to the airport from Carbondale. I immediately snapped my eyes shut to recapture the dream.

It was all still there, every click of his tap shoes, every miraculous sparkle in the eyes of my family—Bucky's ideas brought to life in song and dance. I raised my hand to my face. The skin on my cheek was imprinted with blades of grass. How long had I slept? I remembered knocking on my old front door. How the kindly but ancient lady who now lived there had opened it only a crack and refused to let me in. I'd convinced her to let me walk down to the water, and then I'd followed the shoreline all the way around to the other side of the lake, where I now found myself lying on my side in the sweet-smelling grass under a bright blue sky.

I shook some tiny black ants off my hand. I sat up. I held my arms out in front of me, partly to check for more ants, but also to ask myself, who am I? Am I the self-assured and buoyant actress I'd just seen performing on-stage? Or am I the crepe-skinned, sleep-deprived middle-aged woman snoozing in the grass covered with ants?

Rob was right. I could imagine so much, but manifest nothing. I was the living embodiment of Lilly Tomlin's soul destroying quote, "I always knew I wanted to be somebody. Now I realize I should have been more specific."

This new picture of me became clear. Instead of focusing and seeing projects to the end, I quit. I took the easy way out. I had done it again and again. When I couldn't get help paying for college, I could have figured something out, but instead I gave up. When I left journalism for advertising, I gave up. I had tried everything. Poetry. Blogging. Academic lecturing. In each new endeavor, I had started out with great enthusiasm, but then had either gotten bored or distracted by the next sparkly thing to come along. And now here I was, in the grass, with the ants, drooling in my sleep about playwriting, singing, and dancing—when I wasn't the least bit talented at any of those things.

What was wrong with me?

I flopped down on my back and looked up at the puffy white clouds. There was a word for people like me. What was it?

Dilettante?

Dabbler?

Dreamer?

All of the above?

I watched a pair of red-winged blackbirds swoop down in front of my face and land in the cattails, causing the stalks to bounce up and down, as if the birds were doing it for fun. Nature's way of playing, on display just for me.

What had I been thinking about? Why was I so easily distracted? I watched the birds bounce up and down, trying to remember my previous train of thought. Unable to do so, I had a painful epiphany.

I was broken. I was nothing but a spoiled semi-rich white woman who had managed to marry well and then had spent her entire adult life wringing her hands in self-pity about the planet. Never doing anything. Just thinking about it. For the first time, I understood why I hadn't been able to produce even a smidgeon of the magic I could dream up. I lived in a fantasy world. I made excuses, never actually finished anything. If I was a dog, I'd circle the rug forever, never able to get comfortable enough to settle down on one thing. It was my fatal flaw, the widening crack in the empty vessel I had tricked Bucky into filling.

The tears I'd been holding back poured down my face. I rolled over and let them water the grass. A water bug scrabbled up the stalk of a cattail. A school of minnows darted by below me in the water, casting tiny shadows on the sunlit sand. The crazy blackbirds chirped from somewhere high up above me, and then, in the mud, near the cattails, there appeared the face of a miniature painted turtle. Striped in brilliant reds, yellows, and greens, its tiny face was lit by the sun. It looked right at me and froze.

I had come full circle—from nothing back to nothing again. For Chrissakes, I was staring into a turtle's face, looking for answers. I was losing it. Nothing made sense. I couldn't lay there any longer. I disgustedly picked myself up, brushed the grass off my slacks, and trudged back to the car. There wasn't a cloud in the sky on that bright and warm afternoon, but I didn't care. I didn't even bother to put the top down.

Hours later, on the plane, I cracked open the book I'd bought at the festival, *American Dreamer* by Scott Eastham. I had always read everything I could find about Bucky, forever hoping someone else might have successfully shared his ideas so that I wouldn't have to.

I came upon a passage that washed over me in a wave of relief. Eastham wrote that understanding Buckminster Fuller would require a whole damn committee of experts:

1. a historian to place him in context,

2. an architect or engineer to unearth the principles with which he created,

3. a mathematician to outline his synergetic geometry,

4. a philosopher to understand his often-upsetting pronouncements,

5. a theologian to ponder and pontificate on his spiritual concepts,

6. a social critic to weigh his claim that western society is organized on specious premises,

7. a literary critic to evaluate his mental mouthfuls, and

8. an artist to render it all into something understandable.

I had exactly zero of these eight required professional credentials and definitely did not have all of them at once, so I decided to officially let myself off the hook. Who was I to do something nobody else could do? My self-appointed task was utterly futile. This was the best excuse yet. As I closed that book upon touchdown, I also closed the book on Bucky. It was time to get on with my life.

When I walked in the door that evening, I learned that Heidi had fallen terribly ill. Her kidneys were failing. I went to see her in her bed. Her eyes were vacant. She was panting for breath but still gave me a smile and a lick to welcome me home. Rob and the girls had made plans with the vet to put her to sleep in the morning. It threw me into a tailspin. Nobody slept much that night.

SETH AND THE SHAMAN

2012

Sometimes I think we're alone. Sometimes I think we're not.
In either case, the thought is staggering.
— Buckminster Fuller

After another restless night (three in a row, but who's counting) everyone was a teary-eyed mess over Heidi, which gave me cover to let down and cry about everything else. The sheer volume of tears I shed over the next couple of days — mostly while locked in the bathroom and running water I shouldn't have been wasting during a drought — convinced me I needed help. I dragged myself back to see Dr. Austin.

Maybe it was time for some real meds. Half of America was on Prozac. Why not me? I'd had yet another epiphany in the hot tub that the world was either going to get fixed or not, that it didn't matter one iota what I did or didn't do. All my anxieties seemed suddenly ridiculous, the product of a hijacking by an outsized ego, some brazen obsessive-compulsive character who lived inside of me and worked like the devil to bamboozle the rest of me into believing I had some important mission to fulfill. Preposterous. It was time to shut it down.

Dr. Austin had squeezed me in at the last minute. He looked concerned. "So, how's the Adderall working? Are you doing okay?"

"Wow, Adderall seems like ages ago. It worked fine for a while and helped me focus, but it left me feeling strung out, so I quit taking it."

"That happens. It probably means you don't need it. So how's the Bucky work coming along?"

"Ugh."

"What does that mean?"

I shifted uneasily, not sure I even wanted to talk about it. "Sometimes things feel wobbly, like the universe is playing tricks on me."

"Meaning...?"

I picked at my cuticle. "Well, to start with, somehow I got myself into the preposterous position of believing I needed to communicate things I don't fully understand, ideas nobody seems to fully understand. Nobody can tell me the real significance of the discovery of the carbon 60 molecule, which Bucky predicted the existence of all the way back in 1929. But I know it's a big deal. Some researchers say it may be a key building block of all life on earth. It exemplifies nature's design principles; it came from elsewhere, probably the result of a star exploding. Does it sound crazy if I say these molecules may even contain the secret to free energy? And that this may be why certain fossil fuel interests seem so invested in burying away Bucky's synergetic geometry?"

Dr. Austin's jaw went slack. He shook his head. "I gotta say this all sounds rather fabulous to me, but as we've recently learned, just because something seems insane doesn't mean it's not true."

"Exactly, and just because you're paranoid does not mean they're *not* out to get you."

"Huh? So what's up? What's going on?"

I did not feel like talking. This was a first for me. I'd been diligently trying not to think about anything serious. All I wanted to do was to find my off switch and become a normal person. But he looked disappointed, which made me feel bad, that I owed him an explanation.

"Well, let's see," I said. "Where to start? I went digging through his archives at Stanford, and the most important thing I learned is that the fossil fuel industry is still behaving despicably. They came together decades ago and have worked in collusion ever since, a dark and evil collaboration to perpetrate the greatest crime ever committed against humanity."

He nodded. He was taking notes.

"These executives, these human beings, also knew that the sooner we made the switch to clean energy the cheaper it would be in every way, and that less loss of life would result. But still they didn't give a damn. Publicly they persisted with their lies, knowing the reverse was true, knowing that fossil fuels were to blame, yet they still decided to protect their measly mortal profits."

Tears rimmed my already red eyes. I reached for a Kleenex.

"And they're still doing it. Their lies are still forcing humanity down the path toward extinction, or something close to it."

He looked up. "I know this concerns you. You've told me this before."

"Sorry, I don't want to keep repeating myself." I sat back. What good did it do to know something when you were powerless to do anything about it? I just wanted to put out the fire. I wanted Prozac or a lobotomy or whatever it would take for me to turn everything off once and for all.

"Maybe I should try Prozac."

"Why Prozac?"

I snatched another Kleenex from the box and squeezed it against my finger to stop the bleeding of my stinging cuticle. My mother had been right. Taking care of yourself was job enough.

"I had an epiphany last week," I said. "I'm good at dreaming things up, but that's where my ideas stay. And maybe that is enough. I've raised three awesome kids. I do lots of little things to reduce my carbon footprint. We pay extra for deep green energy from our community energy cooperative. I drive as little as possible. I haven't eaten meat in years, even though I've craved hamburgers my whole life. All of this is going to have to be enough. I do not have the skill or the will to make anything else happen."

He sat back in his chair. "Okay, I'm getting that you are feeling some stress right now?"

Duh. This therapy thing was wearing thin.

"Uh, yes, but I'm pretty sure once I stop dwelling on all this pie-in-the-sky Bucky stuff, it will go away. I'll be a better mother, wife, and friend. I've been fretting long enough. I just want to be happy and not worry so much."

"Is that really what you want to do? What you should do?"

I clasped my hands together. "I'm tired of the shoulds. I'm done."

His brow furrowed. "How are you going to feel if you give up?"

"That's where I thought Prozac could help. I've been reading about it. Maybe I have some kind of chemical imbalance?"

"Well, it's possible I guess, although Prozac has some troubling side effects."

"I know already. It's next to impossible to have an orgasm, and you feel like you're on autopilot. But I've decided I can live without orgasms, and an autopilot is exactly what I need to steer me clear of crazy obsessions about things over which I have no control."

He pulled out his little black book. I hoped he would write the prescription quickly so I could get out of there, but instead he fished around for a business card.

"Before we go all the way to Prozacville," he said, "I would like you try something. I don't normally go for this kind of stuff, but I think maybe a shaman could help you."

"A shaman?"

"Shamans claim to interact with the spirit world on behalf of those who aren't able to. I met this gal at a conference. She specializes in Reiki, which is about tapping into your energy fields to open any logjams. Maybe you are blocked in some way."

"Uh, yeah, I guess you could say I'm blocked. Like a boulder has rolled on top of me."

"I've never recommended a shaman before, but if you're seriously thinking of medicating away your passion, it's worth a try. She might be the real thing, if there is such a thing."

I wasn't sure what I thought. Human energy fields and other metaphysical possibilities hadn't exactly been on the front burner while raising children and living in the real world. The last interaction I'd had with anything paranormal was that crazy night decades ago after Bucky died, when I had sent the spirits on their way, telling them to leave me alone, and they had whimpered at me for not playing along.

Maybe it was time to invite them back. Maybe there was something to the idea that we're all overlapping series of energy events, that life was but a dream, and that maybe I should keep my mind open. He was surely right about one thing. At this point I had nothing to lose. His words "medicating away your passion" had struck me as a pitiful truth.

"At this point, Dr. Austin, I don't care where the answers come from — real world, spirit world, outer space, anywhere. I'm desperate."

I took the business card and called up the shaman the moment I got home.

She picked up my call before it rang. "Hello? This is Margrita. May I help you?" Her voice chirped like a bird.

"Yes, I was referred to you by Dr. Austin in San Rafael. My name is Patricia."

"Yes, Patricia. The doctor emailed me about you. He says you want to better understand your life's mission by communicating with Buckminster Fuller?"

Whoa, wait, I hadn't even thought of it that way, that I might have a chance to chat with Bucky again. And something else was off. She sounded oddly dismissive, as if she'd heard it all a million times. Like I was ordering a pizza. What I wanted to say was, "Look, this isn't just important to *me*. The world has lost some great thinking, and bringing it back would help everybody." But instead, in my newly depressed state, I could only stammer, "Uh, sort of, yeah, I guess."

She snapped at me. "Please explain further."

I was liking her less and less. "To be honest, I'm confused, and sometimes I feel a little desperate. Every day I awaken with an anxious feeling that I'm supposed to be doing something, that I'm supposed to be on some mad dash to somewhere, solving something, doing something important."

"What are you running from?"

I swallowed hard. It hadn't occurred to me I was running *from* anything. "Well, uh, I don't know. I don't have the slightest clue."

"You must open yourself to the energies of the universe and the answers will come to you," she chirped matter-of-factly. "Can you come tomorrow at two? Perhaps I can help you."

I said yes, hung up the phone, and drifted out to the garden in a fog of conflicting emotions. My hands mindlessly clipped the most beautiful blossoms they could find. We had a plan to spread Heidi's ashes under the oak tree after dinner.

▽▽▽

The next day, Google Maps led me to a small purple door in the Marina district. A tiny dark-haired woman with piercing black eyes opened the door and led me up a narrow stairway to a candlelit room.

Margrita asked me to sit up on the massage table, where she said she would work on my energy fields to remove any obstructions. She described how the human body was an electrical system, that only by attending to my chakras could I harness the energy I needed to fully tap my own potential.

Native American flute music played softy in the background. Something smoky burned in the corner. Her tiny hands began to snatch at the air around me, as if she was trying to capture it. She walked over and opened a window, explaining that she was casting away my negative energies.

"We must remove all of your impurities," she chirped, making me feel like a delinquent teenager in the principal's office or someone who had passed some particularly smelly gas.

It took an embarrassingly long time for this apparent housekeeper of human souls to complete her elaborate sweeping and flinging routine. Finally, she shut the window, had me lie down on my back, pulled a sheet up to my chin and told me to close my eyes. She rubbed her hands together then held them over the center of my stomach. I thought she was about to begin a massage, but instead of touching me, she simply held her hands above me.

My stomach started to feel warm, even hot. I cracked my eyes to peek again, thinking she must have something in her hands—a hot stone, maybe—but there was just her hands, palms down, hovering above my stomach. Burning hot. Uncomfortable and getting worse.

Just when I thought I couldn't take anymore, she whisked her hands away and a gust of cool wind raced through the room.

"Now, Patricia," she said, "I want you to keep your eyes closed this time and think of a special place, somewhere you feel safe... Somewhere in or around your home..."

Her voice sounded empty, not at all like the chirping bird that had greeted me moments ago.

"... somewhere you feel warm and protected."

I panicked to realize there was no such place. Not at my house. Not anywhere I could think of. I felt vulnerable, alone...

An image popped into my mind.

"The steps in my garden," I said. "The top step."

"Where is this place? Tell me."

"It's outside the kitchen, where I take a break when I garden." The top step was a large rectangular slab of gray slate that used to be our coffee table back when I was a kid. My father had bought it at a cemetery the same month I was born, justifying its exorbitant cost to my mother by promising to let her bury him under it. Instead, when he died, Rob and I had taken his ashes to England and had them buried next to his father at my mother's insistence, even though his own wishes by that time were for his ashes to be sprinkled over the Pacific Ocean.

"To hell with his wishes," Mummy had said. "Put him next to his father. Old Jack will keep an eye on him and make him behave."

I had forgotten all about the origin of that slab which was now serving as the top step of my garden. But one day I had plopped down onto is cool rough surface to take a break from some heavy-duty weeding and mulching. I wiped the sweat off my forehead, looked up and saw Rob through the kitchen window, making a pie with blackberries I'd picked from the yard. He saw me watching him and smiled. No matter our differences, the metaphysical gravity between us was as real as ever, and just like Bucky had said, love was progressively exquisite. The longer we were in it, the stronger it had grown.

Rob had put up with so much from me: My constant emotional outbursts about the environment, my frayed nerves which sparked and flailed around like downed electrical lines in a storm. Yet I knew he still loved me for who I was, not for what I might or might not accomplish in the world.

Ralph Waldo Emerson said that a worthwhile life required either doing something worth being written about, or writing something worth being read. It now looked pretty definite that I was not going to accomplish neither, and for the first time that was going to have to be okay. I was loved. That was enough.

"Stair steps are good." Margrita's voice brought me back to the room. She took several deep breaths with her eyes closed, as if she were trying to visualize them herself. "I want you to see this place now. Envision it as it is, at this very moment." She waited. "Do you have it?"

I nodded. "Yes. I can see it."

"Good. Now hold onto this vision. This will be the special place you will go to reconnect with your highest and best self. You must sit on the very spot you envision now and ground yourself there. Sit tall and honorably, and call upon your highest self to support your desires to do right by the world. The universe should open up to you on this."

This of course was also Bucky's theory, that alignment with positive universal energies will make everything else fall into place. But while I had dabbled in group meditation and yoga, I wasn't sure I would be able to do this on my own. It took a village to pull me down into the beta waves so I could sit still for any length of time.

"If you stay open, mindful, and authentic, you will receive all the help you need. Sacrifices are being made for you now." Her voice sounded a million miles away.

She drew in a deep breath through her nose and exhaled through her mouth so noisily it was almost a growl. The heat grew intense. My eyes flew open. Hers were still closed and her hands were again poised just above my belly, as if she were pushing something downward into me. She explained she was working on my power chakra, chakra number three, where I apparently was having a malfunction.

This was not the first time I'd heard this. A Native American medicine man named Art Running Bear in Santa Rosa had diagnosed this once before at a weekend retreat

I'd attended with Alyssa on a lark. "There's a hole in your aura," he had said, "caused by a problem in your third chakra." His words turned into a new twist on an old song: *There's a hole in my chakra, dear Liza, dear Liza, a whole in my chakra, dear Liza, a hole!*

Then, like now, I felt like an old car or a washing machine in need of repairs. The sensation of heat in my stomach intensified. Again I was sure she must be holding some hot stones, but each time I peeked, I saw only her tiny unadorned fingers swaying over me in a slow circle, pouring heat into my being, apparently welding my broken aura back together.

I was about to cry out from the heat when she whisked her hands away in a dramatic sweep. Another cool gust of shattering wind blew out the candles and threw the room into darkness.

The door clicked open and she chirped, "I will see you in the parlor when you're ready."

I lay staring up at the cracked plaster ceiling, willing my eyes to adjust to the dark, trying to understand what had happened. It was all too bizarre to categorize, unlike anything I'd experienced. I rose from the table, got dressed, and wrote a check to Margrita.

"Next step for you," she said. "I would like to recommend a brief session with a spirit entity named Seth. He speaks quite fondly of Buckminster Fuller."

I wrote down Seth's phone number, thanked her, and stepped outside into a brilliant late-day sun. A heavy scent of jasmine floated above me. Another aromatic wave of roasting coffee wafted past me. Floating back to the car, my feet hovered just off the ground. My brain felt newly sharpened, like it had been scraped out, polished up, and reconnected to something bigger. Like I'd had a tune-up.

When I pulled into the driveway at home, I was relieved nobody else was there. I wasn't ready to tell Rob or Michaela what had happened. How would I ever explain it?

Never had the house felt emptier. How I missed Heidi's tail whip of a greeting and her toothy grin whenever I said the word "treat." I dropped my things on the dining room table next to Rob's spectacular homemade lemon tart, then I kept going straight through the kitchen, out the back door and across the patio to the garden steps. I wanted to sit on Daddy's slab again to think through all that had happened.

My white roses gleamed iridescently. The garden looked electrified under the late day sun.

I stopped short. There was something on the top step.

In the very place where I had imagined myself sitting and meditating less than an hour ago, there lay a dead bird. And it wasn't just dead, but it was all broken up and coated with feathery goo, made of sticks and leaves, as if it had been part of some bizarre sacrifice in *The Blair Witch Project*.

Sacrifice. She had said sacrifices were being made for me. A reasonable person might conclude that a small bird had indeed randomly died on the same spot at the same time as a magical bird-like shaman had said that sacrifices were being made. But I had been launched into a place beyond reason. I could not fathom this bizarre overlapping series of energy events. I steadied myself against the garden wall, feeling like I had stumbled into some alternative universe—where searing heat came from human hands, where cold air blew through closed windows, and where a sacrificial bird now lay dead on what was supposed to have been my father's gravestone.

I found a garden shovel and gently scooped up the poor thing and buried it next to a rose bush—one more story I would never be able to tell Rob or the girls. They would think I was losing my grip on reality. And maybe they would be right. What the hell was going on?

KARMA

Love is compassionately attuned to other than self.
Love is progressively exquisite.
— Buckminster Fuller

The next morning, the squawk of a crow awakened me from yet another dream about Bucky.

I was about thirteen. In addition to my freckles, glasses, and frizzy hair, I now had ghastly metal braces on my teeth, thanks to sucking my thumb so much it shrunk my mouth and required the dentist to extract four back teeth before putting the braces on. I felt the wild part ripped out of me the day they took those teeth.

It was good to see Bucky pop up again. In his camel hair coat and Burberry scarf, the ancient genius hovered like a drone at the foot of my bed and convinced me to go with him across the lake to see the future.

By now Bucky was like an old friend. As a kid, he had come dancing down his staircase dozens of times. He always came at night, always when I started my period, or any time I was upset. He would rap his cane like a cranky professor to get my attention. Once he knew I was listening he would gently tap out inexplicably beautiful rhythms on the stars, across the water, and my soul would lift to know I was on the brink of some great understanding. The mystery was intoxicating, but any hope of figuring things out was always vaporized by dawn.

Bucky lifted me up and over the lake with his warm weathered hand, his ancient owlish eyes catching mine to make sure I saw the brightly painted turtles swimming across the surface in a perfectly symmetrical pattern like an M.C. Escher drawing. I saw everything now, just like he did. He pointed to the water. "It's all about patterns. Pattern integrities of nature have always held the secret to humanity's future. Go back to that lesson of mine about the knot in a rope. What is it? It is a pattern integrity. Pattern integrities are the key to it all. Humans are about to figure that out."

I felt a wave of relief. "They did? We did?"

"Yes," he said, "It all worked out just fine. As soon as humans decided to go for utopia, they did it. Just like I said they would."

We drifted down toward the ground and landed on a tree-lined sliver of beach. Children played along the water's edge and searched for fossilized bones and shells in the sand, while older people rested in colorful hammocks under great sail cloths that blocked the sun.

Glowing holographic signs floated in midair along the shoreline, proclaiming *Turtles Are King* and *The Winner of the World Game is Everybody*. Next to the beach, a sprawling green lawn the size of a football field was draped in an elaborately colored Dymaxion map of the world. Families sat together in their respective countries, some playing at computers, others on tablets and wristwatches, still others racing around from country to country to negotiate with one another face-to-face. The bleachers were full of onlookers cheering on their chosen teams. The scoreboard kept track of who was helping the greatest number of people win.

Bucky and I sat like yogis in the grass and he explained it all.

Just as he had predicted, an entirely rational and non-judgmental computer called the Geoscope had helped to bring the world together. The Geoscope was a perfect marriage of nature and technology, he said, and like all good marriages, it was based on love. It enabled global collaboration to provide for the good of all humanity without environmental harm. Humans might not be able to trust each other, he said, but they would come together in mutual trust of an objective computer, just as they had already done for decades with air traffic control.

Thrilled at the unexpected news that humanity had finally chosen utopia over oblivion, I untangled my lotus position, jumped up and ran down to the shoreline, where dozens of beautiful women hung in yoga postures on colorful silk trapezes draped from the trees. I had been watching them wistfully while Bucky lectured. Some of them were laughing and talking with each other while stretching, while others hung upside down, long and lean in silent meditation, like bats.

I spotted an empty purple trapeze right next to the sparkling shoreline and I hoisted myself up onto it as I had seen the others do. I bent backwards to attempt an inversion pose, but a crow squawked at me from the branches above. I lost my balance, tumbled upside down, and awakened in my own bed in a tangled mess of sheets.

My feet tingled painfully. They had fallen asleep. I shook them awake.

Another day, another useless dream. I stumbled out of bed to prepare for my scheduled phone call with the spirit world, which I never believed in first thing in the morning, when everything felt so dismal and flat.

A dull headache pressed at the front of my skull as I flipped on the shower. Rain clouds were gathering over Mount Tamalpais. The same old terrifying sensations washed over me. Scientists were begging for people to cry out in protest. Deniers in the fossil fuel industry were still diligently and diabolically prioritizing their profits over everything else.

People like me, who knew better, were still saying and doing nothing.

There must be millions of us by now, maybe even billions. What would it take to make people do something or say something that would make a difference?

At the appointed hour, I sat at my desk with a cup of my best home-grown chamomile to help calm me down, and I dialed up the spirit known as Seth. I had to make the call from the landline, which of course made no sense at all.

Heidi's bed sat empty beneath my desk. I missed her and the way she had buffered the world for me. I was nervous about making the call, knowing I was playing with forces I didn't understand, one of them being the way Rob would react when he saw I had prepaid $125 to talk to a spirit on the phone.

An ancient throat cleared itself on the other end of the line.

"Hello? Who is there?" asked a hollow replica of a human voice.

"Um, hello, Seth, my name is Patricia Field, and I have some questions for you about Buckminster Fuller?"

There was silence, then a weary sigh. "A name is just a name. Symbols you insist on using. So I will use them, too. Yes, this is Seth. I am here, speaking through my friend Mark Frost." There was another long scratchy pause — like some type of metaphysical interference. "You say Buck-minster Fuller is your interest? What is your interest in Buckminster Fuller?"

"I, um..."

"He is not around here much anymore. He has moved on to other planes."

"Well, you see, I met him years ago and promised to help with something, but my notes were lost. He said to watch for signs, which have come and gone, and it may be too late to do anything, but I'm stumped. Was he just too complex for mere mortals to understand?"

"What did Buckminster Fuller say to you? What can you hear him saying?"

"He talked about the need for humans to evolve con-sciously beyond selfishness and greed, to realign ourselves with nature, and to work hard to share resources. He lam-basted the fossil fuel industry, which he said was commit-ting the greatest crime ever against humanity—"

"You are already getting the information. It comes in tele-pathically. You are in his over-soul. The goal was to spin you off, to reframe your thinking."

I gripped the edge of the desk to steady myself. I am in his oversoul? He spun me off? What kind of crazy cosmic surfing was this?

"You are blocking it. You are conflicted. You have some kind of self-esteem issue from your childhood that is pre-venting you from accepting the communications coming to you."

His words had the light of truth, but understanding them was like grabbing at air.

I heard a distant rumble. Thunder? It came from my feet. I felt warmth and looked down. It was Heidi, or at least her spirit, whimpering her concern for me. Goose bumps washed down my arms and legs. I sipped my tea to ground myself, to prove I was still present in the room.

Seth continued without pause. "You are not stuck in time like some fly in a closed bottle whose wings are rendered useless. You already know everything you need to know. You simply must find the courage to express yourself. Do not forget you have far more knowledge when you are dreaming than when you are awake. Take note of your dreams. Keep your mind clear of drugs and alcohol to receive this higher level of conscious evolutionary thinking."

Maybe the nightly glass of wine or two wasn't such a great idea.

"Until you realize that you are the creator, you will refuse to accept this responsibility, but it is upon the smooth functioning of your subconscious self that your well-being depends."

Heidi barked at my feet, jerking me back to the room.

"Shh," I said to the empty dog bed. I rubbed my feet into it, almost feeling Heidi's silky fur.

Seth had stopped talking. Hoping to keep him engaged, I asked, "Okay, but how does any of this relate to Buckminster Fuller?"

"Buckminster Fuller understood everything. But he grew tired of Earthians so caught up in making money that they stopped making sense. But do not worry. As Bucky said, Earth will carry on. It's only the humans who will—"

"I know, once humans are gone, the rest of the planet will be fine. But isn't there still something humans can do?"

The line went silent. I sensed he was gone.

"Wait," he said, "I am getting something on you." The static had returned to his voice, as if he were somewhere far away.

"You have done this before." He sounded angry, even disgusted.

"Um, no, I don't think so. This is actually my first time with this sort of thing, other than a psychic in Toronto once who—"

"No, I mean in another lifetime. You called yourself a scribe and took notes for a dying alchemist. You volunteered to record his wisdom for future generations."

"I did?"

"You took copious notes and promised to pass on the information, but then you left town, saying you had to care for your ailing parents."

I gulped my tea. The story did sound oddly familiar, but I preferred to give myself the benefit of the doubt. "I don't think I would have done that—not intentionally, anyway. Maybe I honestly meant to help. That sounds like me. I'm sure I had good intentions."

"Intentions are not all that matter. Actions matter."

So now I wasn't just a dreamer, but a willful plunderer of humanity's great secrets? Great. What would I find out next, that I am the Antichrist? I felt something crack open inside me, and not in a good way. My soul was a pile of feathery goo, and Seth wasn't done with me yet.

"Years later, you returned and claimed the alchemist's notes had been lost in a flood." His voice was booming now like an angry Greek god about to hurl thunderbolts.

The boxes in the basement. This was getting creepy. "A flood?"

"You were chased out of the village, your life spared only because people had forgotten their anger. Nobody grieves much over vanished wisdom, since it is impossible to grasp what has been lost. This is why earth's current dark age has been such a great crime against humanity. It is a crisis, which by its very nature is unknowable to all but a few. But you knew. You had the information. You kept it to yourself."

He paused to let it sink in that I was, officially, a big-talking good-for-nothing—and not in just one lifetime but in at least two. The sting of his words was almost unbearable. I tried to focus on my breathing so I would hold it together, determined not to blather like a baby.

"This is your cycle," he said.

"My, uh, cycle?" I reached for my tea, but my hand shook so much I had to put the cup down. I could still feel Heidi, her furry tummy warming my feet, her tail thumping to absorb the horrific news of atrocities I had committed in previous lifetimes.

"Your karmic cycle." His patience was wearing thin. "If you wish to move on beyond the harmful pattern you have created, this is the lifetime in which to do it. You must break this destructive reverberation."

I was beginning to feel light-headed from my deep breathing, and I wasn't sure how much more of these accusations I could take. Had I really been such a terrible person, in multiple lifetimes?

"You are looking for a way out. Your ambivalence follows you from life to life. You must choose between family obligations and higher ones. You must complete your magnum opus."

"Ha!" I nearly choked. The phrase brought to mind Mozart, Bach, Charles Dickens, Jane Austin... Certainly not me.

A powerful surge swept through me. I could feel that Seth was gone. The line went dead. I wiggled my feet under the desk, but Heidi was no longer there either. All the energy had been sucked out of the room. I felt more alone than ever before.

My head snapped up at the sound of rain slapping against the window. Yet as I looked outside, the sun broke through the clouds for the first time all day. Millions of brilliantly lit raindrops danced in front of me, glittering in the midday sun, shimmering against a backdrop of brilliant green grass.

I smiled at the memory of how much Bucky had loved the dance of the sun and the rain together. It's like humanity's condition right now, he had said, unbearably bleak and yet iridescently promising. The light was having its way with the darkness.

And then I felt Bucky sit down beside me. His words came into my mind: *Humanity has extraordinary potential. Just you wait and see.*

I knew he was talking about me.

The End.

1. Embrace abundance, not scarcity.

Humans are falsely conditioned by the notion of scarcity promoted by Charles Darwin and Thomas Malthus. The idea of survival of the fittest sets up an us-versus-them mentality. If we believe there is not enough for all, over-consumption and greed are natural results. Only by embracing abundance and setting out to prove there is enough for all can we achieve Bucky's overriding objective, "To make the world work for one hundred percent of all humanity in the shortest possible time, through spontaneous cooperation, without ecological damage or harm to any individual." In other words, whether we think we can or think we can't, we are right.

2. Realign with nature.

Cocooned in our clothing, homes, cars, and offices, humans have become detached from nature. Reconnecting and realigning requires that we return to nature as often as possible and spend as much time within nature as we can, sleeping outdoors, sitting under trees, going barefoot. Realigning with nature's design principles also requires weaning ourselves off fossil fuels. This is humanity's most critical task. Trust that you are part of something bigger than your conscious mind can comprehend.

3. Demand true democracy.

In a 1972 *Playboy* interview, Bucky predicted that a true real-time democracy was on the way. "One day soon," he said, "we will be able to click a thing on our wrist to say 'I like it' or 'I don't like it,' and that will be our vote." Bucky's ideas generally came about fifty years in advance of reality, which means real-time democracy should arrive by about 2020. Considering recent political events, another Bucky thought to ponder is this: "When something is broken, don't try to fix it. Create a new model that renders the old one obsolete."

Bucky said successful global air traffic control is proof that we can cooperate despite our differences. "You may ask how we are going to resolve the ever-accelerating dangerous impasse of world-opposed politicians and ideological dogmas," he said. "I answer, it will be resolved by the computer. While no politician or political system can afford to yield understandably and enthusiastically to their adversaries and opponents, all politicians can and will yield to the computer's safe flight-controlling capabilities and bring all humanity in for a happy landing."
Surely there will soon be an app for that.

4. Know your individual power.

"The future of humanity rests upon individual integrity." How can an individual be more powerful than any corporation or government entity? Only the individual has total freedom to act on passion and principle. Humans have always unknowingly affected all of Universe by every act and thought. Realistic, comprehensively responsible, unselfish thinking does absolutely impact human destiny.

Bucky often expressed this with his trim tab analogy. A trim tab is a tiny flap on the rudder of a boat. Although very small, it is the only thing that changes the direction of even the most massive ocean liner. Know that you are that trim tab, he often said; know that individual integrity is the most powerful energy on earth.

5. Understand what needs to be done, and then do it.

Man knows so much but does so little. Bucky wrote this advice in 1970 to a ten-year-old boy who asked whether Fuller was a doer or a thinker: "The things to do are: the things that need doing, that you see need to be done, and that no one else seems to see need to be done. Then you will conceive your own way of doing that which needs to be done—that no one else has told you to do or how to do it. This will bring out the real you that often gets buried inside a character that has acquired a superficial array of behaviors imposed by others on the individual."

6. Evolve consciously.

Humanity must qualify to survive. For this to happen, the time will come when humans will have acquired enough knowledge of generalized principles to permit a graduation from a class two (entropic or selfish) evolution into a class one (syntrophic or cooperative) species. Thereafter, we will begin to make all the right choices for all the right reasons.

Stay tuned to your own stream of consciousness, so that you can continue to grow in your syntrophic capacities. Focus on your own conscious evolution, and on the evolution of your own consciousness, and you will be helping humanity evolve to a higher level.

7. Remain comprehensive.

We live in an age that rewards specialization, believing it to be logical, natural, and desirable. Yet specialization has bred feelings of isolation, futility, and confusion, and has resulted in a disregard for big-picture thinking and responsibility.

Bucky called himself a comprehensive anticipatory design scientist. Whether you look back at the great captains of ships at sea or at today's modern CEOs, you will see that those who rise to the top to direct and manage others are those whose knowledge is comprehensive. They know a little bit about everything.

8. Speak the truth.

Our survival depends not on political or economic systems but on the courage of individuals to speak the truth and go along only with the truth. Our future depends upon our courage to express what we know and feel is the truth and on our ability to do this with kindness and compassion. Our greatest vulnerability lies in the amount of misinformation and misconditioning available to humanity. These mistruths are one of the greatest obstacles we must overcome.

You'll find the author's blog at **BuckyIdeas.com**. Please visit there to read about Buckminster Fuller's ideas for today and for news about upcoming events and books.

To understand the math and science behind Bucky's thinking, read *A Fuller Explanation: The Synergetic Geometry of R. Buckminster Fuller* by Amy Edmondson. This book explains how Synergetic Geometry can save our species.

For information, tools, toys, and other resources relating to R. Buckminster "Bucky" Fuller and design science, check out the **Buckminster Fuller Institute** at **bfi.org**. And of course, the mother lode of information is tucked away in the **R. Buckminster Fuller Collection** in the **Green Library at Stanford University**. You can reserve specific documents at **collections.stanford.edu/bucky**.

Books About Buckminster Fuller

Bucky Works: Buckminster Fuller's Ideas for Today, J. Baldwin, 1996, Wiley.

Your Private Sky: R. Buckminster Fuller: The Art of Design Science, Joachim Krausse, Claude Lichtenstein, 1999, Lars Müller Publishers.

Bucky: A Guided Tour of Buckminster Fuller, Hugh Kenner, 1973, William Morrow.

Pilot for Spaceship Earth, Athena V. Lord, 1979, Macmillan.

R. Buckminster Fuller: An Autobiographical Monologue/
Scenario, Robert Snyder, 1980, St. Martin's Press.

Artifacts of R. Buckminster Fuller: A Comprehensive
Collection of His Designs and Drawings (4 vols.), James Ward,
ed., 1985, Garland Publishing.

Cosmic Fishing: An Account of Writing Synergetics with Buckminster Fuller, E.J. Applewhite, 1977, Macmillan.

Geodesic Math and How to Use It, Hugh Kenner, 1976,
University of California Press.

An Introduction to Tensegrity, Anthony Pugh, University of California Press.

Synergetics Dictionary: The Mind of Buckminster Fuller (4 vols.),
E.J. Applewhite, ed., 1986, Garland Publishing.

Wholeness: On Education, Buckminster Fuller, and Tao, Alex Gerber Jr, 2001, Gerber Educational Resources.

Your Private Sky: R Buckminster Fuller: Discourse, Joachim
Krausse, Claude Lichtenstein, eds., 2001, Lars Müller
Publishers.

"50 Years of Design Science Revolution and the World Game,"
historical documentation (articles, clippings) with commentary
by Fuller, 1969. Available at www.bfi.org.

Earth, Energy and Everyone: A Global Energy Strategy for Spaceship Earth, Medard Gabel, 1975, Doubleday.

Hoping: Food For Everyone, Medard Gabel, 1975,
Doubleday.

Buckminster Fuller's Universe: His Life and Work, Lloyd Steven
Sieden, 1989, Plenum Press.

New Views on R. Buckminster Fuller, 2009, Stanford
University Press.

You Belong to the Universe, Jonathon Keats, 2016, Oxford
University Press.

Books by R. Buckminster Fuller

4D Timelock, self-published, 1928 (1970 reprint by The Lama Foundation)

Nine Chains to the Moon: An Adventure Story of Thought, 1938, J.B. Lippencott. (1971 paperback, Anchor/ Doubleday)

The Dymaxion World of Buckminster Fuller, 1960, Reinhold.

Education Automation, 1962, Southern Illinois University Press.

Ideas and Integrities, A Spontaneous Autobiographical Disclosure, 1963, Prentice-Hall.

No More Secondhand God, and Other Writings, (poems and essays), 1963, Southern Illinois University Press.

Operating Manual for Spaceship Earth, 1969, Southern Illinois University Press.

Utopia or Oblivion: the Prospects for Humanity, 1969, Bantam.

I Seem to Be a Verb, 1970, Bantam.

Buckminster Fuller to Children of Earth, 1972, Doubleday.

Intuition, 1972, Anchor/Doubleday.

Earth, Inc., 1973, Anchor/Doubleday.

Synergetics: Explorations in the Geometry of Thinking (with E.J. Applewhite), 1975, Macmillan.

Synergetics2: Further Explorations in the Geometry of Thinking (with E.J. Applewhite), 1979 Macmillan.

And It Came to Pass—Not to Stay, 1976, Macmillan.

Critical Path (with Kiyoshi Kuromiya), 1981, St. Martin's Press.

Tetrascroll: Goldilocks and the Three Bears, A Cosmic Fairy Tale, 1982, St. Martin's Press.

Grunch of Giants, 1983, St. Martin's Press.

Humans in Universe (with Anwar Dil), 1983, Mouton De Gruyter.

Inventions: The Patented Works of R. Buckminster Fuller, 1983, St. Martin's Press.

Cosmography: A Posthumous Scenario for the Future of Humanity (with Kiyoshi Kuromiya), 1992, Macmillan.

Books to Kindle a Revolution

Drawdown—The Most Comprehensive Plan Ever Proposed to Reverse Global Warming, Paul Hawken, 2017, Penguin Random House.

This Changes Everything, Naomi Klein, 2014, Simon and Schuster.

Oil and Honey, Bill McKibben, 2014, St. Martin's Press.

The Hidden Geometry of Flowers, Keith Critchlow, 2012, Floris Books

Utopia for Realists, Rutger Bregman, 2017, Bloomsbury.

1. The author/protagonist of this story grapples with a responsibility she accepted long ago to inform the world about something. Can you relate to her situation? Why or why not?

2. R. Buckminster Fuller was and is a controversial figure. Some say he was brilliant, like a modern day Leonardo da Vinci. Others say his head was in the clouds, that he was annoyingly repetitive and sometimes made no sense. Which opinion is true and why?

3. Why does the author go back to her childhood on the lake at the beginning of the story? What does she want us to understand about nature and her fascination with Fuller?

4. During her two days of interviews, Patricia takes copious notes. What role do these notes have in the story? What makes their disappearance so important to the narrative?

5. What role does Patricia's therapist play in her dilemma? Why was his reversal of his diagnosis of her important and why did he make it?

6. She tries again and again to come up with various ways to live up to her promise. Even though she meets with some success, she never focuses on one thing, but

instead keeps coming up with new ideas. Why is this behavior important to the story?

7. There are several metaphysical, paranormal, or otherwise other worldly events that happen, even though it is called a true story. Is this possible or not? Is the narrator reliable or not?

8. One theme running through this story is the role of fossil fuel corporations in obstructing understanding of climate change and the transition to clean energy, which Fuller called "the greatest crime ever committed against humanity." Was this a valid complaint back in 1982? How have things changed (or not) since then?

9. At the conclusion of the story, the author includes a summary: *Eight Bucky Ideas to Save the Planet and Your Sanity*. Which of these, if any, seem important? Do you think it is possible for humans to make these subtle shifts in their thinking? Is this just simple common sense, or is there something important to be learned from these ideas?

ACKNOWLEDGMENTS

My deep gratitude is owed to two early supporters, John Ferry of The Buckminster Fuller Estate and Harvard professor Amy Edmondson. Their belief in the value of Bucky's ideas convinced me I was not crazy. My professors in UCLA's online writing workshops, Sharon Bray and Lynn Hightower, appropriately decimated my early writing in a vacuum, just as real readers would have done. Writing instructor Leslie Keenan at Corte Madera's Book Passage was first to say my story gave her goose bumps, which then became my goal. Enthusiasm from early readers Roger, Sheila, Kappy and Heather, along with the expertise of an editor who fell from heaven, Lisa Poisso, kept me going. The day I learned Bucky's daughter Allegra liked the manuscript, I knew I was almost there. My own family was also supportive, especially once they realized I might actually finish something. In production, Kit Foster and Ruth Schwartz made a great team. And I can't forget my mother. While she does not believe a book like this can make a whit of difference in the world, Barbara Eileen Field, at 94, is still as sharp as a laser and excited to see how it all turns out. Still a British citizen, she deserves to be knighted for her patience.

Thank you to all who have supported me in this project, and sincere apologies to all I endlessly harangued and lectured until I finally stopped talking and started writing. I hope every reader will be inspired by Bucky's wisdom and by one ordinary person's struggle to live up to her promise.

ABOUT THE AUTHOR

In her multi-faceted career, Patricia Ravasio has won awards in advertising copywriting, radio reporting, real estate sales, and community volunteerism. She was named Citizen of the Year by her small northern California town where she led the creation of a new community café. She wrote a long-running weekly column for her town's community newspaper and occasional guest opinion pieces and essays, but this is the first book for the mother of three grown daughters who lives with her husband and two dogs in Northern California.

CPSIA information can be obtained
at www.ICGtesting.com
Printed in the USA
FSOW02n2131030917
38263FS